MUSSOLINI

Was Mussolini really the power-crazed cynic that many see him as? Was he a true revolutionary? Although he could be both ruthless and opportunistic, Benito Mussolini was also driven by ideology and his desire to make Italy great. But conservative forces in the Italian establishment and factional warfare in his own Fascist Party were stumbling blocks to his policy, and ultimately Italy never became as fascist as Mussolini would have liked.

Peter Neville presents a new assessment of the life and times of the famous leader. This study places the Fascist movement in its historical context and assesses its theoretical base. It examines the formative influences on the young Mussolini, his turn away from socialism by 1914, his domestic and foreign policy as a leader, and his historical legacy. Clear and engaging, this book is key to the understanding of one of the most fascinating of twentieth-century European dictators.

Peter Neville teaches history at the University of East Anglia. He is the author of *Appeasing Hitler: The Diplomacy of Sir Nevile Henderson 1937–9* (2000) and of short studies of Churchill and Neville Chamberlain. He is also a Fellow of the Royal Historical Society.

ROUTLEDGE HISTORICAL BIOGRAPHIES

SERIES EDITOR: ROBERT PEARCE

Routledge Historical Biographies provide engaging, readable and academically credible biographies written from an explicitly historical perspective. These concise and accessible accounts will bring important historical figures to life for students and general readers alike.

In the same series:

MUSSOLINI

Peter Neville

Routledge
Taylor & Francis Group

LONDON AND NEW YORK

First published 2004
by Routledge
11 New Fetter Lane, London EC4P 4EE

Simultaneously published in the USA and Canada
by Routledge
29 West 35th Street, New York, NY 10001

Routledge is an imprint of the Taylor & Francis Group

Typeset in Garamond and Scala Sans by Taylor & Francis Books Ltd
Printed and bound in Great Britain by MPG Books Ltd, Bodmin

British Library Cataloguing in Publication Data
A catalogue record for this book is available from the British Library

Library of Congress Cataloging in Publication Data
Neville, Peter, 1944–
  Mussolini / Peter Neville.
      p. cm. – (Routledge historical biographies)
Includes bibliographical references and index.
1. Mussolini, Benito, 1883–1945. 2. Heads of state–Italy–Biography.
3. Fascism–Italy–History. 4. Italy–Politics and
government–1914–1945. I. Title. II. Series.
  DG575.M8N48 2003
  945.091′092–dc21

                                                              2003012386

ISBN 0–415–24989–9 (hbk)
ISBN 0–415–24990–2 (pbk)

CONTENTS

Plates

ACKNOWLEDGEMENTS

I am indebted to a number of people. Robert Pearce was a consistently supportive and helpful series editor, and Vicky Peters at Routledge was patient and understanding when the manuscript was delivered later than I had hoped. Paula Bartley suggested the idea of the book in the first place, and was supportive throughout its genesis, while Philip Morgan at the University of Hull gave me the benefit of his great expertise about Italian Fascism. I am also grateful to Professor Tony Lentin at the Open University and Dr Andrew Crozier at Queen Mary and Westfield College for kindly reading and commenting on parts of the manuscript. Carol Willis contributed invaluable secretarial assistance, while my wife as ever put up with the demands Mussolini made on my time with admirable stoicism.

It is a truism to say that the remaining faults in the book are my responsibility but of course they are.

CHRONOLOGY

	Personal	Political	General
1883	Birth of Mussolini		
1909		Mussolini appointed Socialist Party Secretary of the Chamber of Labour in the Trentino	
1910	Mussolini marries Rachele Guidi. Edda born		
1911			Italy invades Libya
1912		Mussolini appointed Editor of *Avanti!*	
1913		Mussolini elected town councillor in Milan	
1914		Mussolini leaves the Socialist Party over intervention in the First World War	Outbreak of the First World War
1915	Mussolini joins the Italian army		Italy enters the war. Treaty of London signed

	Personal	*Political*	*General*
1916	Vittorio Mussolini born		
1917	Mussolini invalided out of the army		Collapse of Tsarism in Russia. Bolsheviks in power. Catastrophic Italian defeat at Caporetto
1918: November	Bruno Mussolini born	Mussolini denounces Wilson's 14 Peace Points	First World War ends
1919: March		Mussolini sets up the *Fasci di Combattimento*	
June			Treaty of Versailles signed
September		D'Annunzio seizes Fiume	
1920		Fascist agrarian terrorism in operation	
1921		Setting up of the Fascist Party. Mussolini elected to parliament	
1922		Mussolini appointed Prime Minister. The March on Rome	

	Personal	Political	General
1923		Passing of the Acerbo Bill	The failure of Hitler's uprising in Munich
1924		The murder of Matteotti. The Aventine Secession	Lenin dies
1925: January		Mussolini defies parliament and sets up his personal dictatorship	
November		Zaniboni attempts to assassinate Mussolini	
December		New press law introduced	Treaty of Locarno signed
1926: April		Gibson assassination attempt	
October		Zamboni assassination attempt	
November		Powers of the Italian police strengthened	
1927	Birth of Romano Mussolini	Italy returns to the gold standard	
1928		Start of the 'battle for wheat'	

	Personal	*Political*	*General*
1929	Birth of Anna Marie Mussolini	Lateran Pacts between Mussolini and Pope Pius XI	Wall Street Crash initiates global depression
1930		Mussolini secures naval parity with Great Britain and France	
1931	Death of Arnaldo Mussolini		
1932		Dismissal of Dino Grandi from the Foreign Office	
1933		Mussolini proposes a 'Four Power Pact'	Hitler comes to power in Germany
1934		Assassination of Chancellor Dollfuss. Mussolini rushes troops to the Brenner frontier	
1935: April		Mussolini attends Stresa conference	Nuremberg Laws passed in Germany
October		Italy invades Ethiopia	
1936: July		Spanish Civil War	
November		Rome–Berlin Axis	

	Personal	Political	General
1937		Mussolini visits Nazi Germany	
1938: March		Mussolini agrees to Austro-German Anschluss	
September		Mussolini attends the Munich Conference	
1939: April		Italy invades Albania	
May		Pact of Steel with Germany	
August		Mussolini tells Hitler that Italy is unready for war	Nazi–Soviet pact signed
September			Second World War begins
1940: March		Meeting between Mussolini and Hitler	
June		Mussolini declares war on Britain and France	
September		Italian offensive starts in Africa	
October		Mussolini invades Greece	

	Personal	Political	General
1941: March		Italian fleet defeated at Cape Matapan. German intervention in Greece and Yugoslavia	
June			Hitler invades the USSR
August		Mussolini meets Hitler at Rastenburg	
December		Mussolini declares war on the United States	
1942: November		Axis forces defeated at El Alamein	
1943: May		Surrender of Axis forces in North Africa	
July		Mussolini is dismissed and arrested	
September		Mussolini rescued from captivity by German paratroopers	
October		Setting up of the Republic of Salò in Northern Italy	

	Personal	Political	General
1944: January		Mussolini orders execution of his son-in-law Count Ciano	
February		Verona Manifesto	
April		Mussolini visits Hitler in Germany	
June			D-Day invasion
July			Attempt on Hitler's life
1945: April		Mussolini's interview with Cardinal Schuster. His flight, capture and execution by Communist partisans	Suicide of Adolf Hitler in Berlin

INTRODUCTION

On the afternoon of 28 April 1945 a man in his early sixties, together with his young mistress of long-standing, was taken by Italian Communist partisans to a house called the Villa Belmonte near the town of Dongo on the road up to the Swiss frontier north of Milan. They both knew that this would be a last journey, one which would end in their execution. For the man was the former Italian dictator Benito Mussolini (1883–1945) who had taken Italy into the Second World War in June 1940 with catastrophic consequences. The woman was Claretta Petacci who had loyally opted to stay with her lover as he vainly tried to escape into neutral Switzerland in a German airforce lorry.

Shortly after their arrival at the Villa Belmonte the bullet-riddled bodies of Mussolini and Petacci were taken by van to Milan, which had been the starting point of Mussolini's political career decades earlier. There the bodies were hung upside down in a well-known square, and subjected to verbal and physical abuse by the very same Milanese who had once greeted Mussolini as a hero. Mussolini's origins, as will be seen, were humble and his death was both violent and tawdry. But it was the sequel to a long process of decline and humiliation which had begun the moment he decided to take Fascist Italy to war in 1940. This was to culminate in his overthrow in July 1943, and a further period as a puppet ruler in a Fascist enclave in northern Italy which was utterly dependent on the German army to sustain it. By the end

Mussolini himself came to realise that he had become an irrelevance, but his internal enemies on the Italian Left would never forgive him for the crimes of the past, and the Communists in particular could be relied upon to deal out summary justice if he fell into their hands. Even had he survived, Mussolini would have faced a war crimes trial in post-war Italy. Fascism had become synonymous with all that was odious and bestial in Italian and European society. In part, this was Mussolini's own personal achievement.

Mussolini's claim to fame rested, in his own eyes, with the foundation of the Italian Fascist Party in 1921 after he had swung violently away from the socialism of his youth, and left the Italian Socialist Party in 1914. In doing so Mussolini betrayed the socialist heritage of his father, and exchanged a concept of international brotherhood and class division for one of violent and intolerant nationalism. His experience as a soldier in the First World War only appeared to sharpen his nationalist tendencies, allowing him to utilise the mood of post-war disillusionment in Italy and achieve power in 1922. Thereafter Mussolini faced a conflict between the demands of political power and the radical agenda of many Italian Fascists. In many ways he was a pragmatist, being prepared, for example, to arrange a compromise with the Catholic Church, which he had purported to despise, because circumstances demanded it in 1929. But it is too easy to dismiss Mussolini as a cynical opportunist obsessed only with personal power. However ineffectively he tried to impose it upon Italians between 1922 and 1943, Mussolini did have a vision of what Fascist Italian society should be like. In a real sense, therefore, Mussolini's story is the story of how he tried to resolve the tensions between Fascist ideology and the demands of government, when his power was constrained by powerful independent forces such as the monarchy, the Church and the army. Ultimately, it was the disastrous plunge into war in 1940 which destroyed him when his régime had some positive achievements to its credit. Fascist intolerance and violence was seen at its worst in the wartime context.

But to understand the career of Benito Mussolini and the forces which he helped to unleash in Italian society, an historical context is required. Mussolini was a creature of his time, but it was the condition of Italian society in the early twentieth century which made it susceptible to the dynamic of Fascism.

THE *RISORGIMENTO*

The first point that needs to be made is that Italy was a young nation state. The Austrian Chancellor Metternich had familiarly referred to Italy as being merely a 'geographical expression', in the sense that before the 1860s it consisted only of a series of states such as Piedmont, Naples, the Papal States and so on. Humiliatingly, the 1815 settlement which ended the Napoleonic Wars had placed the two large provinces of Lombardy and Venetia under Austrian rule. Having seen the expulsion of Napoleon and the French, the Italians found themselves under the control of yet another foreign power.

Map 1 Italy in 1815

In the years between 1815 and 1848, Austrian influence was predominant. Apart from the direct rule over Lombardy and Venetia, the Austrian House of Habsburg was also linked by marriage to the rulers of the small central Italian Duchies of Parma, Lucca and Tuscany. And successive Popes in Rome (who themselves ruled over a sizeable portion of Central Italy) relied on Catholic Austria to crush any signs of dangerous nationalism and anti-clericalism.

Yet despite the efforts of the forces of reaction, Italian nationalism began to be a potent force. There were miserable disasters when revolts failed in 1821 and 1830–31, but the desire for some form of Italian unity grew from the 1820s onwards.

The question was, who could lead the process of *Risorgimento* (Unification)? The Pope was one possibility and briefly, between 1846 and 1848, it seemed that the Italians had found in Pio Nono (Pius IX) that most unlikely of beings, a liberal Pope. But Pius IX proved to be a major disappointment and ultimately sided with the Austrians in the great revolutionary years of 1848 and 1849.

A second possibility was a republic and this was the solution advocated by one of the great nineteenth-century Italian nationalists, Mazzini. His main objective was the expulsion of the Austrians from his homeland, but he was strongly opposed to the setting up of any kind of Italian monarchy. Mazzini's movement, 'Young Italy', lobbied and fought for an Italian republic throughout the 1830s and 1840s, but although republics were briefly set up in Rome and Venice in 1848–49, Austrian and French military strength ultimately destroyed them. Mazzini's great disciple was the military leader Guiseppe Garibaldi, who played a leading role in the defence of the Roman Republic, and was to be a leading player in the events leading to the achievement of unification in the 1860s. Garibaldi was a dashing, romantic figure with whom Mussolini, when a youthful revolutionary, liked to associate himself, before his politics swung violently to the Fascist Right.

The last option for Italian nationalists was unification under one of the larger Italian states such as Piedmont or Naples. Piedmont was the more attractive possibility, although its king, Charles Albert, was humiliatingly defeated when he tried to take on the Austrians in 1848–49. His slogan that Italy 'could save herself' proved to be an illusion, and one of the lessons of the great revolutionary year 1848 was that foreign assistance would be required if the Austrians were to be expelled.

The English poet Meredith was to write of the process of Italy's unification:

> We think of those
> Who blew the breath of life into her flame:
> Cavour, Mazzini, Garibaldi. Three:
> Her Brain, her Soul, her Sword; and set her free
> From ruinous discords...

Certainly the third member of the triumvirate, Count Camillo di Cavour, fully deserved the accolade of being called one of the creators of Italian unity. Cavour was determined that the power and influence of his master, the King of Piedmont, should be increased (he did not envisage a united Italy until favourable circumstances arose) and that Austrian influence in Italy should end. His great achievement was to secure the help of the French Emperor, Napoleon III, to expel Austria from Lombardy and Venetia. This was achieved as a result of two wars in 1859–60 and 1866. At the same time, Cavour was able to persuade a reluctant Garibaldi to hand over his conquest of Naples and the Two Sicilies to King Victor Emmanuel II of Piedmont in 1860. In an epic campaign Garibaldi and his 'Thousand Redshirts' had smashed the Neapolitan forces and driven up towards Central Italy.

In parallel with a successful foreign policy, Cavour had been able to modernise Piedmont, giving it an efficient army, a proper railway system and a favourable trade balance. But his premature death in 1861 prevented him from seeing the achievement of *Risorgimento*. Nevertheless by 1866 all of Italy, with the sole exception of Rome, was unified, with Pope Pius IX obstinately holding out in the capital city. Then the Franco-Prussian war of 1870 forced Napoleon III to withdraw the French garrison from Rome (it had been there since 1849), and the process of unification was complete. In just twelve years Italy apparently had been transformed from a profoundly disunited country into a united one.

This unity was in fact an illusion. To begin with, Pope Pius IX and his successors refused to recognise the legitimacy of the Italian State which they claimed had stolen its lands and property in Rome and the Papal States. This so-called 'Roman Question' bedevilled Italian politics until Mussolini himself made the Lateran Pacts with Pope Pius XI in

1929. Successive popes were effectively telling their flock that the authority of the Italian State, established in 1870, was illegitimate. This had profound consequences in post-unification Italian politics.

The socio-economic impact of the *Risorgimento* was also limited as 'the masses were notably absent from the events which brought about independence and unification'.[1] The achievement of unity was the work of a tiny élite and the great masses of Italian peasantry were not consulted. Not until 1912 was the franchise extended to give most Italian males the vote, and virtually nothing was done about the crucial question of land reform. The historian Seton Watson has made the distinction between 'legal Italy', which consisted of the King and Parliament centred on Rome, and the 'real Italy', which was the country of the peasant masses.[2]

AFTER UNIFICATION

There was also a chasm between the richer, industrialised North and the impoverished, rural, backward South. Indeed, during the years immediately after unification known as the 'Great Brigandage' organised gangs of ex-soldiers and criminals made sure that the government writ did not run in the South at all. Such brigands were joined by peasants trying to escape either conscription or the taxes imposed upon them after 1871 which were higher than prior to unification.

It is clear that the 'economic handicaps of the south in 1871 were overwhelming'.[3] All sorts of problems plagued its agricultural development, from an arid soil, to malaria and absentee landlords who neglected their estates. Government was based in far-off Rome, which saw to it that expenditure was concentrated overwhelmingly in Central and Northern Italy. Between 1862 and 1897, for example, some 267 million lire were spent on land reclamation in the North and a further 188 million in Central Italy. Just 3 million lire was allocated to the desperately poor South. Small wonder that people spoke of 'two Italies'. The so-called 'Southern Question' – the economic disparity between North and South – continued to bedevil Italian society well into the twentieth century. Mussolini was thus born into an Italy where regional divisions were acute, and most of the population felt excluded from the political process.

The politicians in the newly united state did not help the process of nation building. An alliance of Northern and Southern ruling élites kept governments in power, even though this led to the rigging of elections, especially in the South. One result of this was that the practice of colluding with the Mafia in the South was eventually to pass into national politics. Given this atmosphere of corruption, it is unsurprising that by the 1890s radical alternatives such as socialism were proving attractive to the working classes. This brought the threat of social revolution to an Italy where only 2 per cent of the population had the vote in 1900 and forced the more intelligent members of the dominant Italian Liberal Party to consider concessions and consensus.

The leader of the Liberal Party was Giolitti, who recognised the need to try to accommodate 'legal Italy' with 'real Italy'. The masses had to be brought into the political system and Giolitti sought to do this through a combination of electoral reform and reform of working conditions. He also tried to bring in the Italian Socialist Party from the political cold, so that the representatives of the working class would be integrated into the political system. This integration was, however, to be limited; the Socialist leaders were to be bought off and absorbed into the existing system (as were the leaders of other potentially hostile groups such as the Catholics and the Nationalists) rather than allowed to exist as an important independent force.

In this sense, Giolitti merely adopted the existing system of so-called *Transformismo* which had dominated Italian politics since the 1880s. This was a system whereby factions in Italian politics were 'transformed' from being opponents of the existing government by being offered jobs and favours. Giolitti merely tried, and ultimately failed, to reach some sort of agreement with the Socialists. He was, as one historian has written, 'a clear-headed and rather cynical Liberal, not a democrat'.[4]

CATHOLICISM AND POLITICS

The other important change that took place in the years when Mussolini was growing to manhood was the reversal of the Catholic Church's political strategy. While Pius IX was alive (he died in 1878), Catholics were discouraged from taking any active part in the political process in Italy. A slow process of change followed under his successor Pope Leo XIII, who issued an important encyclical (a statement) on social and economic policy in 1891. Entitled *Rerum Novarum* (New Things), it actually condemned capitalism, and argued in favour of concepts such as a 'just wage' which would allow workers to save and buy property.

The State was, Pope Leo argued, justified in intervening to safeguard workers' rights and Catholics were positively instructed to try to transform existing society. Even trade unions, which would have been anathema to Pius IX, were approved as long as they did not become a vehicle for class struggle (the Papacy maintained its aversion to atheistic Marxism with its doctrine of the inevitability of class warfare). Even though traditional Catholics found Leo XIII's 'Social Catholicism' controversial, the encyclical did help to sponsor growing Catholic involvement in mainstream politics. The government responded to this apparent threat by banning hundreds of Catholic associations in 1897. But Giolitti was more cautious. He spoke in 1904 about the Church and State being 'two parallel lines, which should never meet', but this was one of his very few statements about Church–State relations. He needed Catholic support against the Socialist threat, and Catholic fears about this threat provided him with their votes. In exchange, Giolitti dropped in 1904 a proposed divorce bill which was bound to antagonise Italy's large Catholic population. As it was, Leo XIII's successor, Pius X, was less enthusiastic about 'Social Catholicism', and the Catholic emphasis changed from national to local politics (arguing, for example, for regional autonomy for Sicily).

The Italy, therefore, into which Mussolini was born in 1883 was in most senses barely democratic. Most Italian males only received the vote in 1912 (women being, of course, totally excluded from the franchise in line with the thinking of the time), and the divide between the political élite and the people was alarming. The sharp North–South divide accentuated tensions (many Southerners made the ultimate protest by emigrating) and the atmosphere was also poisoned by ultra-tense Church–State relations. Italy had been united so quickly that there had been no chance for the fault lines in society to mend.

It was in the exploitation of such tensions that the political career of Benito Mussolini was founded. Even before he came upon the scene, the Nationalist Right was exploiting Italian yearnings for a large colonial empire and definitive status as a great power. The fact that Italy lacked the resources to play the role of a great power was ignored and, in 1911, nationalist pressure forced Giolitti to become involved in a colonial adventure in Libya, which proved to be a heavy financial burden as the Italians were obliged to keep 50,000 troops in the country. Such national sabre rattling and adventurism was already pointing the way to Mussolini's Fascism. And the need for violence was a constant theme of Mussolini's own writings.

HISTORIOGRAPHY

There has been a considerable corpus of literature about Mussolini's life. A starting point is the Duce's personal writing, but such works have to be approached with a good deal of caution. Mussolini's *My Autobiography*, for example (published in English translation in 1928), was largely the work of his brother Arnaldo and another Fascist sympathiser. The book is a fascist polemic designed to highlight the virtues and achievements of Mussolini. Similar caution must be exercised with the so-called *Mussolini Memoirs* covering the period 1942–43 (first published in 1949) although this biographical fragment does contain some useful insights into Mussolini's state of mind at a time when he was coming to terms with the loss of power. A very important source, subject to the same caveat, is *Opera Omnia di Benito Mussolini*, published in Italian in forty-four volumes between 1951 and 1960, a massive exploration of Mussolini's letters and papers. Italian diplomatic documents, published under the title *I documenti diplomatici italiani* (especially *serie* 7, 8, 9 and 10), are often useful for the nitty-gritty of Italian diplomacy under Mussolini, although the series is incomplete owing to the conservatism of the Italian authorities in releasing documents.

As far as the secondary literature is concerned, the pre-war study by G. Seldes, *Sawdust Caesar: The Untold History of Mussolini and Fascism* (1936), is critical, whereas the biography by his ex-mistress Margherita Sarfatti, published in 1925, can be largely dismissed as hagiography. A number of competent biographies appeared in English in the 1960s. *Mussolini* by Ivonne Kirkpatrick (a former diplomat in Rome and later Permanent Under-Secretary at the Foreign Office) appeared in 1964 and was a solid, if uninspiring, piece of work, while Christopher Hibbert's *Benito Mussolini: The Rise and Fall of Il Duce* (1962) has much of the author's characteristic liveliness and use of colourful anecdotes. It failed, however, to deal adequately with the domestic aspects of Mussolini's régime after power was secured in 1922, the emphasis being largely upon war and diplomacy.

From the 1970s onwards, the historiography was dominated by Renzo de Felice's multi-volume biography running to over 5,000 pages.

De Felice has been by far the most sympathetic of Mussolini's biographers. Mussolini, in de Felice's eyes, was not a cruel man but someone who was forced into war against his inclinations by the failure of Britain and France to co-operate. De Felice's massive sprawling work about Mussolini, published in the 1970s and 1980s, was thought by critics to be uneven.[5] In the early volumes, de Felice seemed to suggest that Mussolini was guided by instinct rather than by any systematic programme (indeed, he made much of the fact that there was no Fascist version of *Mein Kampf*), but from volume four onwards Mussolini suddenly became an ideologue who wanted to create a new Fascist man. Mussolini now wanted 'a third road' between communism and capitalism which would offer a solution to the crisis facing Western civilisation after the coming of the Depression in the 1930s. Yet it was hard to find in de Felice's work any real explanation about *why* this transformation had taken place.

As regards domestic policy, Mussolini was claimed to have achieved a consensus with the working class in the early 1930s, a suggestion by de Felice which was strongly attacked by Italian Marxist historians who found little evidence for this. Another oddity about de Felice's work (for a historian focusing on a régime which glorified war and conflict) was the absence of any systematic use of archive material on colonial and military policy. This was doubly odd, indeed, for a historian and biographer who claimed to be creating a massive factual base for this work before embarking on interpretation. In fact, de Felice began to offer interpretations before he had completed his research in these areas, but he and his followers (such as Rosaria Quartararo) were also involved in a wider political debate about how the political establishment which emerged from the Italian resistance movement of 1943–45 had allegedly distorted the history of Fascism. Ultimately for de Felice, Mussolini remained a hero, and he saw it as his task 'to remove, with a tender loving care that at times makes one smile, all negative elements from the man's portrait'.[6] The fact that most other historians, be they Italian or English speaking, have sharply disagreed with this portrait may help to explain why this massive work has never been translated into English.

The definitive work in that language for many years was Dennis Mack Smith's *Mussolini*, published in 1981. Acerbic in style, and scathing in its insights into Mussolini's personal weaknesses, Mack Smith nevertheless found him to be a superlative propagandist who did have positive achievements during the early years of Fascism. And despite his catastrophic flirting with militarism, Mussolini was able to claim that 'no-one, friendly or hostile, could understand the modern world without taking Fascism into account'.[7] Mack Smith's book was not in fact as critical of Mussolini as some critics have suggested. His positive features are as readily acknowledged as his weaknesses. He was also careful to acknowledge in his preface the importance of de Felice's work, which has been supplemented in Italian by E. Gentile's work on the Fascist Party and its ideology.

Mack Smith's position as the pre-eminent biographer of Mussolini in English has now been challenged by R.J. Bosworth. His *Mussolini* (2002) is an avowedly anti-Fascist study which sees the essential duality of Mussolini's career. 'He was at one and the same time,' writes Bosworth, 'a charismatic Fascist dictator and a trimming and cynical politician.'[8] Bosworth discounts the idea that Fascists could be seen as 'working towards' their Duce, as Professor Kershaw has suggested Nazi officials needed to do because of Hitler's elusiveness and reluctance to commit himself to the dull grind of day-to-day government, in favour of the idea that Mussolini was really working towards the Party and the people. Unlike Hitler, Mussolini was a dictator who did work office hours (even if they were not as long as he liked to pretend), and had to work harder at making himself popular because Italy was a more divided and varied society than the more homogeneous Nazi Germany. Such comparisons contradict de Felice's assertions that Nazi Germany was so different from Fascist Italy that comparison is profitless.

In Bosworth's view, the German alliance was a disaster, not just in the obvious sense that it led to a sequence of military disasters, but because it forced Italian Fascism to present a more coherent definition of itself than it was capable of doing. Mussolini is revealed, warts and all, as a dictator who could be ruthless enough when the occasion demanded it (as in Ethiopia) but who was ultimately a colossal failure. Bosworth, like Mack Smith, highlights the difficulty in uncovering Mussolini the private man behind the layers of deceit and bombast with which Fascism surrounded itself.

The mainstream biographies of Mussolini have been supplemented by other studies which throw a helpful light on Mussolini's career. The now ageing books by Elizabeth Wiskemann (*The Rome–Berlin Axis,* 1966) and F.W. Deakin (*The Brutal Friendship,* 1966) on relations with

Nazi Germany are still valuable, but more recently MacGregor Knox's 1982 *Mussolini Unleashed* placed a new importance on ideology in the Duce's foreign policy. Additional work by Knox has emphasised the fact that Mussolini did have a programme. There are also important studies on relations between the Fascist Party and the Vatican from John Pollard (1985) and the PNF itself from Philip Morgan (*Italian Fascism*, 1995) and Alexander de Grand (*Italian Fascism: Its Origins and Development*, 1982).

This book will attempt to keep Benito Mussolini at the forefront, while also acknowledging the importance of those non-biographical studies in helping to form a picture of what Italian society was like in the years when Mussolini was ruling Italy. In this sense, it has to be a political rather than a personal biography while hopefully paying sufficient attention to the formative influences in Mussolini's life. He himself wrote a good deal, finishing with a series of no less than nineteen articles in a newspaper concerning the events of 1940–43 when his régime began to slip towards catastrophe. All of his work has to be treated with considerable caution, but we do also have the important *Ciano's Diary* (English version, 1949) as a counterweight, albeit one written by an ambitious, impatient son-in-law who has been criticised for being a political lightweight. Unlike other political personalities who left no diaries or memoirs, Mussolini left a welter of material which, however infected with egotism and dogmatism, does give us some limited insights into his personality. The fundamental problem, and the one on which this volume will focus, is to discern what really drove Mussolini and to assess the sincerity of his political opinions against his obvious desire to exercise great power. He liked to think of himself as a master of politics, but part of the biographer's task is to evaluate Mussolini the statesman, the domestic reformer and the military leader.

THEMES AND CONTENT

The book takes a chronological approach although themes are highlighted and examined in an analytical way. This allows subjects such as the Fascist régime's treatment of women (a subject neglected in other biographies of Mussolini) to be addressed within the context of this largely biographical approach.

It has been said that Mussolini personified the confused Italian iden-
tities which emerged from the *Risorgimento* in the 1860s and 1870s. He
was born in 1883 to a dedicated, political leftist father, who became his
political mentor, and a devoutly Catholic mother. From the outset,
therefore, the traditional and the revolutionary were at war in
Mussolini's personality. It may be argued that Mussolini's later deference
to Catholicism was purely cynical, but it represented an acknowledge-
ment of its importance nonetheless. On the political side, Mussolini was
to progress through anarchist leanings towards socialism, extreme
nationalism and eventual Fascism. His was an unruly youth, punctuated
by affairs, periods of imprisonment, foreign exile and indebtedness
before he became a journalist and politician of substance.

Mussolini married Rachele Guidi (but only after years of cohabita-
tion) and together they had five children. He was a flagrant womaniser
– one estimate suggests that Mussolini may have slept with as many as
400 women – but the relationship was an enduring one, Rachele seeing
the flaws in her husband's character all too clearly. On one occasion she
described him rather contemptuously as 'a poor chap', but she never
tried to share the political limelight with him. Mussolini was to hold
her up as the ideal Fascist woman who stayed at home and did what her
husband told her. This was not quite the case. Rachele was a tough-
minded individual.[9]

Such distortions were typical of Mussolini the propagandist, as this
study will show, and Mussolini's experience as a journalist was to be
invaluable in his political career. The big breakthrough came when he
became editor of the Socialist newspaper *Avanti!* (Forward) in 1912
when still just under 30. At this point in his career, Mussolini was an
avowed socialist who opposed militarism and imperialism (denouncing,
for example, Italy's invasion of Libya in 1911), but there are difficulties
involved in discerning what was genuine and what was not in
Mussolini's ideological genesis. An important aspect of the book will be
its analysis of how and why Mussolini broke with the Socialist Party in
1914 over the issue of Italian entry into the First World War, which
finally occurred in the following year.

Like his contemporaries, Mussolini served in the Italian army during
the First World War, rising to the rank of corporal, and there is nothing
to suggest that he was not a brave soldier. As one of the 'trenchocracy',
however (the generation of young men who survived the bloodletting in

the war), Mussolini was quick to see the potential in exploiting the disillusionment of ex-soldiers with pre-war politicians such as Giolitti. While the ideas behind Fascism can appear to be an intellectual rag bag, there is no doubt that the war experience was a crucial core in holding together the disparate elements which formed the Party founded by Mussolini in 1921.

Mussolini's particular skill, which is duly acknowledged in this text, was in holding together the amalgam of Futurists, Nationalists and Radicals which made up the new Fascist Party which appeared in 1921. He also showed considerable political acumen in the lead up to the achievement of political power in 1922, by playing off the conservative factions in Italian politics against each other. The problem with Mussolini, which will be a central theme here, is the degree to which making Italy Fascist, as against furthering his personal ambition, dominated his actions. There can be no doubt about his ruthlessness, which was demonstrated by the elimination of the Socialist critic Matteotti in 1924, although Mussolini was undoubtedly shaken by the protests sparked off by the murder.

Mussolini, like Hitler, was threatened by his own 'Second Revolution',[10] the danger that Fascist radicals would seize control of his 'revolution' and even eject him from personal power. He seems to have dealt with this threat adroitly so that by 1929 the threat from the Fascist radicals had virtually disappeared. There were also other genuine achievements in this early phase, such as the 1929 Lateran Pacts with the Catholic Church which regularised relations with the Vatican in a way no other Italian government had been able to do since 1870. Mussolini was now at the zenith of his power, and well able to see off the claims from disgruntled radicals such as Farinacci that he had sold out the Fascist revolution to the Italian political and religious establishment.

And yet there were flaws even during these years of achievement before the Ethiopian War of 1935–36. Historians have doubted whether Mussolini's régime ever achieved a real consensus with the industrial working class, and focus attention on the issue of whether the régime ever had anything more than the reluctant, passive acceptance of the Italian people. Mussolini himself was genuinely popular, at least until 1936–37, yet he relied on an army of informers and secret policemen to protect his power base.

Even so, his régime might have survived had not Mussolini chained himself to the German alliance from 1936 onwards. In the 1920s, he had been pragmatic in his foreign policy, conscious of Italy's need to placate wartime allies such as France and Britain, but in the late 1930s a discernible change seems to take place. It is too easy to dismiss this as the cavorting of a 'Sawdust Caesar',[11] mesmerised by Nazi power, and the book will try to determine whether, in fact, Mussolini was really driven by an ideological imperative during those years which saw Britain and France as degenerate nations, where Nazi Germany and Fascist Italy were new, thrusting dynamic powers. Can we, for example, make a link between Mussolini's adoption of anti-Semitic policies in 1938 and his friendship with Hitler? The consequences of the German alliance are well known and can be followed in the vivid pages of the diary of his son-in-law, Count Ciano.[12] The Duce becomes a shadow of his former self by 1942, ageing and wracked with pain from his long-standing stomach ulcer, unable to make decisions and suspicious of his entourage. His overthrow by King Victor Emmanuel and conspirators within his own Fascist Party in July 1943 follows a melancholy series of military disasters and embarrassing dependence on Germany. Attention will be paid to the question of how far Mussolini was aware of how his country and régime were sliding towards disaster and whether he seriously attempted to reverse this process.

Finally, we are left with the tragic sequel to Mussolini's career between October 1943 and April 1945, when he ran the so-called 'Republic of Salò', a Fascist mini-state existing only because of the support provided by German bayonets. There are suggestions that in this last phase Mussolini reverted to the radicalism of his youth, and the validity of such an analysis will be addressed in the book. There will also be an examination of Mussolini's legacy in post-war Italy and Europe.

Mussolini was born in 1883 and died in 1945. It has been claimed that, because of him, no one seeking to understand the twentieth-century world can ignore the phenomenon of Fascism. The book will seek to establish the validity of this thesis, in the context of Mussolini's life and times.

1

THE SHAPING OF A POLITICAL LEADER, 1883–1919

YOUTH

Benito Amilcare Andrea Mussolini was born on 29 July 1883 in the commune of Predappio in that part of Italy known as the Romagna. It was an impoverished area, which lacked amenities such as railways, and the nearest large town Forlì was some 15 kilometres away.

Mussolini was named after three left-wing heroes. One was the Mexican revolutionary Benito Júarez, the other two Amilcare Cipriani and Andrea Costa being heroes of the Italian Left. The choice of names was his father Alessandro's and reflected his left-wing political views. Alessandro was a potent influence on his eldest son and took him to political meetings while Benito was still a young boy. He, according to one of Mussolini's biographers, was 'stocky, dark-haired and dark complexioned, with a friendly face cut by a pair of soldierly moustaches, and short square hands'.[1] He was a blacksmith, lacking formal education but fiercely committed to socialism, even admiring the Russian anarchist leader Bakunin. Alessandro served time in prison for his political beliefs and was regarded locally as a dangerous firebrand. His son was to inherit this rebellious streak.

The contrast with Mussolini's mother Rosa was sharp. Where Alessandro was an atheistic rebel, Rosa was religious and conformist. She attended mass regularly and was a qualified elementary teacher. To a degree, therefore, she had married beneath her, but believed that education would be the means of lifting her children out of rural poverty (Mussolini's brother Arnaldo was born in 1885, and his sister Edvige in 1888). Rosa taught school in a room in the small family house which was turned into a granary in the summer vacation. To enable her to teach, Benito's grandmother lived with the family and looked after the children.

On his own admission in his autobiography, Mussolini was a difficult child. 'I was,' he wrote, 'unruly. And I was sometimes indiscreet. Youth has its passing restlessness and follies.'[2] Mussolini's 'restlessness' in fact involved wild and bullying behaviour towards his younger brother Arnaldo, an amiable fat child, and a tendency to dominate other village children. Sanitised later versions of Mussolini's childhood suggest that he was popular with his peers. This seems unlikely as the young Benito had a strong vindictive streak. He reportedly spent hours sharpening a stone so that he could stab another boy who had provoked him. He was always getting into fights, a fact which distressed his mother, so that Benito went to some lengths to try to disguise the cuts and bruises resulting from his various schoolboy scrapes.

As a child, Mussolini must have felt divided loyalties. His loyal Catholic mother ensured that he attended mass regularly (although the incense reportedly made him sick), while his socialist father, who was overfond of alcohol, took him to taverns. Later the dictator Mussolini was to write of how his father's heart and mind 'were always filled and pulsing with socialistic theories. His intense sympathies mingled with doctrines and causes.'[3] Alessandro was an atheist, but although his choice prevailed in naming Benito, it was Rosa who was to decide what sort of education their son received. Mussolini was to claim that his greatest love was for his mother, who was 'quiet, so tender, and yet so strong ... I often thought even in my earliest appreciations of human beings, of how faithful and patient her work was. To displease her was my one fear.'[4] Such filial devotion did not, however, prevent Benito's escapades, his fights or his theft of fruit and birds' eggs in the locality.

The adult Mussolini conceded that he was a bad boy. But he was not without intelligence. Initially, he had some difficulty in learning to speak (an irony for one who was to found a career on loquaciousness) so that his parents feared that he might be dumb. In fact, he proved to be intellectually sharp, but troublesome at his primary school (he crawled under the desks in the classroom to pinch the bare legs of other pupils!).

The son of the devoted Catholic Rosa was also guilty of throwing stones at children on their way to Sunday school. It was this sort of anti-social behaviour which persuaded his mother to send Benito to the Salesian school at Faenza in 1892 at the age of 9.

The Salesian Order's founding father was Dom Bosco (who reputedly had visions of the Devil). He preached a doctrine of non-violence towards pupils but also believed that the child, although to be cherished, should be kept under observation at all times. Such a régime was bound to be irksome to a rebellious youth like the young Benito Mussolini. He grew to hate the Salesian fathers, and one of his teachers was later to say that he had never had such a difficult student. Mussolini was a loner at Faenza, having only one real friend, 'a boy with a skull so thick that he let Benito amuse himself by hitting him hard with a brick'.[5]

Part of the problem was that Benito was obliged to accept the Salesian practice of making boys sit at three tables according to the amount of school fees they paid (Mussolini knew that his parents had difficulty in finding the fees). This meant that he had to sit at the table of the poorest children in the school, and not with the majority of his class-mates. Economic circumstances, therefore, deprived her son of the status which Rosa Mussolini's lower middle-class origins would have marked out for him. Although Mussolini claimed later that he was proud of his family's poverty from which he was to free himself, the evidence suggests otherwise.[6] He fiercely resented this social slight, and other irksome rules such as the requirement to remain silent at mealtimes and observe absolute silence during Easter week. He was still a rebel who led his fellows in a strike over bad food during his second year at Faenza and was then expelled for stabbing another boy at supper. Subsequently, the Salesians sued his family for the payment of fees. Neither of these facts is mentioned in Mussolini's own account of his schooldays. He recorded merely that at Faenza, 'I studied, slept well and grew'.[7]

For some months thereafter in 1893, the 10-year-old Mussolini was educated, with his mother's assistance, at home. He was then sent to school at Forlimpopoli which was also in the Romagna. This had several advantages as far as the restless Benito was concerned. It was not run by priests or nuns and attendance at mass was voluntary rather than compulsory. The food was better too, and the discipline less rigorous than that of the Salesians at Faenza.

Yet even this more liberal régime did not reform the young tearaway. Benito continued to bully other pupils and to get involved in fights. This behaviour led to suspension and to his being sent home for short periods when he was impertinent and (yet again) stabbed another pupil. It says something for the long-suffering staff at Forlimpopoli that Mussolini was allowed to return to school and complete his education six years later. Although he liked to pretend that he had been at the top of his class (he did show some aptitude for literature, language and music), Mussolini seems to have been only an average student. He was disliked by his fellow students as a bully, but some indications about his character were emerging.

The flamboyant dictator of the future played the trombone in the school band at the age of 17 (a characteristically noisy instrument perhaps for the later braggart public speaker). And in his last year, 1901, Mussolini received his first public recognition. He was asked to make a public speech about the composer Verdi before his entire school. Significantly, it was the socialist newspaper *Avanti!* (Forward), which would have been aware of his father's leftist links, that commented on the young man's performance. 'Last night,' wrote the paper's correspondent, 'the comrade student Mussolini commemorated the Swan of Busseto [a Verdi opera], delivering a much applauded speech.'[8]

Despite his stormy school years, Mussolini finished his education at Forlimpopoli with an elementary schoolteacher's diploma, the same qualification which his hard-working and conformist mother had obtained years before him. He was by now able to argue with his father's socialist friends in the family forge, and his education had produced some interesting pointers for the future. On his own admission, Mussolini was already a fervent admirer of the Roman Empire, and enjoyed history lessons about it. Lazy, fiery and ill-disciplined, he had frustrated his teachers and frightened his peers, but he was already a strong personality resentful about his humble origins and, like his father Alessandro, an instinctive socialist. One of Mussolini's biographers describes the 18-year-old student as having a 'pale face and his wide, black piercing eyes gave him the appearance of a poet or revolutionary, and he liked to think of himself as both'.[9] Mussolini was about to embark on the first part of his political apprenticeship.

He had also embarked on a sexual apprenticeship, and began to boast about love affairs. At 17, he was already visiting brothels in Forlì, a fact omitted from his sanitised 1928 English language autobiography, and his attitude towards women was chauvinistic. A passage in his posthumous 1947 Italian language autobiography is revealing about an early sexual experience. Mussolini wrote:

> I caught her on the stairs, throwing her into a corner behind a door, and made her mine. When she got up weeping and humiliated, she insulted me by saying that I had robbed her of her honour and it is not impossible she spoke the truth. But I ask you, what kind of honour can she have meant?[10]

Even allowing for the chauvinistic Italian culture of the turn of the last century, Mussolini's cynicism about sexual matters is striking. Throughout his life he was to regard women as little more than sexual playthings. By contrast, and surprisingly for a man who later claimed to encapsulate martial masculine virtues, Mussolini had virtually no male friends and gained something of a reputation in Predappio for being a misanthrope who rarely left the family house except at night.[11] He stalked the streets reciting parts of Dante's *Inferno* out loud (he had a very good memory) to disturb the sleeping bourgeoisie.

THE SOCIALIST

In February 1902, Mussolini got a job as a teacher in a school at Pieve Saliceto in the commune of Gualtieri. It seems likely that he got the job because the local socialist councillors preferred his brand of politics to that of the other candidates. Mussolini himself had a low opinion of his employers, regarding the local socialists in Gualtieri as being 'weak and flabby as spaghetti'.[12] He saw himself as a Bohemian intellectual who wore a broad-brimmed black hat and a floppy cravat, but he was too restless to be happy as a provincial schoolmaster.

Mussolini was also in financial difficulties. His salary at the school gave him just 56 lire a month and, of that, 40 lire went to cover board and lodging. This did not, however, prevent the young man from playing cards in local inns and getting involved in fierce political discussions. Fragments of the early autobiography suggest that Mussolini and other young tearaways were involved in raids on dance halls. Predictably the hot-tempered Benito also got into fights over girls (although these escapades were airbrushed out of later autobiographies).

In Gualtieri Mussolini had his first mistress, and his 1928 autobiography boasts of a wild and fierce love. In fact, he reverted to type and stabbed the woman in the thigh with the knife which he always carried with him. How he subsequently escaped prosecution remains a mystery, but a pattern of bullying and abusive behaviour towards women had been well established. Such behaviour was tolerated in Italian society of that time in a way which would be unlikely today.

On the positive side, Mussolini was marking out the beginnings of a career in politics when in March 1902 he was elected by the local teachers' association to represent them at an educational congress in Bologna. Despite his frequently wild and aggressive behaviour, Mussolini was still able to impress with his dynamism, which helped to cover up moral and intellectual weaknesses in his character. Nevertheless, this success in Gualtieri was not enough for the young man. In June 1902 he wrote to a friend telling him that he had decided to emigrate to Switzerland. But the year in Gualtieri was important, Mussolini wrote later, because his experiences there had made him decide, after the year teaching, not to return home to the Romagna. Predappio was, he wrote, 'a narrow world for me, with affection to be sure, but restricted'.[13] The journey to Switzerland began a two-year period when the young Mussolini drifted from country to country outside his homeland.

In fact Mussolini had little choice about leaving Gualtieri itself in the end. In characteristic style, he had become involved in a violent row with the local mayor and been forced to leave the school, bizarrely leaving his academic gown in part payment of the rent at his lodgings.

There may also have been another important reason why Mussolini decided to leave for Switzerland. Shortly after he made the decision to go, he would have become liable for military service, and there is at least an implication here that his decision to leave Italy was not a coincidence (the parallel with Mussolini's fellow dictator Adolf Hitler is an interesting one – Hitler fled his native Austria in 1913 for Germany to avoid being called up).[14] As is so often the case with Mussolini, it is hard to disentangle the truth from the lies and distortions of his propaganda machine. As he himself suggested, he may well have just been short of money or fled from the over-possessive mistress in Gualtieri.

Whatever the reasons, the move to Switzerland marked an important watershed in Benito's life. Even the news that his father had been arrested, which Benito received at the border town of Chiasso while waiting for his train to Switzerland, did not change his mind (Alessandro had become involved in a socialist campaign of smashing ballot boxes at Predappio in protest at unfair elections). His official 1928 autobiography makes no reference to his father's arrest, referring only to financial difficulties and 'the urge to escape' from Predappio.[15]

Mussolini arrived in Switzerland in July 1902 with just 2 lire in his pocket. In a letter to a friend, he described his struggle to survive as he was forced to take work as a hod-man for a builder:

> I made one hundred and twenty-one journeys with a hand-barrow full of stones up to the second floor of a building in the process of construction. In the evening the muscles of my arms were swollen. I ate some potatoes roasted upon cinders and threw myself, in all my clothes, on to my bed, a pile of straw.[16]

Mussolini also claimed to have become so impoverished in Switzerland that he had to hide out in a public lavatory and under a bridge.

Such stories need to be treated with caution. The letter quoted above, for example, is to be found in a biography of Mussolini by his one-time mistress and admirer, Margherita Sarfatti. Certainly contemporary photographs of him show someone who is reasonably well dressed and not the skeletal figure described by Mussolini later. Such exaggerations were doubtless designed to create the impression that the 19-year-old future dictator had shared the sufferings of the workers.

What seems beyond dispute is that Mussolini held a lot of different jobs while in Switzerland. He was variously a butcher's boy, an errand boy for a wine shop and a worker in a chocolate factory, as well as a hod-man.

POLITICAL INFLUENCES

Mussolini's chief interest was still in politics. While living in the Swiss city of Lausanne, he met Angelica Balabanoff, a young Marxist from a middle-class family in the Ukraine. Balabanoff, who knew Mussolini for a dozen years, was a genuine left-wing revolutionary (who also knew the Russian Communist leader Lenin). She provided us with a revealing description of the young Mussolini who had turned up at a socialist meeting she was addressing in Lausanne. Balabanoff was struck by Mussolini's appearance: 'I had never seen a more wretched human being ... he seemed more concerned with his inner turmoil than what I was saying'.[17]

Balabanoff tried to help him with a translation of a German pamphlet for which he had been offered 50 francs. But she noticed the essential egotism of the man and the fact that, in intellectual terms, he was completely undisciplined. She believed (rightly) that Mussolini's radicalism and vociferous anti-clericalism were more a product of his early environment than of any real conviction or understanding.

Nevertheless, under her influence Mussolini apparently (although some doubt remains) began to attend lectures by the influential political scientist Vilfredo Pareto at the University of Lausanne. He also dabbled, in intellectual grasshopper fashion, with the ideas of Nietzsche, the German philosopher, the French theorist Sorel and Buddhism.

In public, however, he remained a braggart. An attempt to heckle a visiting Belgian socialist during a lecture resulted in a humiliating rebuff for Mussolini. By this time his provocative opinions were attracting the attention of the Swiss authorities, who expelled him from Lausanne.

Mussolini then took refuge in the town of Annemasse on the French–Swiss border and began an affair with the wife of a local official, before moving on to Zurich. He again moved in local socialist and Marxist circles and became impressed by the Germanic trait of discipline (Zurich was in the German-speaking part of Switzerland), which he was later to claim that the Italians lacked. This was ironic given his own lack of that quality, but his political activities were sufficiently provocative to get him expelled from Zurich, although a brawl in a restaurant was the immediate cause.

After a brief period in Germany working as a mason, Mussolini returned to Switzerland in 1903 and settled in the city of Berne. By now he had become known as a contributor to socialist journals and as a speaker at meetings. It was clear also that Marx was the single most important intellectual influence in his life, although Fascists in Italy later tried to deny this.

This period is rather glossed over in Mussolini's autobiography, probably because it ended ingloriously with his expulsion yet again from Switzerland, this time for stirring up industrial unrest amongst Italian migrant workers. In July 1903, Mussolini was arrested in Berne and handed over to the Italian police, who had to release him for lack of evidence that he was an agitator, although they opened a dossier on him and his activities. However, Mussolini knew that young men of his age were due to be drafted into the army in January 1904, so he promptly re-crossed the border into Switzerland. He had forged the passport which he presented to the Aliens Registration Office in Geneva to make it appear that it expired in 1905, but it was such a crude forgery that he was re-arrested and expelled from Geneva in April 1904. Mussolini's refusal to do military service was, he claimed, not the result of cowardice but because he was not prepared to fight for the corrupt system of Giolitti in which he did not believe. Nevertheless, Fascist accounts later tried to disguise the fact that Mussolini, the macho dictator, had avoided military service as a young man. Mussolini also claimed, in an attempt to sanitise this episode, that he had encouraged other soldiers to desert.[18] His statement in the autobiography that the Swiss had deported him because of 'some intemperance in my words'[19] crudely disguised the fact that his violence of language and threatening behaviour over a period of years had made him, in the eyes of the Head of Police and Justice in Geneva, a dangerous foreigner who needed to be removed from Swiss soil.

Yet once back in Italy, Mussolini faced the unavoidable fact that if he refused to do his military service, he would be imprisoned. At this point, pragmatism triumphed and he presented himself for service with the 10th Bersaglieri Regiment in Verona. Like his future fellow dictator, Adolf Hitler, Mussolini enjoyed military life and did not try to rebel against military authority as he had invariably done at other stages of his youth. He was also allowed to take periodic leave during his eighteen months in the military, and to visit Predappio, where he helped his father in the forge. The two men apparently read Machiavelli's famous book *The Prince* aloud together, and Mussolini endorsed the author's low opinion of the human race in general. Machiavelli's merciless analysis of Renaissance politics may also have served to sharpen the men's distaste for the existing Italian political system, but it is interesting that Alessandro still played such an active part in his son's intellectual life.

It was at this point in his life, one of relative stability, that Mussolini suffered a shattering personal blow. In February 1905 his mother Rosa died of meningitis, her errant son arriving only just in time to be recognised by the dying woman. Rosa was only 48 years old, and there is no reason to doubt the genuineness of Mussolini's grief, increased perhaps by the knowledge that he had often been a sore trial to her. 'From me,' he was to say later, 'had been taken the one dear and truly near living being – the one soul closest and eternally adherent to my own responses.'[20]

It is dangerous perhaps to indulge in overt psychological analysis of the impact the early loss of his mother had on Mussolini's character. If he took after either of his parents it was his father and his capacity for violent, reckless action. He shared too his father's obsession with politics, if not his capacity to remain loyal to a cause. Nonetheless it is easy enough to appreciate that for a volatile, unstable personality such as Mussolini, his mother's death, when he was only 21, represented a genuine trauma.[21]

Yet again, Mussolini reverted to his earlier profession of schoolmaster, obtaining a post at Caneva in the commune of Tolmezzo in the Venetian Alps. He had completed his military service in September 1906, but did not join his father when Alessandro was forced to move out of the schoolmistress's house in Predappio to make way for the new teacher. All his biographers, and Mussolini himself, agree that he was not a good teacher. The children (forty of them in the class) liked him, but he could not control them. He swore at them but they were not afraid of him, and he was reduced to giving them sweets to keep them in order. This makes the nickname the children gave Mussolini, *il tiranno* (the tyrant), somewhat ironic. Neither did his personal appearance do him any favours. He was often dirty with unlaced shoes and long, straggling hair (the famous bald pate came later).

Haphazard intellectualism was still a strong feature of Mussolini's character. He took Latin lessons from a local priest (while also lampooning the Church), studied Indian arithmetic and German philosophy and literature. His personal life remained chaotic. He drank too much, borrowed money and (as ever) chased women (one of the reasons for his prolonged stay in Predappio was that he was having an affair with a local woman). Even he was to write later that his nine months in Tolmezzo were a period of 'moral deterioration'.[22] It was during this period that Mussolini also contracted syphilis and had to be treated for it at a local hospital (to begin with he had, in typically melodramatic fashion, threatened to shoot himself). An affair with his landlord's wife went in parallel with police charges against him for alleged blasphemy in the classroom. Under the circumstances, it is hardly surprising that the local authorities did not renew Mussolini's contract at Caneva at the end of the academic year. He had been identified as a potential troublemaker when he started work at the school, and the police had kept him under constant observation.

Mussolini was, therefore, forced by circumstances to move into his father's new house near Predappio. Late in 1907, he passed an examination in French which allowed him to get a post as a French teacher at a private school at Oneglia on the Italian Riviera. In Oneglia, Mussolini renewed his political activities. Indeed, he appears to have written entire editions of the small local socialist newspaper under various pseudonyms. The local police already had him under observation and he was ordered to leave Oneglia in June 1908 when they were alerted to a series of savage attacks he had made on the Catholic Church.

Once more the young man had to return to Predappio, where later that year he was given a short jail sentence for disturbing the peace and making seditious speeches. It seemed as if the blacksmith's son would never settle down to achieve anything of real significance. Alessandro's comments on his son's escapades are unrecorded; but as a man in his fifties, he must have found Benito's behaviour something of a trial.

Then, at last, Mussolini's socialist links secured him an important post. In 1909 the Party in the Trentino offered him the post of Secretary of the Chamber of Labour (the province was actually in a part of Italy still under Austrian rule). The post carried with it the responsibility for running a small four-page weekly called *L'Avvenire del Lavoratore* (The Worker's Future) and for organising the local socialists. It was an opportunity for Mussolini to develop his journalistic and organisational skills. But he made little effort to develop the latter, nor did he like the area. Instead, he polished his French and German written language skills in the superior Austrian libraries.

INTELLECTUAL INFLUENCES

Mussolini was now moving into a phase of his life where political journalism was the dominant feature, and it is useful at this point to examine more closely the main intellectual influences upon him. Understandably his later Fascist biographies make no reference to the impact of Marxism on him. This would have been an embarrassing admission for a Fascist dictator. Indeed, with the exception of Pareto, there is no real reference given in Mussolini's autobiography of any major intellectual influence. Angelica Balabanoff thought that he was not a true socialist revolutionary at all, and the characteristic of his early years as a political activist was a belief in the use of violence. He despised the middle classes as insipid and advised his fellow socialists to boycott the institutions of the bourgeois state, represented as they were by men such as Giolitti.

Mussolini did acknowledge a debt to the Frenchman Georges Sorel, who criticised Marxism for creating a form of utopia which could not lead to real revolutionary change. Sorel also hated constitutional politics with its parliaments and elections, and preached the need for the 'energising power of a dynamic myth',[23] and myth was certainly to be a prominent feature of Mussolini's Fascism. To some extent also the Italian experience after 1870 was based on a myth – the idea that Italy could be a great power comparable with Britain, France or Germany.

Mussolini was also influenced by Pareto's theory of élites and his anti-parliamentarianism, but it is likely that he was mostly swayed by his own instincts which favoured the aggressive over the consensual. This was what attracted him to the German philosopher Nietzsche, who also influenced Hitler. Nietzsche's contempt for the Christian virtues of love and forbearance appealed to the wild, anti-clerical young man, as did his concept of the superman, the heroic leader who dominated the masses. These were profoundly anti-democratic, anti-egalitarian influences, odd bedfellows for a man who was supposed to be a socialist. Socialism was meant to be about protecting the rights of the working class and ultimately, in its revolutionary Marxist form, about seizing power for the workers. From his earliest years, however, it is clear that Mussolini's personality and preferences made a belief in such concepts skin deep. Later, indeed, Mussolini was to write that between 1903 and 1914 his experience of socialism 'was not a doctrinal experience. My doctrine during that period had been the doctrine of action.'[24] The quotation lays bare a central component of Mussolini's character: his anti-intellectualism and essential contempt for theory. What counted increasingly was action, and the more violent the action, the better. Yet he could continue to admire individual intellectuals.

THE JOURNALIST

Mussolini's experience as a journalist was very important because it was to reveal to him the importance of propaganda. He soon became bored with his post in the Trentino and, after six months, changed jobs and went to work for Cesare Battisti, the Chief Editor of the newspaper *Il Popolo d'Italia*. Mussolini was effusive about Battisti (a nationalist who was executed by the Austrians during the First World War), whom he described as a 'noble and proud soul'.[25] But he only actually worked for Battisti for a month. Nevertheless, it was an invaluable apprenticeship, providing Mussolini with the technical knowledge of journalism he needed. *Il Popolo* was a well-known local newspaper, not just the sort of news-sheet he was responsible for in the Trentino.

This seven-month period as a journalist was also characterised by what had become the norm in Mussolini's behaviour. His language in print was unrestrained and violent, and resulted in imprisonment on several occasions as the Austrian authorities were outraged by his extremism. He did not, however, as he later claimed, get expelled from the Trentino because he wrote that it should be Italian and not Austrian. In fact, he deemed such an annexation impractical in 1909. What brought about his expulsion was the revolutionary language in his newspapers, which contrasted with the milder language of his social-ist colleagues. They preferred 'reformist' socialism which sought to improve the conditions of the workers rather than support outright rev-olution and the bloody overthrow of the existing capitalist system. It seems likely that Mussolini's fellow socialists were glad to see the back of him when he was expelled. Most of them were reformists rather than the sort of international revolutionary socialist that Mussolini posed as. Their differences with him did however reflect the major division in the socialist world which had come with the reformist revolt against revolu-tionary Marxism in 1900. This followed the publication of a book by the German Bernstein, the father of revisionism and therefore of social democracy, in 1899, under the title of *Evolutionary Socialism*. Mussolini rejected such heresy as a betrayal of international socialism, just as he then regarded patriotism as a petty bourgeois vice (although this made his relationship with the nationalist Battisti somewhat odd).

The period between 1909 and 1914 saw Mussolini's views change slowly. In 1909 he was still an international socialist following the

Marxist line that patriotism was a middle-class vice and that socialists should be working for the liberation of the international proletariat. It was ridiculous, Mussolini argued in his newspaper, that Italian peasants were impoverished while the country wasted valuable resources on military spending and colonial adventure.

Giolitti's decision to attack Libya in 1911, in a misguided attempt to appease Italian nationalists on the political Right, was a godsend for Mussolini. He attacked the invasion ferociously, claiming that it was a crime against humanity (more than twenty years later, the same man would be responsible for the gassing and slaughter of thousands of defenceless Ethiopian tribesmen). His articles equated patriotism with imperialism and militarism.

At the Socialist Party Congress at Reggio Emilia in 1912, a ragged-looking and already slightly balding Mussolini made a fiery and impressive speech denouncing the Libyan invasion and moderate socialist leaders such as Bissolati, who adopted bourgeois policies. Bissolati's particular offence had been to visit the royal palace to congratulate King Victor Emmanuel on surviving an assassination attempt. Mussolini regarded this tugging of the forelock to the monarchy as unacceptable for a socialist. He had argued that the successful assassination of King Umberto by an anarchist in 1900 was justified as an act of protest.

Mussolini's speech went down well with party activists, and his motion to expel Bissolati was carried by a large majority. At the age of only 29, Mussolini, together with his mentor Angelica Balabanoff, found themselves members of the dominant grouping in the party directorate. A few months later, Mussolini's first great triumph as a demagogue was followed by his appointment as editor of the socialist newspaper *Avanti!* He now had a national platform, but he ran the paper like the dictator he was to become. No dissent was tolerated, and he ruthlessly sacked older journalists who might not agree with his particular line. The reformist line of people such as Bissolati was roundly denounced but Mussolini's vivid, aggressive tone sold newspapers. He was able to double *Avanti!*'s circulation as he boasted in his autobiography (for once, the boast was true).

In electoral terms, too, Mussolini's hard-line, anti-reformist position seemed to pay dividends. In the 1913 Italian general election, the Socialist vote went up to almost a million and the Party got 53 seats in parliament. Mussolini himself tried and failed to get elected in his home seat of Forlì in the Romagna but was subsequently elected as a town councillor in Milan, marking a move for him to a bigger urban industrial stage. What was clear by now was that Mussolini was no democrat; his speeches rammed home the point that the masses needed only a blind faith in the dynamic leadership of ruthless charismatic leaders such as himself. He told a lover at the time that he was going to be a man of destiny. When she asked, 'Like Napoleon?', he replied with his usual bombast: 'No, greater than Napoleon'.[26]

For a man walking with destiny, in his own eyes at least, Mussolini gave an impression of nervous indecisiveness in the so-called 'Red Week' of June 1914 when massive street demonstrations rocked the government. Smaller towns were even taken over by Socialist and Anarchist militants, tax registers destroyed and railway stations occupied. All this was in response to the killing of three anti-militarist demonstrators in the town of Ancona. Even the fairly conservative CGL (the Socialist Trade Union Confederation) joined in and supported the demand for a general strike.

'Red Week' appears to have been totally spontaneous. But Mussolini was taken by surprise. He saw the potential for revolution in the mass disturbances, but, unlike other socialist leaders such as Nenni, he stayed at his editorial desk. Mussolini, the advocate of violent action, took part in just one mass demonstration. His readers could not have been very impressed.

THE COMING OF WAR

Luckily for Mussolini, his reputation was saved in the short run by the advent of the First World War in July 1914. Ostensibly, Italy should have entered the war at once, as she had joined the Triple Alliance of Germany, Austria-Hungary and Germany in 1882, but the Italians argued that Austria-Hungary and Germany had provoked the war, and that the Treaty was defensive only in character. Many Italians, however, saw Austria-Hungary as the traditional enemy, whereas Britain and especially France had actively assisted the *Risorgimento* in the 1860s. There was also the question of the Austrian-administered Trentino, considered by most Italians to be rightfully theirs.

In July 1914 Mussolini was consistent in his demand for Italian neutrality. Like all Marxists at the time he saw the war as a bourgeois imperialist adventure which the international working class should boycott. Mussolini maintained this position for several months but soon came to see it as untenable. Partly this was because it was clear that the international working class had only rallied around the national flags (in Germany, for example, the large avowedly Marxist Social Democratic Party had, with a few notable exceptions like Rosa Luxemberg, backed the war effort). But it was also because Mussolini could see that the issue of intervention was likely to split the Party. Some Party comrades had already defected over the issue.

Slowly Mussolini began to alter his position to one whereby he conceded that involvement in the First World War might indeed be possible. There was the hope, too, that war might lead to international revolution and the overthrow of capitalism. Subsequently, Mussolini was to distort the chronology of his move towards interventionism. He stated that, inspired by nationalists such as Battisti and Corridoni, he was able to 'drag with me a fraction of the Socialists in favour of War'.[27] It is certainly true that on 18 October 1914 Mussolini came out in favour of Italian entry into the war against Austria-Hungary and Germany, arguing that Italy could not remain on the sidelines when such crucial events were taking place (by then, Germany's drive to end the war by defeating France in six weeks had failed). He did this without consulting colleagues on the editorial board of *Avanti!* and, when the matter was debated, he found himself in a minority of one. Mussolini, therefore, resigned. His lengthy flirtation with socialism had effectively ended, and Mussolini the extreme nationalist was emerging. He had also discovered that he was a vibrant and persuasive speaker.

MARRIAGE

The years 1909 to 1914 had also been important in Mussolini's personal life. In 1912, just before he took up his post as editor of *Avanti!*, his father, who was such an important influence upon him, died at the early age of 57. His son's respect seems to have been genuine enough.

In 1910, Mussolini the philanderer married, threatening to shoot himself if his bride's parents did not agree to the marriage. His wife Rachele was, in fact, the daughter of Alessandro Mussolini's mistress. She did not share her husband's interest in politics and her focus was overwhelmingly on the family. Rachele had good reason to be jealous about

Mussolini's persistent womanising but she proved to be a loyal wife. Mussolini's hypocritical statements about the importance of family life can be treated with scorn. He was never faithful to his wife although they were to have five children together. Yet Rachele had as much insight into his character as anyone, saying that her husband 'seemed like a lion, but was in reality a *pover'uomo*, a poor chap'.[28] His children, Edda, Vittorio, Bruno, Romano and Anna Maria (born as late as 1929 when Mussolini was 46), saw very little of him and Mussolini conceded that he was not the best of fathers. It was fortunate for the children that Rachele proved to be a dutiful wife and mother, although she disliked Rome and would not travel there after her husband came to power, unless forced to do so. According to Edda in an interview given in 1995 (which has only recently come to light), even Rachele was driven by her husband's inattention into taking a lover.[29] Mussolini, although apparently surprised, was hardly in a position to be critical. Those who knew them, in any case, observed that he seemed to be rather frightened of his wife.

Nevertheless, Rachele could not prevent her husband from having lengthy affairs with Margherita Sarfatti and Leda Rafanelli. Both women were a little older than Mussolini, and, in Rafanelli's case, Mussolini claimed to have found a soul mate although they often quarrelled bitterly.[30] He seemed to be intoxicated by the fact that Rafanelli had spent some time in Egypt and he spoke of her oriental allure. Their affair also coincided with Mussolini's time in Milan with its sophisticated urban chic. But the lovers fell out over the Italian decision to enter the war, which Leda Rafanelli denounced in print.

WAR AND REVOLUTION

Mussolini was both surprised and embittered by the refusal of his socialist colleagues to support his stand on intervention in 1914. His response was to set up his own newspaper, *Il Popolo d'Italia*, which his journalistic flair soon made into a going concern. The paper was still avowedly socialist, but Mussolini took on board some surprising financial bedfellows, an early indication that in his ambitious drive for power he was drifting further and further to the Right. Those who funded the paper included the industrial giant Fiat (which would clearly gain from Italian entry into the war), agrarian interests and foreign powers such as Britain and France who were keen to get Italy involved as well. It has also been suggested that the Italian government itself funded the paper after eventual entry.[31] Mussolini angrily rejected accusations made at the time that he was taking bribes. His already clear commitment to Italian intervention in the war also made it unlikely that the editorial position of his newspaper was actually influenced by those who funded him.

Il Popolo d'Italia (The People of Italy) first appeared on 15 November 1914. Mussolini now argued that war would lead to social revolution in Italy, but also that Italians could not remain 'inert spectators of this tremendous drama',[32] and would show their credentials as a great power on the battlefield. His obsession with the need for Italians to show their military virility became more and more evident in his editorials. Characteristically, Mussolini also claimed that his very first editorial 'turned a large part of public opinion towards the intervention of Italy in the War, side by side with England and France'.[33] This was, of course, a sizeable exaggeration. Italian animosity towards Germany's ally Austria-Hungary was of long-standing and did not need Mussolini's polemics in his newspaper to arouse it, but the campaign in *Il Popolo* was one of many pressures on the then Prime Minister Salandra to enter the war on the side of the Western democracies. But Mussolini's journalistic acuteness made him realise the potency of the Italians' desire for an Alpine frontier, which meant taking the Trentino away from the Austrians.

In political terms, Mussolini was open to accusations of glaring inconsistency. On the one hand, he talked of wars of national liberation against imperialism, saying, for example, that Italy should not claim Trieste and Fiume from a new, independent Yugoslavia because the Yugoslav working class were brothers. But on the other, he now justified the colonial war in Libya in 1911–12, which he had denounced so ferociously at the time. Socialist window-dressing was covering an increasingly aggressive nationalist agenda, but criticism of Mussolini's volte-face needs to be seen in a contemporary context. Britain and France, both more democratic states than Italy, showed no disposition to recognise nationalist aspirations inside their colonial empires, while at the same time offering freedom to the Slav peoples like the Poles and Czechs inside the Austro-Hungarian Empire.

What cannot be denied, however, is the speed with which Mussolini's opinions changed. For as 1915 went on, he moved even closer to the position of the Nationalist Right by demanding the annexation of

Trieste and Fiume together with the securing of an Alpine frontier and Italian participation in the carve up of the Ottoman Turkish Empire in the Middle East which would undoubtedly follow the defeat of Germany and her allies. Mussolini continued to hammer home the point that Italy's national honour demanded that the country's unwarlike image and inferior status in the eyes of foreigners (Bismarck had famously remarked that the Italians had 'a large appetite [for territorial gains] but very poor teeth') be destroyed. There were also shameful reverses to be avenged, for example the humiliating defeat at the hands of Ethiopian tribesmen at Adowa in 1896.

It is perhaps too easy to see Mussolini as the ultimate political adventurer who was prepared to do anything to achieve power. Certain constants did exist on his political map, certainly from 1914–15 onwards. Italian greatness had to be asserted, and a move away from enfeebled democracy towards virile nationalism ensured. At the same time, Mussolini's overriding obsession with personal success remained the dominant feature of his political life.

ITALIAN ENTRY INTO THE WAR

Despite Mussolini's efforts, most Italians were opposed to entry into the First World War until well into 1915. The Socialist Party, which had expelled Mussolini in November 1914, remained non-interventionist, as were most politically active Catholics (encouraged by Pope Benedict XV). Reports to the government by regional officials also showed that the public feared war which they thought would bring the country no benefits.[34]

The decision to enter ultimately owed much to political manoeuvring by the country's leadership. Salandra had initially been a neutralist, like his chief parliamentary opponent Giolitti, but he came to see the war as a means of strengthening his shaky position as national leader. It was also true that the Entente powers (Britain, France and Russia) could make a more enticing offer to bring Italy into the war than could their opponents. On Trieste, for example, Austria-Hungary was willing merely to designate it as a 'free city' while also conceding the right to an Italian university. By contrast, the Entente powers could offer outright annexation of the city by Italy, plus the South Tyrol, the Trentino, Istria and half of Dalmatia (facing Italy across the Adriatic Sea).

Thus it was that on 26 April 1915 Italy signed the Treaty of London whereby she promised to enter the war on the side of Britain and France within a month in exchange for the above-mentioned territories. Ten days later the Italians renounced the Triple Alliance of 1882 which bound them to Germany and Austria-Hungary.

Giolitti was not told about the secret Treaty of London and was furious when he found out about it, but he did not dare to challenge the decision to go to war. King Victor Emmanuel III did not even bother to consult parliament before signing the declaration of war against the Austrians, thus demonstrating the shaky nature of Italian democracy. Neither was the behaviour of the king and Salandra without precedent. Giolitti had not consulted parliament before sanctioning the war with Libya in 1911. He also was aware of an intimidating level of right-wing street violence and thuggery orchestrated by Mussolini and the extreme nationalist poet Gabriele D'Annunzio in Milan and elsewhere. The interventionists consisted of a curious rag bag of Rightists and Leftists (from Marinetti's ultra-violent, nationalist Futurists to reformist Socialists such as Bissolati and excitable young Republicans like Nenni), but they were nonetheless both noisy and effective.

It was an hour of triumph for Benito Mussolini. In 1919 he was to boast that he had started a revolution in May 1915 'which was exquisitely and divinely revolutionary, because it overturned a shameful situation at home'.[35] Nevertheless, his expectations about the war proved to be woefully wide of the mark. He thought that Italy's involvement would tip the scales so that there would be a rapid Entente victory. Instead, Italy fought a bloody and largely inconclusive campaign against the Austrians from 1915 until the final sudden victory (with Anglo-French help) in 1918. Mussolini also believed that Italy's economy was robust enough not to be adversely affected by the war when, in fact, it merely highlighted the country's economic deficiencies. Yet, although he did not know it, the grim attritional war into which Italy had thrust itself was to give Mussolini the opportunity he craved.

Mussolini later tried to pretend in his autobiography that he had volunteered to join the Italian army, saying that he had done so 'as soon as War was declared'.[36] This was not the case. Mussolini expected the struggle to be short, so he remained at his editorial desk, only joining the army when the process of conscription forced him to do so. There is nothing, however, to suggest that Mussolini was not a brave and effective soldier, although the army may have been reluctant to take him because of his record as a political subversive.

He was promoted to sergeant and resented the fact that he was not offered an officer's commission, but could not subsequently resist the urge to make absurd distortions of his military record. These included creating the myth that he had forty grenade fragments taken from his body without an anaesthetic (it *was* true that Mussolini's grenade thrower had blown up!) and that the Austrians had deliberately shelled his hospital because they knew their 'enemy' was being treated there.[37] This nonsense found its way into heroic Fascist myth. Mussolini's distortions were echoed interestingly by Adolf Hitler, his future fellow dictator, then serving in France. Hitler claimed to have been a front-line soldier engaged in hand-to-hand combat when in fact he was a messenger running between different positions. Like Mussolini, he was a brave enough soldier (courageous enough to receive the Iron Cross First Class whereas Mussolini did not receive a similar award), but his role was not glamorous enough for the inaccurate version of his early life presented in his book *Mein Kampf*. As Hitler's acolyte, Josef Goebbels, was to write later: 'When you are going to lie, lie big'. Both Hitler and Mussolini were adept at the practice.

Mussolini's wounds were real enough for him to be invalided out of the Italian army in June 1917. He then returned to his position as editor of *Il Popolo d'Italia* and castigated the government for poor leadership and lack of fighting spirit. At one point it appears that Mussolini and other discontented politicians discussed the possibility of a coup d'état with the then army Commander-in-Chief Cadorna, only for Cadorna to develop cold feet about the scheme.[38]

THE RUSSIAN REVOLUTION

In March 1917 the Russian Tsar, Nicholas II, was forced to abdicate, and in November the Provisional Government which had displaced him was brought down in its turn by the Bolsheviks under their leader Lenin. Mussolini welcomed the revolution in Russia – he had after all expected the war to bring about revolution in his own country – but he was unimpressed by Lenin, whom he regarded as just a new version of Tsar Nicholas. Partly his attitude was dictated by his resentment of Russia's effective withdrawal from the war, which allowed the Austro-Hungarians to reinforce the Alpine frontier. 1917 was also the year of the catastrophic Italian defeat at Caporetto in October which coincided with the Russian Revolution, and which Mussolini blamed on the feebleness of parliamentary government in Italy, socialist anti-war propaganda and poor leadership. 'Never,' Mussolini wrote later, 'have I experienced a sorrow equal to that which I suffered after news of the defeat of Caporetto.'[39] This feeling was probably genuine enough, even if Mussolini looked to the wrong quarters for an explanation. Enthusiasm for the war was much weaker in the army than he liked to pretend (Cadorna blamed the defeat at Caporetto on cowardice and had thousands of soldiers executed).

Mussolini's position had become more and more authoritarian as the war entered its decisive phase in 1918. He was convinced by now that parliamentary government must be swept away and replaced by some form of dictatorship. It was true that in some respects Mussolini was 'a true prophet ... [who] was not far wrong in declaring that democracy had been killed during the war'.[40] He was certainly astute enough to see that the end of the war, which would bring with it the demobilisation of hundreds of thousands of disillusioned army veterans, would offer opportunities to right-wing nationalists like himself. Mussolini had begun to talk about *'trincerocrazia'* or 'government by the trenches' as early as 1916, as he sensed that his fellow soldiers would not be content with the corrupt Giolittism of pre-war days. The common experience of death and privation in the trenches would, Mussolini believed, cut across party political boundaries in setting up expectations about a new, more dynamic post-war Italy.

The war ended with dramatic suddenness in the autumn of 1918, with the decisive event on the Italian front being the shattering Austro-Hungarian defeat at Vittorio Veneto in October. The victory was achieved only with Anglo-French assistance, which had been made available to the Italians after the disaster at Caporetto a year earlier, but this did not dent Mussolini's capacity for hyperbole. Vittorio Veneto was described by him as the greatest victory in world history when, in fact, the decisive struggle was between the Germans and the Anglo-French in the West. Nevertheless, it appeared to provide Italy with the opportunity for territorial aggrandisement which Mussolini had been demanding since 1915. The Adriatic and the Mediterranean were now to become Italian seas, and Italy the dominant Mediterranean power. At the same time, his newspaper dropped any last pretension to be social-ist. Mussolini had, after all, been expelled from the Italian Socialist Party four years before, and was presumably only preserving the illusion of socialist leanings to strengthen his credentials with the working class. Mussolini's rejection of US President Woodrow Wilson's 14 Peace Points, with their commitment to self-determination in Central and Eastern Europe, showed how far the young politician and journalist had moved away from the socialist position.

The war assisted Mussolini in two ways. First, the Italian economy, weak as it was compared with Italy's Anglo-French allies, was more affected by post-war inflation and unemployment. And second, the war brought about a polarisation of Italian politics between the patriotic Right and the Left. Mussolini and his supporters were able to demonise the Left for being unpatriotic, and he also soon realised the potential of anti-Bolshevik propaganda which focused on the threat to Italian life from Russian-inspired communism. Landowners, industrialists and Catholics alike were petrified by the threat from communism in post-war Italy, even though the Italian Communist Party, the PCI, did not actually come into existence until 1921. This fear was partly a result of socialist revolutionary rhetoric, which frightened the middle classes and forced them to look to the Right for a saviour.

The impact of the war in Italy needs emphasising. Italy lost 5.1 per cent of the working male population although this compared favourably with the 10.5 per cent lost by France and the 15.1 per cent of Germans of military age killed. As has been seen, this devastating human loss was combined with inflationary pressures which in turn forced up unem-ployment. This helped to create the pool of the disillusioned which cre-ated recruits for Mussolini, even if Italian unemployment rates were not as high as those in Britain and Germany. But the genesis of the Far Right goes back to before 1914. Corradini's *Il Regno* (1903) provided the Rightists with an influential journal, and increasing dissatisfaction with Giolitti-style democracy brought about the formation of the Italian Nationalist Association in 1910. This right-wing nationalism was anti-democratic, élitist and imperialistic, stances that Mussolini himself had adopted long before December 1917 when he wrote in *Il Popolo d'Italia* of his belief in 'an anti-Marxist and ... national socialism'.

Nevertheless, the pool of unemployed ex-soldiers and the rise in liv-ing costs, together with a lack of faith in Italy's democratic institutions, provided Mussolini and the Nationalist Right with a favourable post-war environment. Especially as the Socialists, too, poured scorn on the existing Italian governmental system.

THE 'MUTILATED VICTORY'

Opponents of the existing system such as Mussolini were further encouraged by the failure of the new Prime Minister, Orlando, to secure the sort of territorial gains most Italians wanted. Orlando cut a poor figure in comparison with the other Allied leaders, Wilson, Lloyd George and Clemenceau. Newspapers may have spoken of the 'Big Four' but the weakness of Italy's position became painfully obvious at the 1919 Versailles Peace Conference. President Woodrow Wilson, who believed that secret diplomacy had helped to cause the war, would not abide by all the terms of the Treaty of London, and the French also opposed cession of territory by the newly established Yugoslav State. This meant that Italian demands for Trieste and Dalmatia would not be honoured. Neither was Italy invited to participate in the carving up of Turkey's Middle Eastern empire, which fell into Anglo-French hands, albeit organised under the League of Nations mandate system. Orlando returned to Italy in disgrace and D'Annunzio talked of a *'vittoria mutilata'* or 'mutilated victory'. Most Italians felt that they had been cheated by their allies.

This was fertile territory for Mussolini. But in the short term he was upstaged by Gabriele D'Annunzio. In September 1919 it was the colourful poet who, together with mutinous units in the Italian army, seized Fiume from the Yugoslavs. Mussolini had apparently spoken to D'Annunzio about such a coup beforehand. D'Annunzio also wrote to Mussolini (according to his version of events) saying: 'The dice are on the table. Tomorrow I shall take Fiume with force of arms. The God of Italy assist us!'[41] But the harmony between the two men described in Mussolini's autobiography is misleading. Mussolini was undoubtedly alarmed that his fellow nationalist had stolen a march on him. Neither did he go and join D'Annunzio in Fiume, with the consequence that the latter called him a coward. In reality, Mussolini was in a difficult position. He had to support D'Annunzio's annexation of the city, but he did not want to be associated with failure. In fact, Fiume had not even been mentioned in 1915 in the Treaty of London so its seizure was totally unjustified (Italian nationalists justified it by saying that there was a majority of Italians in Trieste and its hinterland). But because D'Annunzio's coup was so popular in Italy, Prime Minister Nitti dared not expel D'Annunzio by force. In November 1920 a compromise was reached under the terms of the Treaty of Rapallo, whereby Fiume was to become independent, that is, not Italian but not Yugoslav either. The rebel leader obstinately refused to surrender the city even though by then 'most people had got bored with D'Annunzio'.[42] On Christmas Day 1920, Giolitti, Prime Minister yet again, had to send in the Italian navy to force him into doing so.

The Fiume episode highlighted the weakness of the Italian State, and the popularity (however transient) of dramatic nationalist coups. It was also a seminal event for Mussolini and the Fascist movement which he had set up in March 1919. Many of the artefacts of Italian Fascism first appeared in Fiume with D'Annunzio and his supporters. Thus the 'uniforms and the blackshirts (originally worn by the "*arditi*" or shock troops in World War One), the Roman salute, the "oceanic" rallies ... were plagiarised from D'Annunzio'.[43] But Mussolini would ensure that D'Annunzio, a famous aviator and poet in his own right, never got the chance to upstage him again. D'Annunzio had an international reputation, was a war hero (who had led a daring aerial raid on Vienna in 1918) and was, according to Mussolini's latest biographer, 'a credible national leader'.[44] He was, therefore, a real threat to Mussolini, who regarded him with wary respect. The claim in Fascist propaganda after 1922 that the two men had collaborated over the Fiume occupation was nonsense however.

2

THE ACHIEVEMENT OF POWER, 1919–24

On 23 March 1919, Benito Mussolini had set up a new political movement, the *Fasci di Combattimento* (Fascist Fight Groups) in Milan. He
was 35 years old, which was young for a political leader, yet within
three years Mussolini was to become Prime Minister of Italy. How did
this remarkable transformation in Mussolini's fortunes come about,
especially as the base of popular support for his new movement during
the period 1919 to 1922 was flimsy?

THE GENESIS OF FASCISM

The Fascist movement in 1919 was a rag bag of competing rightist elements. There was the artist Marinetti, with his belief in violence and modern technology (characterised in his vivid yet alarming paintings), who was
leader of the so-called Futurist movement. There were ex-soldiers such as
Captain Ferrucio Vecchi of the famous *Arditi*, or 'Daring Ones', who
chaired the Fascists' very first meeting. And there were pre-war nationalists
who shared Mussolini's vision of post-war Italy. The essence of the new
movement was that it was against the traditional parties and was designed
to draw together the men who had fought in the war who wanted something more than the discredited politics of Giolitti and the Liberal Party.

The experience of the war was the unifying factor in the membership
of the new movement, which was not actually consolidated into the
Fascist Party (PNF) until 1921. Those who had been blooded on the

battlefields of Caporetto and Vittorio Veneto did not need the corrupt old Party apparatus to express their feelings. Mussolini and his followers believed that they transcended the old politics with its divisive class loyalties. But because the new movement resisted the concept of party, it was possible for members to belong to other organisations at the same time. Thus the *Arditi* had their own separate ex-servicemen's organisation which was subsidised by Mussolini,[1] while Marinetti, the Futurist, was also the leader of the *Arditi*.

The Fascist programme which appeared in the summer of 1919 drew from both the Left and the Right of Italian politics. From the Left, the Fascists borrowed the demand for an eight-hour working day, a minimum wage and some sort of social insurance together with taxation on capital and the seizure of excessive war profits (a popular theme with ex-servicemen in Italy as elsewhere who resented stay-at-home businessmen who had done well out of the war). While from the Right, Fascism took its essential patriotic and nationalist rhetoric, its attack on the 'mutilated victory' and its rejection of the PSI (Italian Socialist Party). The programme might open Mussolini to charges of inconsistency but, as one historian has noted, this 'perhaps misses the point'.[2] Fascism was designed to appeal both to the leftist interventionists of 1915 and the ex-servicemen of the *Arditi*.

Initially, however, the Fascists had very little popular support. Fascism was an urban movement in 1919–20, and such support as it had was to be found in Milan, Bologna and Trieste. Membership of the movement at the end of 1919 was less than 1,000, and in the November parliamentary elections the bloc of Fascists, *Arditi* and Futurists won a miserable 4,000 votes in Milan. Mussolini wrote later about the traditional parties in 1919 being 'tawdry and insufficient – unable to keep pace with the rising tide of unexpected political exigencies',[3] but there was little evidence at the time that Fascism's political package could attract meaningful political support. An additional problem which faced the new movement was the appearance of a powerful Catholic party, the Popular Party (*Partito Populare Italiano*, or PPI), which had the tacit backing of the Vatican. The PPI could make it difficult for the nascent Fascist movement to establish a rural support base because it had particular strength amongst the peasantry.

All this meant that Mussolini depended very much on his journalism for the funds needed to keep his new movement afloat. He 'was a born

journalist',[4] and it was *Il Popolo d'Italia* which gave him a national reputation at a time when the Fascists were merely an eccentric right-wing
fringe movement. But the newspaper needed funds to maintain itself
which were obtained, as had been the case during the war, from right-
wing industrialists such as the Perrone brothers. The paper remained
the mouthpiece of all those disillusioned and embittered patriots on the
Right who believed that a radical solution was needed to Italy's international and domestic problems.

It was also as a result of his experience as a journalist, with his feel
for a punchy editorial, that Mussolini knew his readership was not
overly concerned with consistency. So he was able to be all things to all
men, both monarchist and republican, socialist and conservative, and
imperialist and anti-imperialist.[5] Whether this ramshackle approach
would work in the political arena remained to be seen. But Mussolini
was astute enough to impress his financial backers with his opposition
to socialism. He also claimed to have been able to 'put my finger on the
pulse of the masses and suddenly discovered in the general mood of dis-
orientation that a public opinion was waiting for me'.[6]

THE 'RED TWO YEARS'

Mussolini realised that the 1919 parliamentary elections showed a left-
ward swing in Italy. But in the longer term, the so-called 'Red Two
Years' or *Biennio Rosso* from 1919 to 1921 would greatly assist the rise of
Fascism. This was because Italy was paralysed by a wave of strikes and
worker occupations of factories which were linked to a rise in prices and
unemployment, but also to the reappearance of many socialist and anarchist activists after the war following their release from prison. There
was also a massive rise in membership for the socialist trade union, the
General Confederation of Labour, from just over one million in 1919 to
over two million in 1920.

The disturbances began with food riots in Central and Northern
Italy in June 1919 during which granaries were attacked and shops
looted, and went on to include a general strike in Turin (April 1920)
and an army mutiny in Ancona. Reformist gains for the working class
in parliament such as the concession of an eight-hour working day failed
to impress activists, and the Socialist Party itself, despite sweeping
gains in the 1919 elections, was hopelessly divided. The propertied

classes were deeply alarmed by the action taken by socialist councils in raising taxes on wealth and increasing public spending in their areas of jurisdiction.

Most alarming of all to the land-owning and business-owning classes was the mood of defiance in the 'Red Two Years' evident in the peasantry and the urban proletariat. Factory workers in Italy's big firms (such as Fiat in Turin) demanded the setting up of factory councils which carried echoes of the workers' councils (soviets) which had been created in revolutionary Russia. And such councils regarded both the trade unions and the Socialist Party as being either reformist or bogus revolutionaries. The Socialist Party itself, as indicated above, was hopelessly divided between reformists who wanted to obtain concessions for the workers through the parliamentary system, and the Far Left under Gramsci who wanted to carry on the revolutionary struggle outside parliament through workers' councils and workers' control of production. In 1921 Gramsci and his supporters were to break away from the PSI and set up the Italian Communist Party (PCI).

Although the Socialists were the second biggest party in parliament, they lacked strength in the rural South. Catholic peasant leagues dominated the political scene there, but in their own way these were just as militant. The big issues were land for landless peasants and labourers and security of tenure, and many farms were occupied by peasants between 1919 and 1921. Thus throughout the country the violent class warfare which had simmered just below the surface, exploded into what seemed like civil war'.[7]

Table 2.1 provides exact figures for the unrest experienced during this period.

Table 2.1 The 'Red Two Years' in figures

	Number of strikes	Workers involved
1919 Urban	1663	500,000
1919 Rural	208	500,000
1920 Urban	1881	1,000,000
1920 Rural	189	1,000,000

Source: A. de Grand, *Italian Fascism: Its Origins and Development*, p.24.

This widespread chaos in both town and countryside gave Mussolini his opportunity. The Fascists were soon to take on the role of bully boys for the propertied classes who feared that Italy was turning Bolshevik. But before this happened, Mussolini had to do some internal house cleaning.

This was because, at a local level, the *fasci* (groups) knew little about Mussolini himself and therefore followed the local leader. The leaders, or *ras*, took their name from the chieftains in Abyssinia where Italy still retained imperial ambitions after the catastrophic defeat at Adowa in 1896. The *ras* had their own uniformed bodyguards (*squadristi*, who wore black shirts) who were used both to protect them and to run local protection rackets. But the system was chaotic. The *ras* could be republicans or monarchists, clericals or anti-clericals. Mussolini needed to impose his authority on the *ras* and the Fascist *squadristi*. He did this by persuading his motley army of supporters that he alone could make Fascism a national force in Italy. Ultimately, the Fascist Blackshirts owed loyalty to him alone.

In Mussolini's autobiography, the Fascist struggle during the Red Two Years is an heroic one. According to him, 'fear and cowardice have always been typical characteristics of the Socialist Party in Italy'.[8] It was always the Socialists or the Anarchists who threw bombs into crowds or beat up innocent Fascists. This was a completely inaccurate portrayal of events, but the Fascists did succeed in making themselves appear to be the defenders of law and order in the eyes of the middle classes. In Bologna, for example, local tradesmen and industrialists approached the local Fascists to protect them from striking workers and an alleged Bolshevik threat (more apparent than real, as Mussolini conceded later).[9] While in Ferrara, Italo Balbo, who was later to be a key figure in Mussolini's régime, recruited *fasci* from the student population and the sons of the petty bourgeoisie, and received funding from large landowners and industrialists. From there, the Fascist movement was able to spread to Romagna, Emilia, Tuscany and Umbria.

The methods of the Fascist squads were crude in the extreme. Socialists or agrarian trade unionists were made to swallow live frogs and dollops of castor oil. Beatings were administered, with the kidneys being singled out for special assault. It was unsophisticated but effective. In 1920, one million agricultural workers were on strike in Italy. In 1921, the figure had fallen to just 80,000. Mussolini wrote later that the 'iron necessity of violence already had been confirmed'.[10]

The success of Fascist thuggery brought new recruits as well. By the end of the year 1921, there were 834 local sections (*fasci*) and nearly 250,000 members of the Fascist movement. Fascism also became an electoral force for the first time in 1921 with thirty-five seats in the Italian parliament. But the nature of the movement had also changed. Whilst it had not been very successful as an urban movement, 'agrarian fascism was an overwhelming success'.[11] Peasant league offices and co-operatives alike were attacked in a devastating campaign, while the Socialists were demoralised by the burning of their party headquarters and attacks on their members. At the same time, the real forces of law and order in Italy turned a blind eye to Fascist excesses, many off-duty policemen actually taking part in Fascist 'raids' against their opponents. Thus it was that between autumn 1920 and summer 1922, 'the organisational structure of Socialist and Catholic rural trade-unionism was destroyed across much of central and northern Italy'.[12] This was Mussolini's achievement, although in doing so he had to concede a considerable degree of autonomy to *ras* such as Balbo in Ferrara and Dino Grandi in Bologna. In the South, the growth of Fascism was slower but even there membership increased to about a quarter of the national total.

Mussolini's personal responsibility for the violent excesses of his followers was absolute. His brother Arnaldo had long detected a violent streak in his character, and in his writings he constantly urged the use of violence while at the same time trying to pretend that Fascist excesses had been provoked by his political opponents. It was also true that because of their wartime experiences the Fascist Blackshirts had been immunised against moral objections to their violence (just as in Germany, the right-wing *Freikorps* or ex-soldiers were guilty of revolting atrocities against the German Left in 1919–20). Any doubts that they might have had were assuaged by Mussolini's high-flown rhetoric. 'We want to sing of the love of danger,' Mussolini wrote, 'the habit of energy and rashness ... Beauty only exists in struggle.'[13]

THE DEATH OF LIBERAL ITALY

Even when every allowance is made for the success of Mussolini's propaganda and violent tactics, however, he could not have succeeded without the abject collapse of the Italian parliamentary system around him. The return of Giolitti as premier in July 1920 probably marked the last hope for parliamentary democracy in Italy. But the old man was not ruthless enough to deal with someone like Mussolini. He also made the crucial error, common to politicians of the centre-right at the time, of thinking that Fascist violence could somehow be contained within the existing system, and that Mussolini could be persuaded to work with other parliamentary parties. Giolitti had a serious problem in that neither the PSI nor the *Popolari* would co-operate with the Liberals (or each other as they were ideological enemies), but he was naive in his expectation that he could use the Fascists as parliamentary allies. Mussolini, always the pragmatist when it suited him, was happy to accept Giolitti's offer of a political alliance in January 1921. But once elected to parliament himself in May of that year, as one of the thirty-five Fascist deputies, he made clear the intention of his party to vote for the Opposition.

Mussolini expressed some respect for Giolitti as the grand old man of Italian politics but he despised the system he represented. The behaviour of the Fascist deputies in parliament was, therefore, quite outrageous. They took revolvers into the Chamber and, on one occasion, attacked a Communist deputy because he was alleged to have been a wartime deserter. No punishment was dealt out by the government for this piece of thuggery.

Mussolini himself also gained from his new status because his membership of parliament gave him immunity against a charge of trying to overthrow the government by violence. He attended few debates, sitting in ostentatious fashion on the extreme right of the Chamber.

Yet, even as late as 1921 there was evidence that democracy might have been saved in Italy, had the government only had the stomach for it. In July 1921 a small police unit had put a stop to Fascist rioting in the town of Sarzana by firing on the mob. This may have unnerved Mussolini sufficiently for him to make an insincere offer of coalition with the Socialists and the *Popolari*, which was probably intended to be a reminder to the Conservative Right and the centre of how much they needed him.[14] The government, however, failed to learn the lesson of Sarzana (just as German governments failed to learn the lessons to be learnt from the crushing of Hitler's attempted *putsch* in Bavaria in November 1923).

The irony of the Italian political situation was that post-war political reform had actually weakened parliamentary democracy. Orlando's decision to introduce universal male suffrage in December 1918 was laudable enough, but Nitti's decision to bring in proportional representation led to a catastrophic weakening of the system in the November 1919 elections. The Liberal Party only won 114 seats in the Assembly, which was now dominated by two mass parties, the Socialists and the *Popolari*, who between them received more than 52 per cent of the vote. In Northern Italy especially, the anti-government parties triumphed, leaving the underdeveloped, de-urbanised South to the Liberals, themselves split into Giolittian and right-wing factions (162 out of 239 government deputies were elected in the South). This meant that the North–South divide in Italian politics was worsened, and such fragmentation made strong parliamentary government impossible thereafter. Liberal governments could not survive unless they made deals with Socialists or Catholics and (ultimately) Fascists.

Government feebleness was combined with Mussolini's political and economic adroitness. Giolitti's successors, Bonomi and Facta, were no more able to control Fascist violence than he was. Neither did they show much will to do so. And Mussolini was able to win the support of farmers (who were suffering from an agrarian depression in 1921–22) by advocating free trade, while at the same time criticising the government for failing to intervene when iron and steel firms went under in 1921 because of foreign competition. Mussolini spoke in imprecise terms about the need for 'synthesis' between the free market and new forms of working-class organisations. These were the Fascist syndicates, their version of trade unions created by intimidating workers into leaving their socialist unions. Supposedly even-handed, the syndicates were really a way of keeping the working classes under control and demonstrated the bias towards employers that became characteristic of Italian Fascism (excepting those Fascists such as Rossoni who had genuine concern for the workers). At the time however the syndicates seemed to many middle-class Italians to support the Fascist claim that the party transcended the old class divide in the country, as they purported to bring workers and employers closer together.

Another obvious weakness of the Italian State which assisted Mussolini's rise to power was the attitude of the Italian monarchy. Victor Emmanuel III, whom Mussolini later referred to contemptuously as 'the little sardine', became an admirer of Fascism. His instincts were undemocratic and he loathed socialism, but as an anti-clerical he disliked the *Popolari* as much. Initially, Victor Emmanuel hoped that the return of Giolitti would restore stability, but when it did not he came to view Fascism as a potential saviour. The king's attitude was doubly important, for as Commander-in-Chief of the Armed Forces he influenced the attitude of the military which was already impressed by the Fascist emphasis on soldierly virtues. Two of the most important military leaders in Italy, Marshalls Diaz and Badoglio, told Victor Emmanuel in October 1922 that they favoured the Fascists,[15] which meant that the army would not be enthusiastic about intervening should Mussolini attempt to mount a coup d'état. As already noted, the police force contained many Fascist sympathisers. Mussolini, therefore, had comprehensive support in the Italian establishment, even if his basis of popular support was unimpressive (in 1921 the Fascists won only around 7 per cent of the national vote).

When one adds to this the gullibility of political leaders such as Giolitti in dealing with the Fascists, it can be seen that Mussolini's position had become extremely favourable by the autumn of 1922. Giolitti famously remarked that 'those fascists are our Black and Tans', which demonstrated how out of touch he was: the Black and Tans, a paramilitary force used by the British in Ireland between 1919 and 1921 against the Irish Republican Army, were firmly under the control of the Lloyd George government (even though they committed numerous unpleasant atrocities), whereas the same could never be said of the Fascist Blackshirts and Giolitti. And it was Giolitti who invited Mussolini and his Fascists into a governmental coalition after the 1921 elections in his so-called National Bloc, giving them the stamp of respectability. He appeared to be out of his depth.

The last piece in the equation was the Catholic Church. Pope Benedict XV had come to consider the *Popolari* as being too radical, and the Party's leaders never saw themselves as being just agents of the Vatican. Yet Mussolini had long proclaimed himself to be an anti-clerical, and shortly before his election to parliament he had described Christianity as 'detestable'. His immediate volte-face thereafter seems to have been motivated purely by his desire for power and respectability. Thus the Fascists lined up in parliament in support of those who wanted to pass a bill to fund private Catholic schools. As a journalist, Mussolini had already learned that his public would forgive inconsistency as long as it was veiled by a dynamic, noisy exterior. This was the Mussolini who, when asked to define Fascism, replied: 'it is action'.

Despite all his advantages in the years 1920 to 1922, Mussolini also had his difficulties. Although the Fascist Party or PNF had been set up in 1921 by Mussolini to unite a fragmented movement, even he was disconcerted by the sheer level of Fascist violence. This may have been the reason why, in August 1921, he agreed to a 'pacification pact' with the Socialists, which would have put an end to the Fascist squads' terror campaign against them.

He was then faced by what amounted to a mutiny by leading *ras* such as Balbo, Grandi and Farinacci (the *ras* in Cremona), who rejected the pact because they wished to retain their local power bases. To give up violence would destroy the means of protecting such power and also perhaps allow the recovery of socialist trade unions. Mussolini therefore suffered a severe tactical reverse and he temporarily resigned his post as Duce (Leader) of the Fascist Party (the term was in general usage before 1914, but was applied now to Mussolini by the Party). In November 1921 at the Third Fascist Congress Mussolini also had to make a humiliating climb-down and admit he had been in error. The *ras* were allowed to retain their local squads of Blackshirts. This was the beginning of a long struggle between Mussolini and those elements in the Fascist Party who thought him too prone to compromise and not sufficiently radical. He liked to pose as a radical extremist while at the same time reserving the right to make deals with Italy's power-brokers.

THE TAKING OF POWER

It was a central myth of Fascism that political power was seized in October 1922 from the feeble parliamentary régime that preceded it.[16] This is nonsense. Power was presented to Mussolini on a plate. Unsurprisingly, he opted to take it. It is also true that had the parliamentary régime shown any backbone, Mussolini's arrival in power could easily have been prevented. Mussolini for his part played his hand cleverly. A dual policy was adopted. Good behaviour was promised inside a coalition government, but the activities of Fascist terror squads continued unabated.

Prime Minister Facta wanted to believe in Mussolini's sincerity but he lacked the will to do anything decisive about Fascist violence. Mussolini believed that had Giolitti been prime minister, he might have used the army against him if he had tried to seize power by force.

Other politicians such as Orlando and Nitti thought that they could use the Fascists in coalitions headed by themselves. Political ambitions induced myopia. Meantime, Facta pleaded for normality. There was nothing he said 'at all patriotic in one Italian assassinating another'.

Mussolini raised the tempo of agitation. In late October, he told a rally of Fascists that 'either the Government of the country must be given peaceably to the *Fascisti* or we will take it by force'. The threat of an armed take-over of power was implicit in what Mussolini was saying but he continued to show interest in being a coalition partner. The politicians did not know that, at a meeting of Fascist leaders on 16 October, Mussolini had already drawn up plans for an armed uprising. But the two tactics were not mutually exclusive. The threat of violence allowed Mussolini to put pressure on the government to accept the Fascists as a coalition partner. At the same time, Mussolini's talks with other politicians, such as Giolitti and Salandra, reflected his anxieties about staging a coup. He knew that the Fascist Blackshirts were not capable of resisting the army should Victor Emmanuel order it to intervene. Mussolini therefore resisted the demands of hotheads such as Balbo and Farinacci for a wholly insurrectionary strategy. He took steps to reassure the king about Fascist radicalism while the Milan bourgeoisie were told that should the Fascists achieve power, the Blackshirts would be disbanded. Fascist propaganda also went out of its way to praise the virtues of the Italian army.

The decisive period in late October which brought Benito Mussolini to power began badly. During the night of 27–28 October (while Mussolini took his wife Rachele on a rare visit to the theatre in Milan) Fascist *squadristi* occupied key buildings in the provincial capitals of Northern and Central Italy. This action at last forced Prime Minister Facta to act and government ministers agreed to advise the king to use the army against the Fascist uprising. Facta went to see King Victor Emmanuel early in the morning of 28 October to tell him that Fascist disturbances were taking place throughout Rome and in Milan. A decree was prepared to put Rome under martial law.

Meantime, Mussolini's plan was for four Blackshirt columns to advance on Rome led by Balbo, de Vecchi, de Bono and Bianchi, but almost certainly only when Mussolini had been invited to become prime minister or a coalition partner. All the evidence suggests that the army garrison in Rome with its armoured cars and machine guns would have made short work of the Fascists, some of whom were only armed with riding crops and baseball bats. Others had no arms at all.

In fact, the military were easily able to deal with the Blackshirts in Rome, but when Facta went back to see Victor Emmanuel around nine o'clock in the morning, the king refused to sign the decree. Why he changed his mind has been the subject of a great deal of speculation among historians. One reason was likely to have been that as all the leading politicians in Italy seemed to accept that Mussolini would enter the government, there was little point in resisting this eventuality. The king also knew that the army contained many Fascist sympathisers (Diaz and Badoglio have already been mentioned) and might not be reliable in a crisis. Resistance to the Fascists might also have precipitated a civil war for which the king was unwilling to take responsibility. A timorous and indecisive man who admired decisiveness in others, Victor Emmanuel may also have feared that his cousin, the pro-Fascist Duke of Aosta, might have been a candidate for the throne. There was also the fact that Mussolini had threatened the existence of the monarchy itself, should the king resist the so-called Fascist Revolution.

The most convincing explanation, however, is that Victor Emmanuel expected Salandra to become prime minister when Facta resigned after the king refused to sign the martial law decree.[17] Salandra was a right-wing nationalist who was much more acceptable than the Liberal Facta, who was only in office, in the eyes of many, as a surrogate of Giolitti. Salandra did, in fact, try to form a ministry and sounded out Mussolini, who shocked him by refusing to join it. Salandra then ceased his attempt to form a government and the king sent instead for Mussolini.

According to Mussolini's version of events, which as ever has to be treated with caution, he insisted that the telephone message from Victor Emmanuel's aide-de-camp on 29 October be put in writing in the form of a telegram. It read: 'His Majesty the King asks you to come to Rome immediately for he wishes to offer you the responsibility of forming a ministry.' Only then, allegedly, were the Fascist squads allowed to march.

THE MARCH ON ROME

Held in readiness to enter Rome, the Blackshirts were a sorry sight when they got there (it had been raining solidly for two days). There were only about 30,000 of them dressed in a motley collection of uniforms and

348   01/06/2018
Item(s) checked out to
HARROLLE, ANN MARIE

TITLE Let me tell you a story : a
BARCODE   32345065774748
DUE   **01-20-18**

TITLE Mussolini / Peter Neville.
BARCODE   32345030244066
DUE   **01-20-18**

headgear (some even had multi-coloured socks!). Their arrival was followed by attacks on political opponents (a dozen people were killed), the ransacking of shops and the burning of objectionable books. Mussolini led from behind, coming down from Milan by train. He apparently thought about getting off the train early and leading the Fascist militiamen into Rome on horseback but rejected the idea. This was probably wise as he would have cut a bizarre figure dressed as he was in spats, a crumpled black shirt and a bowler hat. Subsequently, the Fascists invented the myth that 3,000 Blackshirts had died in the 'taking' of Rome. There was no need for fighting because on the morning of 30 October Mussolini presented himself at the Quirinal Palace to have his appointment as President of the Council (Prime Minister) confirmed by the king. The next day thousands of Blackshirts were allowed to parade past the monarch in triumph. Mussolini, who should have been there throughout, was, according to one account, indulging in a sexual liaison in his office.[18]

Mussolini had played his hand with a great deal of skill. He had blended the threat of violence with the promise of moderation and stability if, and when, the Fascists came into government. He had profited throughout from the political selfishness of the Old Guard and the unwillingness of his political opponents to co-operate. And the new government created an image of moderation because Mussolini carefully excluded potential rivals such as Balbo, Farinacci and Grandi. He himself took the Foreign Affairs and Interior Portfolios as well as the Premiership. Among the Fascists only Oviglio (Justice), de Stefani (Finance) and Giuriati (Liberated Provinces) received Cabinet posts, and the Cabinet also included members of the *Popolari* and Social Democratic Parties. It would have included a pliable socialist as well had not Mussolini had second thoughts. Rejoicing crowds danced in Rome as Italy's new strong man assumed office. Unlike most pro-Fascist demonstrations, these appear to have been entirely spontaneous.

FASCISM: REVOLUTION OR COUNTER-REVOLUTION?

The apparent pragmatism involved in Mussolini's coming to power in 1922 has frequently sparked off debate about the genuineness of his ideological convictions, and indeed whether Italian Fascism had any real ideology at all. Discussion has also focused around the extent to which

Fascism was a child of post-war crisis, the First World War itself or the challenge to the old order emerging in the years before 1914. To what extent, historians and political theorists have asked, was Fascism 'new'?

Some things about it were demonstrably new. The march pasts, the black shirts, the emphasis on youth and physical virility were all colour-ful and dynamic aspects of the new movement even if Mussolini were indebted to D'Annunzio for some of them. More importantly, so was the emphasis laid by Mussolini on the way his movement transcended the old political loyalties and the old class divisions in Italy. And because it allegedly did this, Fascism was a uniquely new movement in Italian his-tory; "everything within the state, nothing outside the state, nothing against the state" was Mussolini's slogan. He believed that individuals were only valuable when they contributed to the nation or made sacri-fices for it. The experience of the war was central to this conception of the relationship between the individual and the State, but it has been argued that the beliefs of Fascists such as Mussolini, Gentile and the British leader Mosley were the result of a synthesis of pre-war theory and wartime experience.[19]

If this view is accepted, Mussolini was plainly a man who was pro-foundly influenced by the changes taking place in Europe in the late nineteenth century, and especially by the process of industrial and tech-nological modernisation. The intellectual influence upon him of Sorel, Nietzsche and Marx has already been acknowledged, and Mussolini's flair for manipulating the masses also owed a good deal to the Frenchman Le Bon, whose book on the psychology of crowds he claimed to have read many times. This awareness of the way in which propa-ganda and demagoguery could sway the masses was a feature of Italian Fascism which can accurately be described as novel. Mussolini was espe-cially well suited to take advantage of the new technologies such as radio and film which were coming to the fore just at the point when he was becoming Italy's leader.

But was Mussolini a revolutionary? The argument is a finely bal-anced one. Certainly some aspects of Fascism (and one could extend these comments to take in the generic Europe-wide Fascism of the inter-war period) appear to be revolutionary. In Italy, the Fascists wanted to sweep away the old corrupt parliamentary system and replace it by a dynamic charismatic movement headed by a leader who had superhuman characteristics. They wished to create national unity by transcending the old political and class barriers, and in foreign policy they wished to overthrow the 'mutilated' peace of 1919 and replace it with a revised settlement much more favourable to Italy. More than this, the Fascists wanted an expansionist, imperialistic colonial policy to demonstrate Italy's greatness. Mussolini symbolised these aspirations in his own person, and in that sense can be described as a revolutionary, someone who wanted 'palingenesis', or the rebirth of the Italian nation in a more dynamic, unified form.[20]

The problem with this analysis of Mussolini and his movement is that there is equally convincing evidence that Italian Fascism was a counter-revolutionary, reactionary movement. Although attempts have been made to suggest that Fascism's socialist roots (and more particularly its syndicalist roots) are all-important, most historians have emphasised its anti-Leftist credentials. Fascism in Italy and elsewhere rejected the influence of the eighteenth-century Enlightenment and the French Revolution, with their nineteenth-century liberal democratic heirs. Equally, the movement rejected Marxism and internationalism. It was, and this was demonstrably true in Mussolini's Italy, a movement of the ultra-nationalist right. True, Mussolini's Fascists did not manifest the signs of vicious racism based on biological determinism which were a feature of Nazi Germany (anti-Semitism only became a feature of Fascist Italy in 1938), but many authorities have doubted whether Nazism can be fitted into the generic Fascist mould at all.[21] And Italian Fascism was not merely anti-Communist but also an enemy of parliamentary democracy, trade unionism and indeed pluralism in Italian society. Anything which did not accord with the narrowly Fascist definition of Italian-ness was to be destroyed.

A major caveat has to be entered at this point. It is that, in achieving power, Mussolini had to make compromises with those very forces his more radical followers despised. In the Italian context, this meant the monarchy, the Church and the army, without whose tacit approval or passivity the Fascists could not have come to power in October 1922. As has been seen, the Fascist deputies in the Chamber dropped their anti-clericalism to win Church approval just as Mussolini wooed both king and army in the weeks before he came to power. It can, of course, be argued that Mussolini was obliged to make deals to secure power, but the fact remains that these rival conservative power centres remained in play in Italy all through the Fascist era. Thus, Mussolini may have sought to achieve national rebirth in Italy after 1922, but there must be serious questions about the extent to which he achieved a Fascist revolution, and if indeed this was ever going to be possible. Fascism, therefore, can be deemed to be revolutionary only in the sense that it did involve a rejection of the liberal democracy which had come into existence in 1870. This liberal democracy was, in fact, to be destroyed when Mussolini introduced his personal dictatorship in 1925. Thereafter, there are good grounds for saying that Mussolini still never resolved the tensions between his genuinely radical followers and the needs of the Italian State. He recognised these tensions in his very first government by keeping leading Fascist radicals out of office. His struggle to resolve them forms the focus for succeeding chapters. In the meantime, Mussolini was content to act as a mediator between the Fascist Party and its non-Fascist political supporters, such as the industrialists and big landowners.

It has been suggested that during his first eighteen months in power 'Mussolini did nothing to dispel the notion that Fascism could be woven into the fabric of the state'.[22] It could also be argued that he had little choice in the matter in that although Fascism was a mass movement with over 300,000 members, its grip on national power was tenuous and relied upon the support of others. Italy's traditional power brokers, the king, the army, parliament, the Church, industrialists and landowners, remained very much in play and Mussolini's anxieties about his more radical followers have already been referred to. This does not, however, mean that Mussolini, the ideologue, can be dismissed as irrelevant, rather that Mussolini's ambition to 'make Italy Fascist' had to be proclaimed more softly in a context where traditional conservative forces still mattered. In the period between November 1922 and January 1925, in particular, Mussolini had to try and convince his conservative allies that Fascism could be trusted both to restore stability at home and to create a more favourable image of Italy abroad. During this time, the Italian political system 'remained in limbo, a hybrid of authoritarian practice grafted onto the old liberal constitutional forms'.[23]

MUSSOLINI AND PARLIAMENT

When he was an ordinary deputy who led a small minority party, Mussolini had treated the Italian parliament with contempt. It was hardly to be expected, therefore, that he would show any deference towards it once he had become prime minister. He sent away the Blackshirts on special trains before he met parliament on 16 November, but some of the Fascist deputies still appeared in black-shirted uniforms when that body assembled.

Mussolini then flaunted his new power, telling the parliament that he could 'easily have turned this dull and grey hall into a bivouac for my platoons. I could have nailed up the doors of parliament and have established an exclusively Fascist Government.'[24] In doing so, he dangerously ignored his need to establish credentials with the non-Fascist parties (excepting the Communists and Socialists) about Fascism's respectability, because his own conception of power was so authoritarian. Yet, amazingly, he got away with it. Parliament gave him an enormous vote of confidence: only the Communists and Socialists voted against him, and five ex-prime ministers voted for him (they included Giolitti, Salandra and Orlando). And the Senate gave Mussolini an even larger majority. Italy's democrats, it seemed, were only too susceptible to bluster and threats. Mussolini himself well knew that he was in no position to impose 'an exclusively Fascist Government' in 1922, even if some mesmerised senators had asked him to do so. But he had proved his potency as a demagogue.

Mussolini's parliamentary triumph meant that he faced little real opposition in 1923/4. It consisted, such as it was, of Amendola's Liberal Democrats, the Unitary Socialists (the reformist wing of the Socialist Party) and the Communist Party. Amendola's party would not co-operate with the Unitary Socialists any more than they would unite with the Communists. This allowed Mussolini to plot further fragmentation of the Opposition in 1923, by trying to detach the Confederation of Labour from the other Oppositionists.

Parliamentary elections were pending in 1924, which Mussolini was determined to win at all costs. Systematic Fascist violence during the election was to be expected, but Mussolini wanted to rig electoral law to such a degree that a favourable result was a foregone conclusion. His means was the notorious Acerbo Bill of 1923. This would allow a party with the largest vote, as long as it exceeded 25 per cent, to obtain two-thirds of the seats in parliament leaving the remaining third to all the other parties. There was never any doubt that the Fascists would acquire the needed 25 per cent.

But to get the Acerbo Law through parliament, Mussolini had to secure the support of the *Popolari*, the Catholic Popular Party, which was unlikely to be forthcoming. It was here that Mussolini showed his tactical ability. Fascist violence against the *Popolari* was stepped up to include attacks on mainstream Catholic organisations, so that the new Pope, Pius XI, feared that support for the *Popolari* would involve the Church in a full-scale anti-clerical campaign. At the same time, Mussolini dropped the *Popolari* ministers from his government in April 1923, when it became clear that their support could not be relied upon. The result was that Pius XI, who was later to describe Mussolini as 'a man whom Providence has caused us to encounter' (a statement he was to regret), ordered Sturzo, the General Secretary of the *Popolari*, himself a priest, to resign and go into exile. His Party was thus hopelessly fragmented, some right-wing Catholic deputies voting for the Acerbo Law and most of the party abstaining. The measure passed comfortably on 21 July 1923 by 223 votes to 123. Right-wing *Popolari* who sympathised with Fascism even ended up on the Fascist national parliamentary list of candidates in 1924.

Mussolini had sugared the pill for the Vatican by banning PNF members from being freemasons, knowing that successive Popes were almost as fearful of this allegedly atheistic secret society as they were of their particular *bête noire* communism. The government had also slyly introduced the Catholic Catechism, a booklet laying down the basic tenets of the faith, into all Italian primary schools, and insisted on crucifixes being present in schools and government offices. Mussolini thus skilfully had begun the process which was to bring about the normalisation of Church–State relations in Italy six years later. He also knew that Pius XI's dearest ambition was to solve the so-called 'Roman Question'.[25]

THE 1924 ELECTIONS

The scene was therefore set for an apparent Fascist triumph in the parliamentary elections of 1924. The Acerbo Law made this inevitable and the government got 66 per cent of the vote and 374 out of 575 seats. Never, however, had Fascist violence been so blatant in an election campaign, and violence was intermixed with fraud so that Fascist supporters were allowed to register more than one vote. Remarkably though, the Fascists still obtained only 54 per cent of the vote in the industrialised North, although they polled almost 30 per cent more votes in the South.

The old political parties did badly and the 'newness' of Fascism was emphasised by the relative youth of its new parliamentary deputies. Two thirds of them were aged under 40, thus honouring Mussolini's pledge that 'the new Italy would be represented by the trenchocracy', the veterans of the war.[26] But Mussolini had also been careful to cement his alliance with the *agrari* (large landowners) and the industrialists who admired his robust anti-socialism. His main electoral problem was that his Fascists had still been unable to make much impact in the industrial heartlands of the North where Socialists and Communists continued to poll well. He attempted to address this problem by flirting with the General Confederation of Labour. Opposition from the *ras* (now known as 'consuls' in the old Roman style) and the Fascist syndicates prevented Mussolini from bringing representatives of organised labour into his government. This was unsurprising for representation of orthodox unionism might well threaten the position of the Fascist syndicates, founded as they were on violence and thuggery. The issue highlighted the difficulties Mussolini was having within his own movement. He, like many political leaders, was finding that the radicalism of opposition was difficult to accommodate with the realities of government.

This needs to be borne in mind when accusations are made that Mussolini was nothing more than a cynical pragmatist with no real ideology and no objective other than the achievement of power. The ambitious young tearaway of the pre-1914 era was now faced with the subtle political management required to keep the disparate elements involved in Fascism together. Just how fragmented the movement was needs to be emphasised, for no less than five distinctive strands in Fascism can be identified in 1922–24.

1 First of all, there were the *ras* and *squadristi* who wanted an all-out radicalisation of Italian society, and a transfer of power away from the traditional élites to the socio-economic groupings they represented. This aspiration was encapsulated in the phrase 'a second revolution'.

2 The next component was the Fascist left wing which included ex-syndicalists like Rossoni and Bianchi. Its objective was to replace the Old Left of the Socialists and the Communists with a national syndicalist state.

3   Fascist technicians or 'revisionists' like Bottai saw the movement as a modernising force in Italy. Mussolini certainly gave some encouragement to this grouping.

4   The Nationalists who had merged with the PNF in 1923 wanted to move Fascism towards a more capitalist and imperialistic outlook.

5   Conservative Fascists who might, for example, have been drawn from the right wing of the *Popolari* wanted 'normalisation' of Party–State relations and no truck with any 'second revolution'. The status quo in Italy should be preserved.[27]

Mussolini's task was to act as a link and a mediator between those groupings, whom he could also attempt to play off one against another. It was by no means an easy task.

3

CRISIS AND CONSOLIDATION, 1924–29

THE MATTEOTTI MURDER

The intrinsic violence associated with Fascism always meant that it was likely to involve Mussolini in embarrassment in the period before he was able to establish a Fascist dictatorship. Such a crisis arose in June 1924 when a Socialist deputy, Giacomo Matteotti, was murdered by Fascists in Rome.

Matteotti had been born in 1885, the son of a land-owning family in the Po Valley who was converted to socialism while a student. He found Fascism morally distasteful and became its most forceful opponent in the Chamber. More alarmingly from Mussolini's point of view, his anti-Fascist rhetoric was combined with diligent research into Fascist excesses in the recent elections. This research was used to devastating effect in an attack on Mussolini's government in a speech in parliament on 30 May 1924. Mussolini was infuriated by Matteotti's defiance and undoubtedly used phrases (such as 'get rid of him')[1] which encouraged those in his entourage to take violent action against Matteotti. Conversely, no absolutely conclusive evidence that Mussolini gave a direct order for Matteotti's execution has ever been unearthed.

Nevertheless, the known facts establish Mussolini's moral guilt. Matteotti was kidnapped by a carload of Fascists from a street in Rome on 10 June in broad daylight. Matteotti was seen struggling and shouting for help by eyewitnesses. He was never seen alive again, his body being found in a ditch outside Rome in mid-August.

Matteotti's disappearance was immediately attributed to Mussolini by anti-Fascists because he was known to have set up a special squad, called by his opponents the '*Cheka*' (after the Secret Police in Lenin's Russia), to deal with political opponents. This so-called *Cheka* had already administered beatings to Amendola and two dissident Fascists called Forni and Miscuri. Matteotti had obviously been singled out for attention with or without a direct order from Mussolini.

In fact, the execution of opponents by the Fascists had precedents before 1924, even if this were not the norm. A notorious political murder had already taken place, for example, in Ferrara in August 1923 in the area controlled by Italo Balbo. In this instance, a Catholic priest, Dom Giovanni Minzoni, a decorated First World War veteran who had joined the *Popolari*, had clashed with local Fascists. One attempt had already been made on Minzoni's life before he was ambushed and beaten by local Fascists on 23 August, in the course of which attack he sustained a fatal skull fracture. In public, Balbo deplored the murder, but he obstructed the investigation into Minzoni's murder and ultimately the case was dropped for lack of evidence. This behaviour obviously created the suspicion that Balbo had authorised the murder, even though a post-war inquiry concluded that he probably had not.[2] What is certain is that Balbo tried to protect the murderers, and this is exactly what Mussolini did in the Matteotti case.

Mussolini publicly denied any knowledge of the Matteotti murder, but he certainly knew who was responsible. He was also shaken by the news that an eyewitness had come forward to say that a car full of suspicious-looking people had been seen near Matteotti's house for a number of days before the kidnapping. Worse still, the witness had taken the car's number; it was easily traced and bloodstains were found in it. The culprits were Dumini, the leader of the *Cheka*, and another gang member called Volpi. There has been speculation about whether it was actually their intention to kill Matteotti but there was little doubt that the order to abduct him had come from someone close to Mussolini himself.[3] Just as Thomas à Becket was a 'turbulent priest' whom King Henry II wanted out of the way, Matteotti was an irritant whom Mussolini wanted dealt with (the order probably came from his close aide, Caesare Rossi).

It is known that Dumini reported to Mussolini's office on 10 June and told him what had happened, even taking with him a piece of bloodstained upholstery from the car which strongly suggests that he expected official approval for his action. Dumini went to prison for two years subsequently but was paid large sums of money by Mussolini and the Fascist Party to keep his mouth shut. Clearly Dumini was a scapegoat to cover the responsibility of others who were higher in the chain of command, for example Marinelli, another high-ranking member of Mussolini's entourage. Volpi and any other *Cheka* members involved appear to have escaped punishment.

However hard Mussolini tried to distance himself from the murder of his opponent, he could not escape its political consequences. The non-Fascist parties were outraged by the murder, yet only the Communists were prepared to encourage any popular response. Mussolini was immediately faced by an effective boycott of parliament by most of the non-Fascist parties. Known as the 'Aventine Secession' (after a revolt against tyranny in Ancient Rome), this tactic, remarkably ineffective though it turned out to be, seems to have been based on the assumption that King Victor Emmanuel was bound to take notice of the protest and remove Mussolini from office.

The timorous monarch did no such thing. As in October 1922, the king was alarmed by the prospect of further Fascist violence and vastly preferred Mussolini to any of the alternatives on offer. Thus, Victor Emmanuel did nothing. Neither could Mussolini's opponents offer a semblance of the unity needed to form a rival coalition government. Socialists and Catholics would not form a common front, and any remote prospect that they might have done so was undermined by a statement from Pope Pius XI in September warning the *Popolari* against doing any such thing (as has been seen, Pius had already emasculated the Party by ordering Sturzo into exile). Liberals such as Giolitti may have been convinced of Mussolini's tendency to condone the illicit, but they merely hoped that a weakened Mussolini would be obliged to make concessions. Giolitti himself hoped that Mussolini would be able to justify himself in parliament, and encouraged his supporters to stay there. This instruction caused a hopeless division inside the Liberal Party that considerably increased Mussolini's chances of survival. Mussolini won another victory on 24 June in the Senate when only 21 members out of 398 voted against him on the Matteotti issue. But the Conservative Right led by Federzoni of the Italian Nationalist Association had made demands which Mussolini was obliged to accept on 16 June. His immediate aides were removed, a number of Liberals, Catholics and Nationalists came into the government and Federzoni was appointed Minister of the Interior, a post formerly held by Mussolini himself. Mussolini outrageously blamed the Matteotti murder on Jews, freemasons and bankers, but he had to get rid of de Bono, the Director of Public Security, who had been supposedly investigating the murder, and a Jewish Under-Secretary, Finzi, who was smeared with the accusation of some degree of responsibility (he died in 1944 fighting for an anti-Fascist Partisan unit against the Germans). These men were merely scapegoats for a crime which was irrevocably linked to Mussolini himself, even though he never mentioned Matteotti's name again for the rest of his life.

As so often during his early years in power, Mussolini's main problems came from within his own Fascist Party. The consuls such as Balbo and Farinacci were angered by the concessions made to the conservative parties on 16 June, seeing the Matteotti crisis not as an occasion for concessions but rather as an opportunity to smash the opposition. In Ferrara, Balbo organised massive rallies of the MSVN militia to support Mussolini with slogans such as 'Not Fascism but Italy now has a single face ... that of Benito Mussolini'. But in reality, the purpose of these rallies was as much to intimidate Mussolini as to support him.[4] The threat of a 'second revolution' lay just beneath the surface.

The defining moment for the radical Fascists came on 31 December 1924 when Mussolini, who had survived the Matteotti crisis, was given what amounted to an ultimatum in a meeting with thirty consuls in Rome (although Balbo was not present on this occasion). Unless he silenced all anti-Fascist dissent within the country, he would be faced with a 'second revolution' which could result in his own removal from power. The radicals had also been outraged that Mussolini, in his desire to conciliate the moderate Right, had accepted a demand that the MSVN take an oath of allegiance to the king rather than to the Fascist Party leader himself. Faced with such a threat, Mussolini then confronted his critics in his speech of 3 January 1925 in parliament. 'I, and I alone,' he said, 'assume the political, moral and historical responsibility for all that has happened.' He went on to say that 'if two irreconcilable elements are struggling with each other, the solution lies in force'.

Mussolini defied his opponents to remove him from office, but there was no response. He followed up his speech by removing all non-Fascist ministers from his government. At a stroke, Italy was on the way to becoming a one-party dictatorship, shielded from outright totalitarianism only by the continuing influence of the monarchy and Church. Mussolini's hand may have been forced by the Matteotti crisis, but ultimately he had to choose between his Fascist comrades and the semblance of the liberal state which remained in Italy after the achievement of power in October 1922. It was a choice he was reluctant to make, but ultimately his objective was clearly to obtain a near monopoly of power for himself and his movement, although the Fascist Party was to be prevented from carrying its revolution to the extremes the radicals wanted. The crisis nonetheless demonstrated that Mussolini was quite ruthless in despatching colleagues when the defence of his position demanded it.[5]

It is instructive to compare Mussolini's handling of radical dissent within the Fascist Party with Hitler's management of it in the Nazi Party ten years later. The Nazi leader too was faced with an ultimatum, in this case from the German army, about the demands of the SA for a 'second revolution' in Germany. The threat was dealt with on 30 June 1934 in a welter of bloodshed and illegality, but it was crushed far more speedily and comprehensively than was the case in Italy. By contrast, Mussolini, in the short term at least, was forced to accept the radical agenda because he needed the support of the *ras* at a time when Italian opinion had been outraged by the Matteotti murder. Neither did he have the massive popular mandate which Hitler had when he came to power in 1933.

It has been accurately observed that 'Italian opinion reacted with such horror to the murder of Giacomo Matteotti that Mussolini recognised thenceforth the existence of a line that the Establishment would not let him cross'.[6] This did not mean that the Italian Establishment was prepared to jettison Mussolini, however, as the alternatives in 1924 were unacceptable. But there was a distinct difference between dollops of castor oil and physical beatings (albeit with a few cases where beatings resulted in death) and the mass murder of 30 June 1934 which the German Establishment was prepared to condone. President Hindenburg after all congratulated Hitler on saving the German State after his bloody assault on the Brownshirts. Neither was Mussolini's Italy to suffer from the systematic terror inflicted on Germany after the SA had been dealt with. How much of this was due to Mussolini lacking the stomach for systematic terror, and how much to the constraints he faced in Italy, must remain a matter for judgement. He certainly liked to indulge in bloodthirsty rhetoric, as his behaviour during the Matteotti crisis shows. Yet Matteotti's murder seemed to remain on Mussolini's conscience so that the murdered man's widow and children received a large pension. Is this perhaps proof that Mussolini was not capable of 'an act of that cruelty and callousness which other dictators so readily displayed'?[7]

THE CONSOLIDATION OF POWER, 1925–29

Mussolini's speech in January 1925 put a definitive end to the Matteotti crisis, but it also meant the end of Liberal Italy, the Italy which had existed since unification was completed in 1870. Although there were aspects of Fascist anti-democracy present in the pre-1922 Italian State, it is hard to argue that there was a great deal of continuity between Fascism and what preceded it. This was demonstrated by the wave of repressive legislation which Mussolini was to introduce in 1925–26, and the centralisation of power in his hands. If it were patently absurd that Mussolini headed eight government ministries (in practice, nearly all the work was done by under-secretaries in those ministries), it was an absurdity which underlined both Mussolini's overblown conception of personal power and his lack of faith in his Fascist colleagues. By 1928 he had drawn the teeth of the Fascist radicals and had made Italy an authoritarian state fashioned in his own image. Slogans such as 'Mussolini is always right' were to become part of Italy's political culture for a generation.

In January 1925, however, the anti-Fascist opposition still had some hope that Mussolini might be brought down along with his overblown rhetoric. They were soon disabused of this hope, particularly as the agents of its destruction were the conservative ex-Nationalists Federzoni and Rocco (Ministers of the Interior and Justice respectively) rather than the Fascist intransigents who had threatened Mussolini himself in December. Mussolini was astute enough to realise that he had political debts to pay (the Nationalists had stood by him during the Matteotti crisis), while also ensuring that the Nationalists were complicit in his destruction of individual and collective freedom in Italy.

As a former journalist, Mussolini was well aware of the potency of the printed word. And it was the Press which represented the greatest threat to him by the end of 1925, political opposition having virtually disintegrated. Federzoni had organised police raids on Opposition party offices and arrested 100 people in the aftermath of Mussolini's speech of 3 January. Pius XI had abandoned the *Popolari*, the Socialists were hopelessly split, the Nationalists were in alliance with the Fascists in government and the right wing of the Liberal Party had also allied itself to the PNF by the end of 1926. There was opposition in the Senate led by Benedetto Croce, Ruffini and other independent-minded senators but it was the only surviving outlet for real opposition. This was because the new Press Law of December 1925 stated that only registered journalists could be published, and the Fascists controlled the registration process. It was also well known that Mussolini read the papers carefully every day, indeed he spent far too much time reading them, looking out for the most trivial examples of dissent. While it was true that the Socialist paper *Avanti!*, of which he had, of course, been editor in his Socialist youth, was available in Rome and other big cities, it was rigorously censored. Silencing of anti-Fascist personnel was even more effective and Italy's best-known editor, Luigi Albertini of the *Corriere della Sera,* was sacked along with most of his staff. Albertini joined Croce's group of Oppositionists in the Senate, where he had less influence. The Fourth Estate was to become an adjunct of the Fascist régime.

THE ASSASSINATION ATTEMPTS

Mussolini was assisted in his campaign against political opponents by a highly convenient series of attempts on his own life. So convenient were they, in fact, that the Opposition suspected the Fascists might have instigated at least one of them themselves.

The first attempt on Mussolini's life was made in November 1925 by the Socialist Deputy and war hero Tito Zaniboni, and seems to have been provoked by sheer desperation about the authoritarian drift in Italian politics. It was, like all the others, unsuccessful, and Zaniboni was arrested in a room in the Hotel Dragoni in Rome before he could fire his Austrian-made rifle. According to Mussolini, Zaniboni was a drug addict who had been paid 300,000 francs by Czech Socialists to kill him.[8] The entirely innocent General Capello was also implicated in the plot and arrested.

Three more attempts were made on Mussolini's life in 1926, the first by a deranged Anglo-Irish woman called Violet Gibson in April which Mussolini reacted to (generously in his own eyes) by merely having her deported. He suffered some embarrassment because his nose was injured by the bullet and had to be swathed in bandages. The second attempt on 11 September was more serious in that it was occasioned by internal dissent, the assassin in this case being the anarchist Gino Lucetti who threw a bomb at Mussolini's car which, unfortunately for him, bounced back on to the ground, leaving its target unscathed. Mussolini made the unconvincing claim that the French were behind the assassination attempt because Lucetti had just returned from that country.[9]

The final attempt on Mussolini's life came on 31 October 1926 in Bologna. It was allegedly made by a 16-year-old boy called Anteo Zamboni, but there are strong grounds for believing that dissident Fascists themselves may have been involved in the attempt. The sequel was appalling as 'the presumed marksman ... was lynched on the spot by Fascist guards and his body torn to pieces and carried around the town in a horrifyingly macabre ceremony'.[10] Mussolini himself gave two contradictory accounts of what happened, but to cover his tracks he ordered that two of Zamboni's relatives should be given long jail sentences, although there was little real evidence against them.

Whatever the truth about Zamboni's involvement, there is no doubt that, together with the earlier attempts, the episode gave Mussolini the chance to impose an internal crackdown. Federzoni was made a scapegoat for the assassination attempts and dismissed, to be replaced as Minister of the Interior by Mussolini himself, while a new Police Chief, Bocchini, was appointed who remained in the post until 1940. These changes were accompanied by new legislation in November 1926 which gave the police extra powers of confinement for cultural and political offences. The government was also empowered to close down opposition organisations. A further law deprived the Opposition deputies of their seats in the Chamber, and in December the 'Law for the Defence of the State' was introduced which imposed the death penalty for attempts on the lives of members of the government and the Royal Family. More controversially, a Special Tribunal was set up to deal with political offenders, which was staffed by members of the military, thus depriving the accused of the right to jury trial. A secret police organisation called OVRA (*Opera per la Vigilanza e la Repressione Antifascista*) was set up with the task of monitoring the activities of Oppositionists.[11]

When one adds to this list of repressive measures, the suppression of democratic trade unions (also in 1926), the devastating blow to Italian democracy that they entailed is readily apparent. Only the Communists managed to retain a small underground presence in Italy but they were severely harassed by the police and their leader, Gramsci, was given a twenty-year jail sentence (he died after serving only eleven). The other two big opposition parties, the Socialists and the Liberals, could only operate in political exile in France. Police activity was on a much higher level than had been the case in the past, with an average of 20,000 visits to premises being made in an average week for the seizure of literature, arrest of 'subversives' and so on.[12] Mussolini himself was now given massive protection with as many as 500 plain-clothes policemen around him on State occasions.

THE TOTALITARIAN STATE

Italy had been moved sharply in the direction of what was becoming known as totalitarianism. Mussolini himself had first used the term in a speech in June 1925 when he referred to the need for Fascists to apply a 'ferocious totalitarian will' against the fragmented Opposition so that Italy could be 'fascistised'.[13] Later he was to declare that:

> A party governing a nation 'totalitarianly' [sic] is a new departure in history. There are no points of reference nor of comparison. From beneath the ruins of liberal, socialist and democratic doctrines, Fascism extracts those elements which are still vital.

Mussolini's first reference to totalitarianism was in fact picking up on a comment made in March 1925 by the man who had the greatest claim to be the philosopher-king of Fascism, Giovanni Gentile. Gentile served as Mussolini's Minister of Education from October 1922 to July 1924 before returning to academic life, but he continued to influence Fascist thinking into the 1930s.

Gentile believed that the rise of secularism and individualism in pre-Fascist Italy had destroyed the heroic and the capacity for faith. He looked back to the heroic age of Mazzini and deplored the cynicism and materialism of the Giolitti era. Fascism would displace this with its demand for 'total' adherence (hence the word 'totalitarianism') to the national principle and an all-embracing conception of politics which allowed it to enter all sectors of Italian society. Individuals in this society were important only insofar as they were members of the State, whose task was not to remain aloof and non-interventionist, but to inculcate moral values in the people. Such theory underpinned Mussolini's famous declaration of October 1925, 'everything within the state, nothing outside the state, nothing against the state', which was in its way an attempt to define totalitarianism. Yet it was a distinctively different concept from that of the radicals of the *squadristi* who wanted to control *all* the functions and activities of institutions and organisations in Italy. Mussolini did not seek to do this between 1925 and 1929. Rather, he required compliance with, and loyalty to, the Fascist ethic, while leaving institutions such as the Vatican and Confindustria, the employers' federation, some degree of autonomy. His conception of Fascism was 'statist' because for him the State was superior to everything else in Italy, including the Fascist Party itself. The radicals might feel that Mussolini had sold out the Fascist revolution which they wanted, but he recognised the need to create a balance between Fascism and the existing economic and political forces which he had inherited from Liberal Italy.

Was Italy, therefore, ever truly totalitarian under Mussolini? The constraints placed upon his power by the continued existence of the monarchy and the Vatican are obvious, and neither did the régime challenge the power of the army in the way which was to occur in Germany (there was no SS in Italy). It has also been argued that, unlike its Soviet Stalinist counterpart, Fascism

> never projected a state doctrine with sufficient centralisation and bureaucratisation to make possible complete totalitarianism. In its original Italian meaning, the sense of the term was more circumscribed.[14]

If this is accepted, then Mussolini's 'statist' conception of Fascism was a sensible accommodation with the realities of Italian political and economic life rather than a betrayal of the 'second wave'. Nevertheless, Mussolini had to battle with his old party comrades to ensure that his conception of the Fascist State endured.

THE BATTLE WITH THE RADICALS

On 7 April 1925, Italo Balbo made a speech complaining about the régime's conservatism, for which he was rebuked by Mussolini in a telegram.[15] At the time, this may have seemed to be a mere straw in the wind, but it was an indicator of the way things were moving between Mussolini and the Fascist Party.

The immediate aftermath of the 3 January speech was deceptive because Mussolini brought in Roberto Farinacci, the *ras* from Cremona, often described as his 'left hand', as Fascist Party Secretary. Farinacci was known to be one of the most intransigent *ras* who would have been expected to support the radical agenda. In 1925, he had acted as defence counsel for Matteotti's murderers at their trial, and he was also known as a vehement opponent of freemasonry, a favourite target for the *squadristi*. His appointment was actually something of a masterstroke by Mussolini because it would undoubtedly appease the radicals, while still frightening conservatives who were appalled by Farinacci's encouragement of violence against the fragmented *Popolari* in the provinces. Mussolini could, therefore, follow his old strategy of posing as a moderate while actually encouraging Farinacci to get rid of some of the more turbulent elements in the Fascist Party (as he did in 1925). But it was Mussolini, and not Farinacci, who got the credit for this purge of the *squadristi*, and he who stepped in when the squads killed eight Liberals in Florence in October in front of horrified foreign tourists. The Duce (Leader) of the Fascist Party had decided that enough was enough and he ordered the breaking up of the squads, and their expulsion from the PNF if they continued their activities. The threat that the *squadristi* could be re-activated remained however. But Farinacci had served his purpose as the radical who had purged the radicals, and he was unceremoniously dismissed and sent back to Cremona. There he spent an embittered decade spiced by letters of complaint to Mussolini about the direction his régime had taken. Farinacci's successor, Turati, was little more than Mussolini's hatchet man who would do his master's bidding.

In the short term, this meant an expansion of party membership, so in 1926–27 over 300,000 new members were recruited. These people were largely careerists and opportunists who saw a party badge as an investment. And while they were being encouraged to join, the intransigents were being purged. It has been estimated that up to 60,000 squad members and

Fascist dissidents were expelled by 1929. Mussolini also took the opportunity, through his pliant henchman Turati, to rid himself of turbulent Party secretaries such as Giampaoli and Cottini in Milan.[16] But unlike some Fascist leader counterparts, these old fighters for the cause were generously treated. There was to be no 'Night of the Long Knives' in Fascist Italy. Nevertheless, in encouraging Turati's purge and his parallel acceptance of new members, Mussolini was destroying any lingering radical hopes that the Fascists would remain a revolutionary élite. Instead, the PNF was becoming a party of white-collar middle-class careerists, noted for its nepotism and corruption, so that by the late 1930s a joke was circulating that PNF stood for *per necessita famigliari* ('for family reasons'). By 1939 there were more than two and a half million Fascist Party members, nearly nine times the number in 1921.

WORKING WITH THE BUREAUCRACY

Mussolini liked to boast about the degree to which he purged the bureaucracy in Italy in 1926–27, but in reality the reform of the Civil Service was superficial. Most of the cuts actually took place in the period 1922–24, before Mussolini created the authoritarian Fascist State.[17] One of the problems facing Mussolini was the lack of high-calibre Fascists who could usefully be put into high positions in the bureaucracy. Instead the mediocrities and incompetents got jobs in the PNF, which became a bureaucratic monster in its own right.

Surprisingly, Mussolini rejected a proposal from the Finance Minister, De' Stefani, for a more streamlined Civil Service in Italy, remarking that

> we have to adopt a policy of the maximum of jobs in the State bureaucracy, if we don't want an insurrection on our hands, an insurrection caused by the hunger, I repeat hunger, of intellectuals.[18]

This unusual concern for the fate of intellectuals perhaps covered Mussolini's anxiety that the bureaucratic boat should not be rocked too much lest it jeopardise the drive for modernisation which was such an essential feature of Fascism. During the economic slump of the 1930s, mass unemployment created even more need for a bloated bureaucracy, although the regular Civil Service tended to off-load new government tasks on to agencies and 'quangos'.[19]

Mussolini's statist concept of power made him an ally of the traditional Italian bureaucracy. The key government official was the Prefect, and in a circular of 5 January 1927 Mussolini reaffirmed the importance of these officials. The Prefect was 'the highest political representative of the Fascist régime' according to the Duce, yet throughout the Fascist era (which lasted until 1943) most prefects were non-Fascist political appointees. They were needed in the early days to control the *ras* and the *squadristi*, but when this threat had been dealt with, they retained their authority in Italy's provinces. Mussolini's faith in the loyalty of the Prefects is demonstrated by the fact that they were given the extra task of spying on local Fascists on the government's behalf. They were an authoritarian corps of civil servants whose task was eased by the abolition of local councils in 1926, and the fact that they themselves had to be elected. The old democratically elected councils were now run by a municipal state office called the podestà, which was appointed by the Prefect. It was assisted in local government tasks by another appointed body, the consultative council. Considerable care was taken to ensure that the podestà came from the old privileged land-owning or military castes so that the supporters of the 'second wave' were excluded from power and influence. Thus did Mussolini stifle the radical threat in Italy's regions and reassure the old élites that Fascist hotheads would be kept under control.

Mussolini recognised, however, that the Fascist Party had to be given a role. There was the so-called 'Grand Council', which was given the title the 'supreme organ of Fascism' and which was allowed to appoint Fascism's National Directorate. However, beneath it, at federal level, the appointee system dominated and there were no local Party congresses or provincial congresses through which ordinary PNF members could express their views. Instead, the Party was given a cultural and educational role. Under Party Secretary Starace (1931–39), youth was targeted and local Fascists were supposed to inculcate the right manly, military virtues.

The role of the MSVN also shrank as Mussolini asserted his control over the Fascist Party. He knew that the army would be sensitive about any attempt by the Militia to encroach on its role as 'Defender of the Nation', and in August 1924 he moved to place it more firmly under the control of the generals. The following year a career soldier was made Commander of the Militia, and its role became more and more peripheral. It trained young Fascists who marched about on Sunday parades, but did very little else, thus becoming 'the army's appendix – quite useless but occasionally troublesome'.[20] It was a pale shadow of its German counterpart.

THE LEGAL SYSTEM

A key figure in the process whereby Italy was transformed from being a liberal democracy into an authoritarian dictatorship was Alfredo Rocco. Mussolini made Rocco Minister of Justice in January 1925, knowing that he had been a strong supporter of the PNF–Nationalist merger and that as an ex-nationalist Rocco would be an enthusiastic supporter of the process of strengthening state authority. Rocco declared that Fascism would

> not abolish the individual as individuals have abolished society in other more primitive doctrines, but subordinates him to society leaving him free to develop his personality on lines which will benefit his fellow men.

Rocco was responsible for drafting the oppressive legislation that removed individual freedoms and liberties in Italy between 1925 and 1928. However, he was also responsible for the 1931 Penal Code, which was not overtly Fascist and was to remain in force after the collapse of Fascism in the post-war era. The ordinary legal process was largely left alone by Mussolini and Rocco, who dealt with political opponents through the military tribunal set up by the 1926 legislation. It was organised by MSVN consuls and presided over by military judges who applied military law against offenders. In practice, the Special Tribunal was relatively lenient. Few capital sentences were passed down, the judges preferring to use the '*confino*' (internal exile to remote locations) or prison sentences.

Mussolini called Rocco the 'legislator of the Fascist revolution', and even if one can quibble about the use of the word 'revolution', it is an error to underestimate the extent to which Italy was changed during the early years of Fascism. Legislation did allow Mussolini to remove unreliable judges if need be, and both the judges and the police, however superficially autonomous, did have to enforce Fascist laws. Mussolini also intervened personally in cases, usually to insist on the imposition of severer punishments or, in some instances, the maximum sentence.[21] Thus, the legal system ultimately fell under the jurisdiction of the executive in the person of the Duce, whatever Mussolini claimed to the contrary.

The police operated by the same principle. Bocchini was a career policeman who had to implement Fascist laws. He also had responsibility for the operations of OVRA, and it has accurately been observed that Bocchini, through his secret police dossiers, was the one person in Italy who could give Mussolini accurate information about what the average Italian was thinking. It was also true that in its day-to-day operations the police force was only obliged to consult with the MSVN and the local Fascists in the provinces. It alone was responsible for policing the Italian population (once again the Nazi model was to operate quite differently, with distinctive organisations like the Gestapo and the *Sicherheitdienst* operating alongside the ordinary police force).

As has been suggested, it is too easy to underestimate the extent to which Italy was transformed under Fascism in the years that followed Mussolini's defiance of parliament in January 1925. While it is true that Mussolini had effectively crushed the threat from the Fascist Old Guard by 1927, he had brought about significant changes in Italian society which moved it in the direction of totalitarianism. Freedom of expression and freedom of association had been destroyed in Italy by Mussolini (another important victim was freemasonry which had been banned under the 1925 legislation) and with a minimum of opposition. If Italy was only, to coin a phrase, Fascist in parts, these parts made Italian society distinctly different from what it had been like in 1922.

QUOTA 90 AND THE ECONOMY

Mussolini was no economist, and had little real interest in the subject of economics. In December 1925 he stated that he considered 'the Italian nation to be in a permanent state of war', and the management of the economy under Fascism was presented in militaristic terms. Thus there was 'the battle for the lira', 'the battle for wheat' and 'the battle for births' (in Fascist Italy population numbers were linked to power and effectiveness). The currency, in particular, became a matter of national virility, and resulted in the introduction of a draconian deflationary policy after 1926 which had serious adverse consequences for the Italian economy. There were successes, such as the land reclamation schemes of the late 1920s, but Italy was the poorest of the major nation-states and nothing Mussolini could do would alter that fact. He placed great emphasis on producing more, and in some spheres, such as wheat production, the régime succeeded in boosting production but only at a price. It was the ordinary Italian workers and consumers whose standard of living was badly affected by the revaluation of the lira in 1926, and Mussolini was too dependent on industrialists for support to take measures to alleviate the economic suffering of the working class which was a feature of Italian life by 1933–34. In similar fashion, the balance of power in the economy increasingly favoured the employers who had an open channel to Mussolini rather than the workers. The left-wing Fascists who wanted to legislate to protect workers' rights were effectively defeated by 1928.

As in other spheres in Fascism's early years, Mussolini was content in economic matters to rely on technical experts and civil servants. Both his first Minister of Finance, De' Stefani, and his successor but one, Mosconi (1928–32), fell into this category. Alternatively, when the occasion demanded large-scale state intervention in economic policy (as in 1926–27), the Duce would use a minister with strong links with the Italian financial community. Guiseppe Volpi, who replaced De' Stefani in 1925, came into this category. But the policies pursued by all these men were strictly orthodox.

Volpi's policy in particular brought considerable success in the traditional sphere of international debt repayment. The Italians had borrowed heavily from both the United States and Britain during the First World War, but in 1925–26 Volpi was able to secure a favourable loan settlement with the Americans which was linked to a promise of more US investment in the ailing Italian economy. Only Germany benefited as much from American loans as did Italy between 1924 and 1929.[22]

It was at this point that Mussolini made his only decisive intervention in the management of economic policy between 1925 and the coming of the Great Depression after 1929. In his eyes, the crucial factor was the exchange rate of the Italian lira which had been affected by inflationary pressures in 1924–25 and which Mussolini believed had to be stabilised. Other factors were the burden of cheap foreign imports, and a desire to please those Fascists who believed that freemasonry and international Jewry were somehow being allowed to undermine the Italian currency.

In August 1926, in a speech at Pesarò, Mussolini announced that the lira would be sharply revalued. Its value against the pound sterling would be 90 lire (the rate when Mussolini came to power in 1922) and against the US dollar 19 lire (although by December 1927 the exchange rate with sterling had risen to 92.46 lire). This so-called 'Quota 90' (*quota novanta*) was clearly the result of a political decision by Mussolini, as Volpi thought that the measure placed the lira too high and foresaw the negative consequences of such an overvaluation of the currency.[23] In this sense, Quota 90 was a distinctively Fascist policy which emerged from Mussolini's linkage of currency value with Italy's standing as a great power, regardless of the negative impact such an upward valuation of the currency might have on Italian export trade. By 1926, the lira only stood at one-seventh of its pre-war value. Quota 90 was to push it up to one-third of this figure. It is easy to deride such macho economic nationalism, but before doing so it is wise to recall that democratic Britain was guilty of similar folly in returning to the gold standard in 1925 on the advice of Treasury experts, a decision which the then Chancellor of the Exchequer, Winston Churchill, was to regret bitterly.[24] Italy too was to return to the gold standard in December 1927.

Ordinary Italians paid the price for Mussolini's economic nationalism as ordinary Britons did after Churchill's decision. Quota 90 was followed by wage reductions in both agriculture and industry which were meant to align wages with the revalued lira. These cuts, in 1927, were supposed to bring down wages and prices by ending Italy's post-war inflationary spiral, but in reality wages fell more quickly than did prices. Unemployment also went up sharply, especially in agricultural areas in the South. Matters were not improved by Mussolini's ideological decision to limit Italian emigration in the period 1925–27 as a response to the decision by North and South America to put quotas on Italian emigrants. It was the poor South which suffered most from such restrictions, and Mussolini merely succeeded in worsening the so-called 'Southern Question'. Neither did Fascism's demographic policy of encouraging births, and even putting a tax on bachelors, make much sense when traditional targets of emigration for Italy's poorest people were being choked off (as it turned out 'the battle for births' had little real impact).

THE 'BATTLE FOR WHEAT'

In response to the agricultural depressions in the late 1920s, the régime began the melodramatically named 'battle for wheat' in 1928. Volpi had already put a protective tariff on wheat in 1925, and this, combined with the more extensive use of fertilisers, did bring about a big rise in production so that by the end of the 1930s Italy was almost self-sufficient in grain. But protection, as always, was a double-edged sword, and it was the big landowners who gained most from government policy, whereas the high price of Italian grain (excepting that on the international market) hit the less prosperous. A massive Fascist propaganda campaign was mounted to enlist the support of farmers and consumers alike, and the Duce even abandoned his office to be photographed stripped to the waist, allegedly working in the cornfields. Hitler always thought such behaviour degrading, but Mussolini was proud of displaying his torso! Thus did the Fascist propaganda machine try to convince Italians that the 'battle for wheat' was another triumph for the Duce. In reality, it created as many problems as it solved.

PUBLIC WORKS SCHEMES

Another weapon in the attempt to deal with the agricultural depression was the use of public works schemes. The most commonly used method was land reclamation or what the Fascists called 'integral drainage'. In this instance, they used the services of a noted agronomist called Serpieri, although the reclamation policy did bear something of Mussolini's personal imprint. Most famous of all was the draining of the Pontine Marshes near Rome which was the subject of much Fascist propaganda, but land reclamation was expensive. Taxes had to be raised under Finance Minister Mosconi to pay for it, and they continued to rise thereafter, as did the Italian national sport of tax evasion (De' Stefani was sacked in 1925 because his efforts to stop this sort of corruption had made him unpopular.)

It can reasonably be argued that the land reclamation policy, which had its successes, was only window dressing to cover the grimmer economic realities in the South. Fascism, like Nazism, tried to elevate the peasantry to a mythical status, praising the solid virtues of the humble tillers of the soil. The truth, however, was that the régime was engaged in another 'battle' which it wished to disguise from the Italian public. This was to stop the drift from the land, partly occasioned by the consequences of Quota 90, so that Southern Italian towns would not be overrun by unemployed peasants. This policy of so-called 'Ruralism' has been seen (fairly) as an attempt to interfere with economic mobility in Italy.[25] The real beneficiaries of Quota 90 and protectionism were the big Southern landowners (as has been seen), inefficient though they were.

In industry, too, Fascism favoured the big battalions, and mergers were a feature of the Mussolini period. Nevertheless, and despite its obvious drawbacks, the ferocious deflationary policy adopted in 1926 did have its positive points. Revaluation favoured the new electrical and chemical firms as well as importers of raw materials which seemed in line with Fascism's efforts to provide itself with a new shiny image. Conversely though, Italy's exporters suffered because the lira was too high, and textile manufacturers were particularly angered. The financier, Gualino, who had close links with the artificial silk industry, wrote to Mussolini to complain about the revaluation but policy was not reversed.[26] The dangers of treating economic policy as merely an extension of foreign policy were obvious enough for Italian businessmen, and while it is true that Mussolini's involvement in high economic policy before 1929 was limited to a sixteen-month period in 1926–27, the results of this intervention were profound.

LABOUR RELATIONS

The Fascist movement purported to stand for national unity before everything else. Mussolini had abandoned the socialism of his youth, but he was sensitive to the charge that he had betrayed the working class in favour of an alliance with the privileged. The upper classes were grateful to him for ending the mayhem of the 'Red Two Years', but continued to assume that he would protect their interests against working-class militancy.

This created a real dilemma for Mussolini, which could only be confronted by the creation of some sort of mechanism that could reconcile class differences. The tensions between Right and Left inside the Fascist movement also meant that he needed to maintain the pretence, at least, that there was some sort of equality between employers and workers. Between 1922 and 1928 the figure in the Fascist hierarchy who represented the workers' interests was Edmondo Rossoni, an old friend and associate of Mussolini's from the Romagna, who had subsequently spent some years in the United States. After the achievement of power in 1922, Rossoni had been made Secretary General of the Confederation of Fascist Corporations (*Confederazione delle Corporazioni fasciste*), which was renamed the National Federation of Fascist Unions in 1926.

In the mid-1920s Mussolini was still flirting with populism and he described Fascism as 'a method, not an end, if you like, it is an autocracy with democratic overtones'.[27] This allowed Rossoni, a genuine believer in workers' rights, to support strikes in the metallurgical industry, but it soon became apparent that the Fascist syndicates or unions did not command the kind of loyalty given to the traditional democratically elected unions, which belonged to the Socialist Trade Union Federation (CGL) and the Catholic Trade Union Federation (CIL).

On the legislative front, syndicalists such as Rossoni were also in retreat. In 1926, Rocco framed labour legislation which outlawed both strikes and lockouts, but Rossoni and his supporters were not convinced that this created legislative equality. The strike was the primary weapon of the industrial working class while the lockout was but one of several options available to employers. Neither was Rossoni impressed by Mussolini's appointment of himself as Minister of Corporations in 1926 (as usual, the real work was done by the under-secretary, in this instance Bottai), as part of his attempt to create a 'Corporate State' which would submerge class hatred in Italy. The ultimate aim of the system was to create corporations which would represent both labour and management in major industries, which would then, in turn, provide parliamentary representation. The system of corporations was to be extended to the entire Italian economy.

ROSSONI'S FALL

In 1927, Bottai was the prime mover in drafting the Labour Charter together with Rossoni and the right-wing Minister of Justice, Alfredo Rocco (Mussolini himself had played a minor role in the drafting of the Charter). The document promised complete freedom for the syndicates but Rossoni was not deceived. The undermining of workers' rights implicit in corporatism culminated in Rossoni's dismissal in November

1928. His post of Secretary General was abolished and replaced by a sub-division of power amongst seven heads of corporations representing Industry, Agriculture, Trade, Transport, Banking, Professions and Artists, Seamen and Airmen.

There appears to have been a personal element in Rossoni's fall as well. Stories circulated that Rossoni was talking about Mussolini's possible fall from power, and the Duce began to keep a file on his old friend's activities. This contained allegations about corruption involving land deals and his wife having been a Rome prostitute (uncannily similar to allegations about Hitler's Defence Minister, von Blomberg, in 1938, although in that instance the accusation about prostitution was used to obtain von Blomberg's resignation after his unfortunate marriage).[28]

The Rossoni dismissal also raises an historiographical issue about Mussolini's relationship with the industrial working class, and the degree to which Fascism achieved consensus with the workers. On the face of it, the removal of a long-standing syndicalist and influential Fascist such as Rossoni points to an abandonment of any real concern about workers' rights in Italy to appease Confindustria because Mussolini realised that he could never win over the workers. This viewpoint has been contested by Renzo de Felice, a right-wing admirer of the Duce, in his massive multi-volume biography and supported to a degree by the oral historian L. Passerini in her analysis of the Turin working class. But this concept of acceptance of Fascism by the working class has been hotly attacked by other historians, and the evidence for it is unconvincing.[29] Fascism was unable to thrive in a normal democratic context and, in the end, had to create structures which meant that industrial relations disputes were settled outside factories either by the PNF itself, or by arbitration courts associated with the corporations. In practice, Fascist industrial policy was about wage cuts and oppression of the workers, even if this may not have been what Mussolini originally intended. Indeed, it is no exaggeration to say that the trade unions that existed in 1922 had become 'impotent' by 1928 and were unable to combat the massive unemployment which afflicted Italy by the early 1930s.[30] Official sponsorship by the régime was unable to save the syndicates from the same fate as their Catholic and Socialist counterparts.

Nonetheless, there is still some evidence to suggest that Mussolini felt uneasy about an alliance with the employing classes. He did not like the capitalists and could not entirely erase memories of a socialist upbringing, while the capitalists regarded Mussolini as a necessary evil because the alternatives were unpalatable. Corporatism can therefore be seen in part as an attempt to mollify Mussolini's latent socialist conscience, even if the Fascist rhetoric about the Corporate State was increasingly to do with style rather than substance. Employers recognised that force of circumstance obliged Mussolini to favour them, and this is why Confindustria was happy to subscribe to the Palazzo Vidoni Pact of 1925, whereby they accepted that the Fascist syndicates alone could legally represent the workers, and with this measure went the abolition of elected workers' councils, which underlined the extent to which Fascism was the enemy of local industrial democracy. Mussolini's major weakness in industrial policy was his lack of any real popular base amongst the proletariat. There were no 'shirtless ones' in Italy to support Mussolini in the way, for example, that Juan Perón's quasi-Fascist dictatorship was underpinned by workers' support in Peronist organisations in Argentina.

Ultimately, therefore, Mussolini's record in economic policy during Fascism's first decade was patchy. There were spectacular over-hyped successes such as the draining of the Pontine Marshes, and an improvement in the railway system which gave rise to the legend that 'Mussolini made the trains run on time', but foreigners were not always convinced and there are suggestions that the groundwork on the railways had in fact been carried out before 1922. More solid achievement came with Volpi's renegotiation of Italian war debts, and the more positive consequences of Quota 90 and the 'battle for wheat'. But even when due recognition is given to such successes, it is hard to ignore the negative impact of Mussolini's dramatic insistence on Quota 90 and the draconian revaluation of the lira in 1926. Had he left the currency issue to technical experts or financiers like Volpi, the country might have avoided some of the catastrophic results of the Depression which struck Italy and the rest of the world in 1929. Yet Mussolini's leadership style demanded dramatic interventions even in policy areas where he lacked the technical expertise to properly evaluate the consequences of his decisions. In his autobiography Mussolini stated that before his Pesarò speech, Italians were living 'under a régime of giddy and disastrous finance' from which he had freed them.[31] He was equally proud of putting the lira back on the gold standard in December 1927. Nonetheless it was the Italian people who had to pay the price for Mussolini's economic illiteracy in terms of lost jobs and lost markets.

SOLVING THE ROMAN QUESTION

The Italian State and the Papacy had been at loggerheads since the achievement of Italian unity in 1870. Indeed, this unity had only been attained by confiscating Church lands in Central Italy. Thereafter, successive Italian governments had failed to solve the so-called 'Roman Question', and successive Popes had refused to recognise the legitimacy of the Italian State.

It seemed, on the face of it, unlikely therefore that the rabid young anti-clerical Benito Mussolini, who had inherited his father's anti-Catholicism rather than his mother's piety, would succeed where other Italian political leaders had failed. Once in power, however, Mussolini veered sharply away from the vehement anti-clericalism of his youth, and began a process of softening up the Vatican to the point where it would recognise the Fascist State in exchange for accords which would address the financial and religious grievances the Church had after 1870. This process culminated in the Lateran Pacts of February 1929 which secured Papal recognition of the Fascist State in exchange for considerable financial, political and religious concessions. All historians of modern Italy and Mussolini's biographers have agreed that this represented a massive triumph for the Duce and brought him both international and domestic prestige. It can be argued that Mussolini had to concede much to the Church to secure agreement, but he surely gained more, even if accommodation with this most conservative of organisations appeared to undermine his claims to be a revolutionary. But he deemed it better to try and co-opt Catholicism into some sort of Fascist consensus rather than confront the Church directly, something at which even the doughty German Chancellor Bismarck had failed to succeed during the nineteenth century. It remains to examine how Mussolini achieved his greatest domestic triumph.

Mussolini came to power in 1922 in a context of tense relations between the Italian government and the Vatican. Earlier post-war attempts to resolve the Roman Question by Nitti and Orlando had failed, and King Victor Emmanuel III had known anti-clerical leanings. Opinion in the *Curia* (the Pope's Civil Service) was also hostile to the House of Savoy.

Nevertheless, there was soon evidence that Mussolini was prepared to make concessions in order to achieve reconciliation with the Church, despite anti-clerical opinion inside the Fascist Party. He showed this in his personal life by remarrying Rachele in a church in 1925, and having his three children baptised although they were all well past the normal age for such a religious service. More importantly, Mussolini showed that he was prepared to recognise and even strengthen the Church's central role in Italian society. Freemasonry was banned (much to the Church's delight) and the clergy were exempted from taxation. Public funds were used to prevent a leading Catholic bank from collapsing, and the Vatican was additionally gratified by a law against lewd behaviour during Lent. Mussolini's own anti-clerical past was disowned with the suppression of his pre-war pamphlet 'God does not exist'. Even abroad, the Duce championed the Catholic cause by supporting the Vatican's claims in Palestine, and forcing the Albanian Orthodox Church to accept the authority of Rome rather than of the Orthodox Patriarch in Constantinople.

There was, in addition, a marked convergence of policy on social issues. Mussolini, as has been seen, campaigned for a higher birth rate and therefore banned contraceptives in 1924 (despite having made use of them during the excesses of his youth). Fascist attitudes towards women dovetailed with those of the Vatican, even if not to the absurd extent demonstrated in slogans such as 'War is to men as childbirth is to women'. Birth control was also banned as part of Mussolini's 'battle for births', which coincided with Catholic insistence on the sanctity of life. Mussolini even donated the Chigi Palace to the Vatican and gave cardinals free railway passes in his anxiety to placate the Pope. Pope Pius XI reciprocated in turn by preventing any accommodation between the *Popolari* and the Socialists at the time of the Matteotti crisis, and by refusing even to see the wife and mother of the murdered man. Catholic newspapers remained sympathetic to Fascism, even though the movement's thugs were beating up Catholic trade unionists and destroying Catholic co-operatives. Mussolini was clever enough to distinguish between the spiritual and lay aspects of Catholicism, although even Catholic boy scouts were unacceptable in the Fascist scheme of things. Disputes about the role of Fascist and Catholic youth movements continued, in fact, to trouble relations between Pius and the government. Nevertheless, by 1926 the situation was sufficiently favourable for talks to start between the Vatican and Mussolini's government about normalising relations.

THE POPE AND THE DUCE

The two men at the centre of these negotiations had one thing in common. Both were autocrats. Achille Ratti had, at the age of 65, been a surprise choice as Pope, but he shocked his clerical subordinates with the ferocity of his personality. There was only one motto under Pius and this was *'obbedire'* (obey). Woe betide any cleric who failed to live up to the new Pope's exacting standards. He was a stern businesslike Lombard whose hobby was mountain climbing, and his ecclesiastical heights were both uncompromising and articulated in language alarmingly close to Fascism. 'If a totalitarian régime exists,' Pius declared, 'totalitarian in fact and by right – it is the régime of the church.'[32] His greatest fear was not the violent thuggery of Fascism, but the ideological threat from Soviet Communism.

But Pius was no fool. He understood the Fascist threat to Catholic Action, the major Catholic Youth Organisation, and this worry caused him to break off talks in the period between 1926 and 1929 when the two sides were locked into negotiation. On the Fascist side, Gentile, Farinacci and Balbo tried to slow down the pace of the negotiations lest the Duce give away too much to win the approval of the Holy Father.[33] Doubtless they hoped that the Mussolini who had written a novel about a lecherous cardinal in his youth would reappear with a diatribe against 'black microbes who are as fatal to mankind as a tuberculosis germ'.[34] Mussolini may have been a pagan at heart but he recognised that the stamp of Papal approval was essential for his régime.

Pius XI was to have some last-minute qualms about making a deal with Fascism, but he was persuaded to sign an agreement by his influential Secretary of State, Pacelli, later Pius XII. Pacelli's lawyer brother, Francesco, was also involved on the Vatican side, while the pro-clerical Arnaldo Mussolini may have prevented any anti-religious lapses by his brother during the tense final talks in 1928–29. During this final stage, Mussolini himself was directly involved in the negotiations, spending hours reading through the draft agreement.

THE LATERAN PACTS

The day 11 February 1929 has a considerable claim to be the most important in Mussolini's life. For, on that day, he signed the Lateran Pacts with the Vatican, doing so with the heavy gold pen presented to him by the Papal representative, Gaspari. There were massive celebrations throughout the Eternal City. The next day Pius XI greeted a huge crowd of 200,000 in Saint Peter's Square who were chanting 'Long live the Pope of Reconciliation' and was moved to tears. Yet Mussolini was not to be found (even the jaundiced Victor Emmanuel III showed a public face), just as he had been absent on his day of triumph in 1922. The circumstances, however, were quite different. In 1922, the Duce had been indulging his taste for extra-marital sex; now he absented himself from the celebrations lest he be seen to show undue deference to the Holy Father. Fascists had swallowed the agreement with the Vatican, often with ill grace, but they would not stomach the sight of the Duce kissing the Papal ring or bending the knee. He would not, Mussolini told his entourage, 'go to Canossa'.[35]

Mussolini seemed, to some of his supporters, to have conceded too much in the Lateran Pacts, which took their name from the Church of Saint John Lateran. The agreement comprised three components: a treaty, a financial agreement and a Concordat. The Pope received generous financial compensation for the losses sustained in 1870 to the tune of 750 million lire, together with 1,000 million in Italian Government State Bonds. The Treaty created the mini-state of the 'Vatican City' which consisted of 108 acres (44 hectares). The new State had full diplomatic rights and Italian assistance in setting up a radio station. Funding was also provided for a separate railway station.

The Concordat was the most crucial part of the agreement both for Pius XI and Mussolini. Article 43 allowed the continued existence of Catholic Action but only if its development was 'outside every political party and in direct dependence upon the Catholic hierarchy for the dissemination and implementation of Catholic principles'.[36] Furthermore, clergy and religious orders were also prevented from taking part in party politics. In effect, political Catholicism was dead, and the last rites had been carried out with the full co-operation of the Vatican.

On his side, Pius XI secured the recognition of Catholicism as the sole religion of Italy, and Article 34 also accepted the validity of Catholic marriages without any state involvement. But, Mussolini received official endorsement from the Church for Fascist candidates in the elections of 1929 and 1934. Priests might now lead their flocks to the polling booths and might be seen giving a Fascist salute.

Who gained most from the accords? It is hard not to see Mussolini as the bigger beneficiary. At a relatively modest cost, he won immense prestige for the régime both at home and abroad. What Cavour and Giolitti had been unable to achieve, Mussolini had done in only three years.

But Mussolini was not disposed to be generous in victory. He still saw the Church as a dangerous rival and was soon making statements about the subservience of Church to State which infuriated Pius XI. The thorny issue of the role of Catholic Action remained, and it blew up into a major crisis in 1931, which has been described as the point where 'Italo–Vatican' relations reached an all-time low'.[37] The origin of the crisis lay in the Fascist accusation that Catholic Action was organising sports activities and trying to form 'occupational groups' when sport was supposed to be the preserve of the National Balilla Agency, formed in 1926 with the object of indoctrinating Italian youth. Pius XI was angry enough to issue a Papal encyclical (usually known from its opening words), 'We have no need ...' (*Non abbiamo bisogno...*), and warnings that Catholics ought to think hard before taking an oath of loyalty to Fascism.

Ultimately though, both sides had too much to lose from a confrontation and a compromise was reached. The Vatican agreed that Catholic Action would not organise sporting events, and by the end of 1931 Mussolini was saying that he was 'well disposed to the Church'. In 1932 the Duce even visited Pope Pius in person to cement the new friendship.

CATHOLICISM UNDER FASCISM

Pius XI has been accused of throwing away his moral authority by signing the Lateran Pacts with Mussolini. Certainly he had occasion to regret his actions later. Yet the paradox was that Catholicism seemed to grow in strength after 1929. The Catholic Student Organisation in particular, which was subsumed by Catholic Action, thrived in the 1930s and was to produce many of Italy's Christian Democratic post-war leaders. The number of priests grew under Fascism, as did the number of nuns, in this case from 71,000 in 1921 to 129,000 in 1936.[38] Catholicism continued, therefore, to be a state within a state in Mussolini's Italy, and one which could never really be part of a Fascist consensus. Mussolini's 1929 pacts, although they gave Fascism the stamp of respectability, did so at a price. Mussolini plainly believed that in this instance Rome was worth a Mass or, at least in his own case, the pretence that he himself was a regular Mass-goer. Catholicism was too potent a force to be confronted, whatever Fascist radicals may have thought. And in the end, Mussolini could bask in the knowledge that he was the man who had resolved the Roman Question.

By 1929 some of Mussolini's followers might have accused him of becoming a pragmatic trimmer, willing for example to compromise with the very same Catholic Church that he had so despised in his youth. Yet despite such pragmatism, the blueprint for a Fascist society was in place by 1929, with the destruction of freedom of speech and democracy, the manipulation of local government and Mussolini's adoption of the concept of totalitarianism. It remained to be seen how thoroughgoing the Fascist 'revolution' would prove to be in the long run.

4

THE DICTATOR AT HIS ZENITH

MUSSOLINI ABROAD. THE PRAGMATIC PHASE, 1922–32

Mussolini said that 'Fascism should be the watchful guardian of our foreign policy', and he stressed the importance of enhancing Italy's position in Europe and the world. But he also sought to allay foreign anxieties about his fiery new movement by saying, 'Fascism is not for export'. In practice, therefore, his foreign policy in the 1920s mixed Fascist adventurism with traditional diplomatic caution. But it was the latter which predominated.

This reflected the realities of the time. The Duce had to try and maintain a working relationship with Italy's former Anglo-French allies even when strains appeared, especially with the French. Increasingly though, he came to be a revisionist, even if only in a rhetoric which was largely for domestic consumption (observers noticed that Mussolini's speeches were more moderate on the rare occasions when he went abroad). Yet, this rhetoric represented genuine Italian discontent with the 1919 peace settlement which it was thought had failed to recognise Italian aspirations. There is no sense, therefore, that Mussolini was following his own overtly nationalist agenda in the early years of Fascism. That agenda was already there and had been clearly articulated by his Nationalist allies before 1922. Indeed, there is a good case for saying that on issues such as the relationship with Yugoslavia (which focused on the thorny question of Fiume), Mussolini was running *behind* the

Nationalist agenda. He was also, of course, a learner in the international arena in the 1920s, dependent to a considerable degree on the diplomatic expertise of the Foreign Office. Yet it would be unwise to ignore altogether the Fascist gloss which was put on foreign policy after 1922, or to reject the idea that Mussolini did have a programme which he hoped that circumstances would allow him to pursue (in particular, regional aggrandisement in the Balkans and colonial expansion).

MUSSOLINI AND THE FOREIGN OFFICE

As always with Mussolini, perception was as important as reality. One of his first acts on coming to power in 1922 was to move the Foreign Office away from its traditional home in the Palazzo della Consulta in Rome, to the smaller Palazzo Chigi. There, next to Victor Emmanuel's royal palace, Mussolini could pout and posture to his heart's content in the busy centre of Rome. The move was made in only a week at Mussolini's insistence, presumably to reinforce the impression of Fascist dynamism, but it actually caused a good deal of administrative confusion.[1]

Any such impression of dynamism was misleading. Control of foreign policy in Italy remained with the professionals, one of whose early tasks was to teach their master about the niceties of diplomatic protocol, because at conferences abroad he gave the impression of being rather uncouth. As with the Civil Service as a whole, it was a question of preserving the status quo. True, there was the so-called 'Class of 27' when non-Fascist members of the diplomatic corps were removed and replaced by Fascists, but this did not much alter the management of foreign policy even though Mussolini himself held the post of Foreign Minister.

In practice, Fascists in the Foreign Ministry often tended to go native. A good example of this process was afforded by Dino Grandi, who was put into the Foreign Ministry in 1927 as an under-secretary after being under Federzoni at the Ministry of the Interior. Ostensibly, his task was to make foreign policy more Fascist in style, but the reverse actually happened as he adopted the conservative outlook of the Foreign Office career officials. Mussolini made Grandi Foreign Minister in 1929 and he held the post for three years before his alleged conservatism caused his dismissal. According to Mussolini, Grandi had permitted himself to become the prisoner of the League of Nations, had conducted a pacific and internationalist policy, had acted the ultra-democrat and League of Nations man; he had made Italian policy deviate from the straight course of egoism and realism and compromised the aspirations of a new generation.[2]

This was the same Dino Grandi who had been *ras* of Bologna and leader of the *squadristi*, who had terrorised the surrounding countryside in 1921–22, but Mussolini's criticisms were entirely accurate. They left an unanswered question however. Why had Mussolini made Grandi Foreign Minister in the first place, given that he had veered so sharply away from the radicalism of his youth? It raises the issue once more of the extent to which pragmatism outweighed Mussolini's desire to Fascitise Italy's foreign policy.

FOREIGN REACTION

The other European powers reacted cautiously to the arrival of the new demagogue in Rome. Nor did the young dictator make a favourable impression on his first trips outside Italy. He wore spats and a butterfly collar with a top hat and badly pressed striped trousers, causing the aristocratic British Foreign Secretary, Lord Curzon, to remark, 'He is really quite absurd'. Mussolini seemed ill at ease with foreigners despite his claim to be able to speak English, French and German fluently. They were also surprised by his small stature (Mussolini was only five foot six inches), and unimpressed by his blustering attempts to demand equality at the 1922 Lausanne Conference where he spent as little time as possible. The subject of the conference was the Turkish settlement which was of little real interest to the Italians, but Mussolini insisted on being present, surrounded by his Blackshirts and a band which constantly played the Fascist anthem 'Giovinezza'.

Shortly after his return from Lausanne, Mussolini went to the London Conference on German reparations, where his behaviour seemed equally bizarre. He insisted on wearing his Fascist Party badge when visiting King George V at Buckingham Palace and got into an unseemly row at Claridge's Hotel when the French delegation was allocated better rooms than those of his own delegation.[3]

The British were confused. *The Times* commented that there was a good and bad side to Mussolini, and the British Ambassador in Rome thought him an able man if a 'strange' one. In Washington the Harding administration and the business community were willing to give the new Italian leader a chance. The French, knowing of long-standing Italian claims to Tunisia, were suspicious.

In general, foreigners noticed that Mussolini seemed to be more interested in making press statements than engaging in orthodox diplomacy. The British diplomat and historian Harold Nicolson commented in 1923 on 'the exuberant petulance of Mussolini's language',[4] which was certainly far milder abroad than his pronouncements at home, but the former journalist was always looking for cheap propaganda victories. Yet with the passage of the years, and certainly by the time of the important Locarno Conference of 1925, a more restrained Mussolini was beginning to win important foreign admirers. Austen Chamberlain, British Foreign Secretary from 1924 to 1929, was one. Winston Churchill was another, while the US Ambassador to Italy, Richard Washburn Child, was one of Mussolini's most uncritical devotees.

THE CORFU CRISIS

Before Locarno, however, Mussolini had given the international community a fright. The occasion of this crisis was the murder on 27 August 1923 of the Italian general Tellini, who was president of an international commission supervising the demarcation of a new frontier line between Greece and Albania. Italo-Greek relations were already tense, as the Greeks objected to the 1912 Italian annexation of the Dodecanese Islands, and Mussolini refused to accept the Greek explanation that the murder of Tellini (and three other Italian colleagues) was the work of bandits.

At this point, the whole dispute should have been handed over to the nascent League of Nations for moderation. But Mussolini flatly refused to allow this to happen. Instead, he insisted on 3 September 1923 that the so-called Council of Ambassadors (which was still in permanent session in Paris to deal with problems linked to the 1919 settlement) should mediate in the crisis. Mussolini bombarded the island of Corfu and then sent forces in to occupy it. He also threatened to leave the League altogether if it intervened in the Tellini affair.

Mussolini's action was in clear breach of the League of Nations Covenant, and it was a high-risk one because he was warned that should Great Britain act under League auspices, the Italian navy would be unable to counter British naval power in the Mediterranean. But in this instance, Mussolini was lucky. The British Foreign Secretary, Curzon, opted for a pragmatic policy of falling in with Mussolini's wishes and not risking the prestige of the League in a possibly dangerous confrontation with Italy. At the Rome Embassy, the British diplomat Howard Kennard was angered by Britain's appeasement of Mussolini. The Italian leader, he wrote, was 'a man who has no experience of diplomacy or statesmanship' who might continue to take 'some rash and impulsive step which might greatly react on the people of Europe'.[5] As it was, after mediation by the Council of Ambassadors, Greece had to pay Italy 50 million lire in compensation. In exchange, Mussolini ended his occupation of Corfu. Force had prevailed in this instance and Fascist Italy 'was announcing itself on the international stage with what seemed a replica of the *squadristi* raids, so ruthlessly deployed against its Socialist and other democratic enemies'.[6]

There is no doubt that Mussolini's occupation of Corfu had widespread support at home. Even his critic, Luigi Albertini, gave Mussolini full backing in *Corriere della Sera*. And abroad in Britain and France, right-wing politicians who disliked the high-flown pacifist rhetoric of the League thought his action over the Tellini murder justified. The fact remains, however, that Mussolini did not risk any further adventures of this type for the rest of the decade. He continued instead to attack the Treaty of Versailles in his propaganda, saying that it was an 'absurdity' which would 'one day bring about not only revolution in Germany but war in Europe'.

MUSSOLINI'S REVISIONISM

As a dissatisfied power, it was to be expected that Italy would campaign against Versailles and its associated treaties. Relations with Yugoslavia were a particular sore point, and D'Annunzio's occupation of Fiume had only resulted in the unsatisfactory (in Italian eyes) Treaty of Rapallo in 1920. This gave Fiume autonomous status as a city, and obliged Italy to give up much of its claim to Dalmatia in exchange for a land corridor linking it to the city.

The Corfu crisis actually improved relations with Yugoslavia in the short term. A new treaty in January 1924 allowed Italy to annex Fiume in exchange for other territorial concessions, and this was followed within days by a treaty of friendship. But Mussolini failed to take advantage of this opportunity to improve relations with his neighbour. This may have been in part because he was criticised for making too many concessions to the Yugoslavs, but the main reason for a growing coldness was Albania. A civil war broke out there which found the Italians and the Yugoslavs on different sides. Worse, from the Italian point of view, was the fact that they backed the wrong side, although Mussolini was able to bribe the winner, Zog, so that in 1927 Albania became, in effect, an Italian protectorate. The converse was that the Yugoslavs drew ever closer to the Little Entente, a French-sponsored alliance between Yugoslavia, Rumania and Czechoslovakia. Mussolini's response was to try and subvert the Yugoslav State by funding Croat separatism. He also drifted into a revisionist alliance with Hungary and Bulgaria, defeated powers in 1918, who felt they had been victimised by the post-war settlement. In April 1927 Mussolini signed a ten-year Friendship Treaty with Hungary which had territorial claims against both Rumania and Czechoslovakia.

The only issue on which Mussolini was robustly anti-revisionist during the 1920s was over an Austro-German *anschluss* or union. This was specifically forbidden by Article 80 of the Treaty of Versailles, and Mussolini shared his countrymen's view that tiny post-war Austria could not be allowed to be swallowed up by a nationalistic Germany. There was already a sizeable German-speaking minority in the South Tyrol, inside Italy's frontiers.

Mussolini had already adopted the imperialist agenda of his Nationalist allies, but the 1920s were not a productive era for colonial revision in Italy's favour. In Asia Minor, the Graeco-Turkish war had resulted in the appearance of the strong nationalist régime of Kemal Ataturk which ended any Italian hopes there, and the same was true in Africa. Italian interest was centred on Ethiopia, where the humiliating defeat of 1896 was unavenged, but in 1923 Mussolini was obliged to sponsor Ethiopia's independent entry into the League of Nations. The 1928 commercial treaty with Ethiopia merely underwrote Italy's continued interest in that country, but there does seem to have been a good deal of confusion in British policy about Ethiopia's admission to the

League. The official line was that Britain would co-operate with Mussolini to keep the Ethiopians out of the League because they were sponsors of the slave trade. Somehow, the British representative in Geneva failed to go along with his instructions and actually supported Ethiopian admission instead of co-operating with Mussolini and opposing Ethiopian entry. Mussolini's instruction to his League representative was not to oppose Ethiopian entry openly, but to keep in touch with his British counterpart so that together they could demand such major concessions from Ethiopia that its entry to the League would become impossible. But the British representative in Geneva, Cecil, believed that Ethiopian entry into the League would somehow solve the slavery problem, and voted for entry despite his instructions to vote against. Faced with this situation, the Italians did so too, rather than be in a minority of one on the League Slavery Committee.[7]

Despite this muddle and British displeasure about Mussolini's occupation of Corfu, relations between the two states improved after 1923. The same was not true of Italian relations with France. There was a suspicion that France had encouraged Ethiopia's application to join the League to embarrass Mussolini, and the French were also sensitive about the large Italian population in Tunisia which might be used by Mussolini in his propaganda against French North Africa. Conversely, Mussolini resented French influence in the Balkans, most obviously represented by the Little Entente with which France was allied. By contrast, the new British Foreign Secretary, Chamberlain, helped to smooth out the path of Anglo-Italian relations (his wife Ivy became a particularly warm admirer of the Duce). The area known as Jubaland was transferred from British control to that of Italian Somalia, and a small rectification was agreed along the Egyptian–Libyan frontier in Italy's favour.

There were other gains too. Italy had extensive wartime debts in the United States and it also needed American loans to stabilise the Italian lira in the period 1925–26. The debt question was settled on surprisingly generous terms in October 1925 when Mussolini's government was granted a low interest rate. Less favourable to Italy was the US adoption of an immigrant quota policy which reduced the number of economic migrants from its poor South.

The most interesting aspect of Italy's foreign relations during this period, perhaps, concerns its relationship with the Soviet Union. The

Fascist Party had, after all, demonised Bolshevism inside Italy, terrorised its adherents and imprisoned the Communist Party leader, Gramsci. Yet, despite this ideological hostility, Italy was the first major European power to recognise the Soviet Union through the commercial treaty of 7 February 1924. This pragmatism may not have led to anything of substance in trading terms, but it did highlight the extent to which Fascism had accommodated itself to the norms of diplomacy whereby the managers of foreign policy came to terms with the existence of alien components in the international system. In the 1920s, at least, ideology played little part in Mussolini's foreign policy, and this continued to be the case in the early 1930s too.

LOCARNO

In October 1925, representatives of the European great powers met at Locarno in Switzerland to discuss the stabilisation of Germany's frontiers with France and Belgium. Mussolini had wanted the conference to be held in Italy but he failed to secure agreement to this proposal. Always on the lookout for the spectacular gesture, Mussolini arrived there in a speedboat and tried to secure a guarantee for Italy's frontier with Austria along the Brenner Pass. In this, too, he failed, but Italy was asked to guarantee the new Western settlement along with the British. Germany now voluntarily accepted the existing Franco–German and Belgian–German frontiers but nothing was said about frontiers in the East.

Mussolini's role at Locarno was small (it is not mentioned at all in his autobiography for that reason), but it did show that the Fascist leader had achieved a degree of respectability in Europe. The more tawdry aspects of his régime had been made plain days before when Blackshirt thuggery shocked foreigners in Florence, and this led some foreign journalists to boycott Mussolini's press conferences. But in 1925 at Locarno Mussolini posed as a sober member of the European family and showed no desire to repeat the alarms and excursions of 1923.

Nevertheless, it has been justly observed that of all the leaders at Locarno, 'Mussolini was perhaps the most displeased by the outcome'.[8] He had not really wanted the commitment north of the Alps, and came heartily to dislike the sort of collective security arrangements created at Locarno. As has been noted, he subsequently made a nuisance of himself in the Balkans by encouraging Croat separatism in Yugoslavia. On the credit side, he could only point to a new friendship with Austen Chamberlain and the two small territorial gains made by Italy in Egypt and the Horn of Africa. When, later in 1925, Chamberlain, Briand, the French Foreign Minister, and his German counterpart, Stresemann, were awarded Nobel Peace Prizes, Mussolini was left out in the cold and thought of trying to get one for himself to place Italy back in the limelight.[9] Nothing came of this idea.

Pragmatism continued to be the characteristic of the late 1920s. Grandi was installed as Foreign Minister in 1929 and he seemed to have a sensible recognition of the limits of Italian power. He worked closely with the British and his major achievement was to secure naval parity with France in London in 1930 (Italy was allowed the same number of warships and aircraft carriers as the French in the Mediterranean). Then, abruptly, in July 1932 Dino Grandi was sacked, and Mussolini took over the Foreign Affairs portfolio himself once more. It was the beginning of a new, seemingly more aggressive phase of Mussolini's foreign policy. If Mussolini wanted to cut a powerful figure on the diplomatic stage, there are still some grounds for believing that even in foreign policy he was a revolutionary manqué. The evidence for this rests with statements he made in 1925–26 at the very time when he was apparently underwriting European stability. These involved Italy challenging both Britain and France in the Mediterranean so that she could break out of the straitjacket imposed by the peace settlement and achieve both regional and colonial expansion. This thesis stresses the link between domestic and foreign policy and sees Mussolini, in Grandi's phrase, as 'the Pope of anti-democracy'.[10] Existing international constraints might hedge in Mussolini's ambition, but both at home and abroad he wished to challenge the status quo.[11] This view, based on more recent research, challenges the older view of Mussolini's most laborious biographer, Renzo de Felice (a startling seven volumes and 5,648 pages), that whereas domestic policy in the 1920s *was* revolutionary, foreign policy was characterised by cautious realism.[12] Mussolini could be cautious in his management of foreign policy, but it is perilous to take the first decade of Fascist foreign policy out of context. The fact that Mussolini was unable to pursue ideological foreign policy goals in those years does not mean that he did not have such goals.

A fellow Fascist wrote of Mussolini in the last week of his life that he was 'the most complicated and contradictory man I have ever known', and this judgement is more perceptive than the traditional one of Mussolini as a braggart poseur or a 'Sawdust Caesar'.[13] Yet it is hard to shake the well-established image of Mussolini as a superficial, bombastic demagogue, more actor than real political leader, a man more concerned with superficiality than with substance.[14]

This traditional portrayal does Mussolini an injustice. That there were deeply unpleasant aspects of his personality is undeniable. He could be vindictive, cruel and insensitive, but some of his character traits are surprising in a dictator and he was demonstrably not the monstrous tyrant recognisable in Hitler and Stalin. Mussolini showed none of the interest in ostentatious wealth so common amongst dictators, and several biographers have seen this as remarkable in a man who was so keenly aware of how to corrupt others. Neither was Mussolini the kind of idler that Adolf Hitler showed himself to be, reliant on the eccentric notion that 'a moment of genius is worth a lifetime of office work'. True, he had created a grotesque personality cult which grossly exaggerated his virtues, but Mussolini for all his flaws was demonstrably human in ways that the other great twentieth-century dictators were not. It can perhaps be argued that his vices were those of insecurity and vanity, rather than outright evil as in the case of Hitler and Stalin. Nevertheless, his true character continues to elude us, shrouded as it were in layers of self-protective propaganda and self-created isolation.

THE MAN

Mussolini was a man for whom the physical often seemed to dominate the intellectual (despite his pretensions as a theorist of Fascism). He was obsessed into middle age with physical fitness and spent much time riding, running, fencing, playing tennis and football. He insisted on running up and down ranks on military parades, and even demanded that his ministers should run across the vast floor space between his office, door and his desk. Yet observers noted that he did not seem to enjoy physical exercise; to indulge in it seemed to have more to do with an image of Fascist virility than genuine enthusiasm. The exception, perhaps, was riding, which Mussolini seemed to like and which allowed him to take on Napoleonic poses. Swimming was another daily preoccupation, but this manic activity does not seem to have done all that much for Mussolini's general health.

The Duce, like his friend the German Führer, suffered badly from digestive problems. On 15 February 1925 Mussolini, then still only 41, vomited blood in his Rome house at the Via Rastella (which was rented from a sympathetic Roman banker) and doctors rapidly diagnosed an ulcer. The Duce was obliged to take several weeks off away from the public gaze. There were even rumours that he might be replaced by a triumvirate of Giolitti (elderly but still active), Salandra and Federzoni.[15]

There was no coup. Instead Mussolini was forced to accept a drastic new diet. It consisted of a bland combination of milk, as much as three litres a day, and fruit as many as five times a day. Little meat was consumed, and Mussolini had already given up drinking alcohol in 1923 except on special occasions. He had been a heavy smoker but also gave up cigarettes. None of this saved him from considerable pain and discomfort for the rest of his life, and Mussolini suffered another ulcer attack in 1929. Naturally, the Italian people were shielded from the knowledge that their Duce suffered from such human frailties. Mussolini flatly refused to have surgery for his ulcer in 1925, and even his wife was not told about the seriousness of his condition.

In fact, the ulcer condition probably owed a good deal to Mussolini's hectic lifestyle. He boasted that he never spent more than three minutes over a meal or ten minutes eating in a day, and this could hardly have eased the task of his unfortunate bowels. Yet, despite this, Mussolini in middle age was rather portly. The entirely shaven head was intended to hide any signs of ageing, and an aversion to glasses meant that Mussolini's speech notes were typed on a special typewriter with large characters. Even Mussolini's chin, which he liked to jut out in militaristic poses, was starting to sag.

Sexual virility was also part of Mussolini's image, at least until the point when he tried to pass himself off as the ideal Fascist father. All women were fair game and were pounced upon in the crudest fashion at the Via Rastella house. Frequently Mussolini did not even bother to wash before these sexual encounters, merely slapping eau de cologne all over his body.[16] Even after he went through a religious marriage service with Rachele, Mussolini continued to have a string of mistresses. The last one, Claretta Petacci, who began to write admiring letters to him at the age of 14, was the daughter of the Pope's doctor. She was to die with him in 1945.

Observers often commented on Mussolini's chaotic fashion sense. His morning suits were badly fitted and he maintained a strange addiction to spats. His shoes were often unpolished and he wore the same suits for weeks on end. He continued to wear bowler hats until the admired Laurel and Hardy ceased to do so in the silent American films he enjoyed watching. Even the convention of shaving went unobserved before Mussolini attended diplomatic functions. But the truth was that Mussolini had no time for the fripperies and fopperies of conventional fashion. The image of the strong man was all important.

THE FATHER

It was part of Fascist myth that the Mussolini family exemplified the best of family life. This was far from being the case. His sexual exploits apart, Mussolini did not seem to enjoy family life, and not until 1927 did he bring his family to Rome from the Romagna. Two more children were born in Rome, Romano (September 1927) and Anna Maria (September 1929). Mussolini was doing his bit for the 'battle for births', even if his fellow Fascist leaders were not.

It has already been noted that contemporary observers believed Mussolini to be rather frightened of his wife. But Rachele played the role of the obedient Fascist wife to perfection; this at least was the propaganda image. Even in family circles she referred to him as 'Duce', although privately she could be scathing about her partner. She disliked Roman society and preferred the farm, showing no interest whatsoever in her husband's political career. Occasional comments like 'What a character' give us little insight into what Rachele might really have thought about Fascism. She said that Mussolini was a good father, but this sits oddly with comments by Vittorio Mussolini about hardly ever seeing his father during those years.

Mussolini's favourite child was Edda, who was to marry his Foreign Minister, Count Ciano. But her antics in adolescence are reminiscent of Mussolini's own turbulent youth, and in 1928 she had to be sent off on a tour of India to keep her out of mischief. Edda was probably the closest to her father, but even she was not a rival to his younger brother Arnaldo, who has the best claim to being called the Duce's alter ego. Quieter than his brother, Arnaldo was deeply religious (his role in the signing of the Lateran Pacts has already been noted) but he was also a

co-conspirator. As editor of *Il Popolo d'Italia*, Arnaldo was a major contributor to the creation of Mussolini's cult of the personality, and he
also co-authored the Duce's self-serving autobiography. Praised as an
intellectual and writer, Arnaldo was, in reality, a mediocrity. But he
had his brother's trust, and his premature death in 1931 has been seen
by some as the beginning of Mussolini's slide into egotistical fantasy.[17]
Certainly, Mussolini became more isolated the older he got, actively
disliking the company of other human beings and referring to ordinary
people as 'the herd'.

THE LEADER

Mussolini did his best to cultivate an image of omnipotence as Italy's
leader. He took on far too many jobs and appeared to others to be alter-
nately swamped by them or skimping on his duties. The image of the
Duce as a hard-working leader was central to Fascist mythology however, and it was put about that Mussolini worked as many as eighteen
hours a day (fourteen on Sundays).[18] He did not, of course, and lights
were deliberately left on in Mussolini's office late at night to support the
illusion that the great leader was working away for the nation. Analysis
of Mussolini's alleged daily activities, which took in eighteen-hour
working days, voracious reading of newspapers, playing his collection of
rare violins *and* watching his favourite films in his personal cinema,
underlines the element of unreality involved.

Part of the problem was that combined with Mussolini's campaign to
portray himself as the Fascist superman was a profound contempt for his
Fascist colleagues, which made it necessary for him to wear so many
hats in government. When ministers were able, like De' Stefani, they
were likely to be sacked. So too were those like Balbo who had too high
a public profile. In Balbo's case he achieved fame as an aviator, and in
1931 led a squadron of Italian flying boats across the Atlantic (this was
in response to the embarrassment caused by the anti-Fascist de Bobis,
who had showered Rome with leaflets telling people to oppose
Mussolini's tyranny). The exercise was a triumph and Balbo returned to
Italy as a hero. Mussolini came to Ostia airport to meet Balbo, then,
when the propaganda tumult had died down, he sacked him as Aviation
Minister. Mussolini had not yet learnt to fly and he did not want any
competition, even from an old comrade like Balbo. Farinacci, as has

been seen, suffered a similar fate. Loyalty to old comrades was not always one of Mussolini's characteristics, and like many dictators he preferred mediocre sycophants to men of ability.

On the credit side, Mussolini showed a surprising modesty about receiving honours. He even insisted on writing a thesis to justify the conferment on him of an honorary law degree by Rome University. Neither was he interested in money for its own sake, seeing the pursuit of riches as ignoble. Between 1928 and 1943, Mussolini did not take his salary as prime minister, living instead on the profits of *Il Popolo d'Italia* and money made from writing articles for the right-wing American press magnate William Randolph Hearst. He also made a good deal of money from the various editions of his autobiography and the hagiographies turned out by his mistress Sarfatti and Giorgio Pini.[19] Mussolini personally corrected the proofs of the Sarfatti biography, later admitting that it was rubbish published because 'invention was more useful than the truth'.[20]

It would be wrong, however, to suggest that Mussolini lived in the austere style of a Ho Chi Minh. The house in the Via Rastella was spacious and admired in Rome, and Mussolini was also given a castle in the Romagna called Rocco delle Caminate by the province of Forlì, which was restored at some expense to the State. It was said to resemble a museum more than a house, but Mussolini enjoyed the views over the area in which he had grown up (the castle overlooked Predappio). Some family holidays were also spent at the resort of Riccione on the Adriatic coast. But if not austere, Mussolini could be generous. He was often given large sums of money by admirers, and much of this was given to charities without any publicity.

Mussolini's public face rejected such civic virtues. Alongside the absurd domestic sloganising, the cult of *ducismo* (leadership) demanded a favourable image of Mussolini abroad. He went to great pains to win the approval of important foreign journalists such as the American Anne O'Hara and the Englishman Ward Price. To a considerable degree, this charm offensive worked, and Mussolini's foreign admirers included Winston Churchill and his wife Clementine, and both the Chamberlains. Such charm was rarely bestowed on Italians however. For them, the Duce was a scowling, ever-present superman. A ban was even placed on photographs which showed Mussolini smiling.

Many people thought that Mussolini's aggressive posturing was nothing more than an act designed to cover an essential timidity. His addiction to fast cars (which he drove in an alarmingly reckless manner) and aircraft could also be explained in terms of an underlying inferiority complex. This is a seductively easy explanation. This same Mussolini, after all, had been a brave soldier in the First World War, and had impressed Italians and foreigners alike by the cool way he reacted when attempts were made on his life. Mussolini was indeed a complex and contradictory character, who felt the need to confuse in order to protect his status as the leader. He could be reckless, indecisive, charming, abrasive and generous in bewildering succession. He could also, in the case of enemies and supporters alike, be cold-hearted and calculating. But a buffoon he was not.

WORKING TOWARDS THE DUCE?

An interesting comparison can be made between Mussolini and his German counterpart Adolf Hitler. It concerns the way in which Mussolini worked with his colleagues, and the extent to which, as in Hitler's case, the dictator's habits shrouded him in a blanket of charisma and mysticism. In Hitler's case, as Professor Kershaw has so convincingly demonstrated, Hitler's elusiveness and slapdash working habits meant that subordinates were obliged to try and interpret the Führer's will because he was loath to involve himself in the day-to-day grind of government and administration. This also meant that Martin Bormann obtained great power because he was able to act as a filter between his master and his own rivals in the Nazi hierarchy.

Can we discern a similar pattern in the workings of Fascist Italy? In many respects, as Professor Bosworth has pointed out, Mussolini was a quite different animal from Hitler.[21] He had, after all, a traditional family life, albeit one with an array of mistresses in the background, whereas Hitler's sexuality has been a matter for debate over the decades since his death. Also, and again unlike Hitler, he was reasonably scrupulous in dealing with paperwork, working long hours at his desk while also staying within the constitutional constraints placed upon him when he became prime minister in 1922. Even when Mussolini's personal dictatorships began in 1925, he still accepted the role played by King Victor Emmanuel within the Italian Constitution. By contrast, once the aged President Hindenburg died in August 1934, there were really no constitutional constraints upon Hitler's power and he was quick to merge the positions of Reich Chancellor and Reich President into one.

One looks in vain for an Italian Bormann, and although Mussolini did accept the concept of Social Darwinism with its emphasis on the survival of the fittest, there is little to suggest that he had a coherent strategy for encouraging his subordinates to fight out their power struggles so that the 'fittest' would triumph. Mussolini could be manipulative and ruthless (his treatment of the Radical Farinacci bears this out), but he was, if anything, guilty of interfering too much in the government machine and of holding far too many ministerial portfolios. It was not necessary, therefore, for Fascists to 'work towards' Mussolini in the way in which Nazi bosses were obliged to do with Hitler, trying on the basis of hints from the elusive Führer to formulate day-to-day policy. It is also pertinent here to recall that Mussolini, unlike Hitler, never had a mass popular base. He therefore had to work harder at being popular by being more visible and interventionist. Mussolini was never the leader of the largest party in Italy in the way in which Hitler was in the years 1932–33. He did succeed briefly in securing a high level of popularity around the time of the Ethiopian War, but did not risk putting himself before the Italian people for judgement as frequently as did Hitler through a series of referenda (although there was one over the Lateran Pacts).

Where the two dictators did have a good deal in common was in their protection of long-standing and incompetent party colleagues. In Mussolini's case, incompetent veterans such as de Bono were followed by youthful nitwits like Vidussoni (a Party Secretary during the Second World War) in a misguided effort to appeal to Italian youth. But the Duce's movement lacked the sort of hard core of ideological party fanatics who surrounded Hitler. De Bono, Grandi, Balbo and Farinacci (although he was an unpleasant anti-Semite) hardly compare with Himmler, Goebbels, Heydrich and Rosenberg. And although Mussolini's flirting with racism was discreditable and cowardly (as will be demonstrated in later chapters of this book), the Fascist movement lacked the emphasis on crude biological determinism which was such a feature of National Socialism. Yet both movements put their faith in the magnetic leadership qualities of the Leader, who was supposed to represent in his own person all that was good and wholesome about the nation. Fascist slogans such as 'Mussolini is always right' seem absurd from the vantage point of the twenty-first century, but they reflected two needs. One was Mussolini's own personal need to make his leadership a dominant feature in every Italian's life, the other the necessity for a movement with a limited and fragile popular base to focus attention on the Duce's qualities rather than on the patent flaws of the régime. The claims of cultural historians of Fascism that Mussolini was somehow able to turn Italians into real militants and Fascist new men and women fail to convince. He may well have wished to do so, but Italian conditions never allowed him to develop the absolute, fanatical belief in his message achieved by Hitler.

At his zenith and basking in the afterglow of victory in Ethiopia, Mussolini had a real, if illusory, popularity in Italy. But although he became more remote from colleagues and people alike in his later years, Mussolini would never achieve Hitler's Olympian detachment.

5

ITALIAN SOCIETY UNDER MUSSOLINI, 1931–39

Mussolini's aim was to regenerate Italy, and to do this he had to create a new Fascist élite. If this was to be achieved, Italian youth had to be Fascistised, thus the domestic emphasis in the 1930s was on youth. To be old in the new Fascist Italy, according to Mussolini, was shameful, and the régime highlighted youthful achievement be it in sport, aviation or culture.

The new Italy was also crudely masculine and warlike. The role of women, according to the régime, was to be clearly delineated. If not as absolute as the Nazi slogan of 'Children, Church, Kitchen', Fascist slogans still placed women in a limited, subservient position, and their primary function was biological. The demographical thrust of Fascist policy demanded a pliant femininity – if the threat to 40 million Italians from 200 million Slavs and 90 million Germans was to be addressed. In practice, the population policy was hopelessly unrealistic, but Fascist rhetoric eulogised the earth mother who produced numerous children for the nation and did what her husband told her.

As a journalist and propagandist, Mussolini was quick to see the potential of radio and cinema, and the 1930s saw his régime make increasing use of the mass media, albeit not in the sophisticated mode of neighbouring Nazi Germany. All this contributed to the all-pervasive personality cult created by Starace, the Duce's reliable sycophantic tool as Fascist Party General Secretary between 1931 and 1939. Mussolini's personality cult had by now transformed him into an almost godlike

figure imbued with superhuman qualities. A lonely dominance characterised the Duce's life, separating him from the Italian people. As he
told an aide during the early 1930s: 'A chief cannot have equals. Nor
friends'. As the decade went by, there were increasingly dangerous signs
that Mussolini himself was becoming the dupe of the adulatory culture
which he had allowed Starace to create.

WINNING OVER ITALY'S YOUTH

As with any totalitarian régime, the battle to win the hearts and minds
of Italy's young people was a lynch-pin of Fascist strategy. But educational policy was another area where the PNF's tentacles were resisted
by the State, with Mussolini's connivance. Only the GUF, the Fascist
Organisation for University Students, was directly under the Party's
control in the education system proper, although Fascist influence over
children up to the age of 12 was considerable. It was secured by an elaborate system of political education whereby, for example, children as
young as age 6 became 'Sons of the She Wolf' (a reference to the animal
which had allegedly saved the infants Romulus and Remus, who went
on to found Rome), and girls aged between 8 and 14 years became
'Young Italians'. As most primary headteachers were Fascists, recruit-
ment into these organisations, which were subsumed by a national
group called the *Opera Nazionale Ballila* (ONB) in 1926, was quite easy.

At Mussolini's direction, Fascist readers and textbooks became available in 1930, and primary schoolchildren learnt about the perils of
Bolshevism and the masterful character of their Duce. But problems
arose in the secondary sector, where the demands of the academic cur-
riculum restricted the time made available for political indoctrination.
Subjects such as philosophy (which women were banned from teaching)
might encourage non-conformity rather than the consensus which
Fascists sought. The evidence suggests indeed that Italian adolescents
were not enthusiastic Fascists, although there were no signs of obvious
revolt as manifested by the 'Swing Movement' or the White Rose group
in Germany.

Matters were even worse in the universities, where apathy was
widespread amongst the student population. Mussolini realised that the
new Fascist élite would need to be recruited from the ranks of the university graduates, but was reluctant to interfere too much. Farinacci, in

his usual blunt style, actually accused his Duce of crawling to the professors in the universities,[1] and he may have hit a sensitive spot. Mussolini was proud of his right to call himself '*professore*' because of his teacher training, and in this, as in other instances, he was sensitive to charges that he was muzzling free speech. Gentile persuaded him to impose a loyalty oath on university academics in 1931 (few resisted), but that was as far as Fascist interference went until Mussolini's lurch into anti-Semitism in 1938 produced a rethink. Outside the universities also critics like Croce were tolerated and writers such as Moravia were able to publish without censorship. Mussolini was merely gratified when intellectuals like Pirandello endorsed his régime at home, more so when the famous British playwright George Bernard Shaw did so from abroad. In this sense, it is accurate to say that Mussolini 'ruled with a light rein'[2] where educational and cultural matters were concerned. There was no Fascist equivalent of Stalin's relentless bullying of Shostakovich, Prokofiev, Pasternak and Mandelstam.

The problem of winning over Italian youth remained nonetheless. Mussolini seems to have overestimated the extent to which the secondary education system and the PNF youth movements had indoctrinated the youth even after all rivals, for example, the Catholic Boy Scout Movement, had been removed. He did have an alternative strategy, however, which was to use sport as a political weapon. Sport was a Fascist obsession which happily coincided with the priorities of most red-blooded Italian males.

The ultimate role model was the Duce himself, of course, whose interest in sport has already been outlined. But there were plenty of others for Italian youngsters to emulate with the encouragement of the PNF. Italians won twelve gold medals at the Los Angeles Olympic Games in 1932, and the national football team won the World Cup in both 1934 and 1938. It was the same in boxing, where the giant Primo Carnero was world heavyweight champion in the 1930s and towered over Mussolini in celebratory photographs. And somehow it could all be put down to the Duce's inspiring leadership. All forms of sporting participation were encouraged for the greater glory of Fascism. Functionaries such as Under-Secretary Arpinati ensured that they were at the forefront of sporting bureaucracy. He became President of the Italian Football Federation and built a huge stadium for Bologna, his local soccer club. Soccer then, as now, was the pre-eminent Italian sporting obsession.

Fascism also took to the air in its effort to impress young Italians. Balbo's exploit in 1931 has already been referred to and he wrote in grandiloquent terms of his achievement. His soul vibrated 'in harmony'[3] with his Duce, Balbo wrote, as he swaggered about in his black shirt and grey-green jodhpurs. When he arrived back with his squadron in Italy, the old Fascist Marinetti, a poet as well as a painter, broadcast in ecstatic terms about 'The rich music of Balbo and his transatlantic fliers ... The delirious crowd yells: Here he is, here he is! Duce! Duce! Italy! Italy!'[4] Mussolini had to wait until 1939 to get his pilot's licence, but there were other Fascist fliers like his son-in-law, Count Ciano, and his own two sons, Bruno and Vittorio. Fascism seemed to have the modernity which appealed to youth, and such glamorous exploits as that of Balbo concealed the banality of much of its political propaganda.

WOMEN UNDER FASCISM

Mussolini became more of a chauvinist as he grew older. He was dismissive of women's abilities and avoided the relationships with female intellectuals which had been a feature of his youth. Thus, Sarfatti, one-time lover and biographer, was expelled from the Duce's inner circle in the 1930s. He preferred, seemingly, the adulatory letters of teenagers such as Claretta Petacci.

Mussolini's personal attitude towards women was reflected in that of the régime he headed. Some feminists had supported Fascism in the early days, but they were soon put right about the position allocated to women by Mussolini and his Party. Instead, Fascism imposed a 'monolithic stereotype of idealised womanhood'[5] which focused on the virtues of Italian motherhood to the exclusion of almost everything else. Middle-class women were encouraged to do good works for the poor, but they were not encouraged to enter the professions and could not be found (any more than their working-class sisters) in the top echelons of the Fascist Party. Mussolini pretended to encourage 'Latin feminism' and some feminists were converted to Fascism through the nationalist route during the war. Liberal democracy had done little for women so the hope was that Mussolini, with his search for consensus, might do more. It also seems to have been the case that some feminists recognised that they could not easily challenge the Fascist emphasis on the importance of motherhood.[6]

As was the position with men, Fascist propaganda was far less effective with working-class women. The Fascists were unable to break down and penetrate working-class strongholds in the big cities and, it has been argued, their attempts to exclude women from the employment market were more to do with bluster than reality. Quotas were placed on the number of women that could be employed in particular industries, but it is questionable whether the apparently draconian 1938 law on female labour had the impact which some historians have claimed. It seems to have had more to do with defining what women could do rather than stopping them from working altogether.[7] Like the Nazis in Germany, the Fascists found that economic realities, especially during wartime, made the exclusion of women from the labour market a hopeless absurdity. What Fascist propaganda did do, however, was to reinforce the idea that women's work was casual, transient and supplementary to the male role of primary breadwinner.

Mussolini found a useful ally in the Church, which echoed Fascism's opposition to abortion and the importance of the family. Contraception was also made illegal, but although the Duce made a sterling personal contribution to the 'battle for births', the Italian birth rate perversely continued to fall during the Fascist period. Live births fell to 23.1 per 1000 by the late 1930s, despite Fascist support for 'The Day of the Mother and Child' (started in 1933) and the 'Opera Nationale Maternità ed Infanzia' (National Agency for Maternity and Infancy), which provided medical care and subsidised milk for mothers and small children.

In its treatment of women, Fascism also underlined its opposition to real democracy. Mussolini had made sympathetic noises about bringing in a female suffrage bill (women did ultimately get the vote after the Second World War), but he reneged on his promise. His cynicism on the issue was then further demonstrated when, at the point where he conceded the vote to women in 1926, local elections were abolished in favour of a system of Fascist patronage. Mussolini encouraged his supporters to believe that women were too irrational and emotional to be brought into the political process. In this sense, Rachele, who preferred the farm in the Romagna to political involvement, was supposed to be the ideal Fascist woman. If she ever did venture to offer an opinion, following complaints from family friends, Mussolini would tell her that she 'knew nothing about it'.[8] Under Fascism, women were to be seen and not heard, although Mussolini's policies did impact on their lives through his undermining of the collective bargaining system in industry and his alliance with Catholicism which controlled, or attempted to control, their personal lives. It is impossible to demonstrate nonetheless that the Fascists achieved any degree of consensus with the female population. Neither could Fascism make women 'the angels of the hearth' as its propaganda machine demanded.

THE MEDIA

As a former newspaper editor, Mussolini had wasted little time in securing control of the print media when he came to power. It was to be expected, therefore, that he would see the propaganda potential of the new broadcasting and film media as well. Italy, like other European countries, was involved in the radio revolution (its inventor Marconi had after all been an Italian), and by 1938 there were more than a million registered radio sets in the country. In 1937, Mussolini set up a Ministry of Popular Culture (popularly known as Miniculpop), and it controlled the new medium thereafter, blaring forth much inane Fascist propaganda.

The cinema, too, offered important opportunities for propaganda, and the régime set up the Experimental Centre of Cinematography as well as taking over Italy's best-known film studio, Cinecittà, in 1938. Like its Nazi equivalent, Fascism specialised in the cinema of escapism, although some fine films were produced, such as *Luciano Serra pilota* (underlining Fascism's love affair with the air), in whose production the Duce's own sons Bruno and Vittorio were involved. Alongside these stood the standard Fascist propaganda films such as *The Year Seventeen*, which was technically poor in comparison with Nazi propaganda films like the 1934 *Triumph of the Will* as well as banal in content.

Vainly, Mussolini tried to counteract the influence of Hollywood, even though he, like most Italians, loved Laurel and Hardy. He provided the Italian film industry with heavy financial subsidies after 1934 and tried to censor American films, but he was no more successful in counteracting the influence of Hollywood than was democratic Britain with its failed 'Quota Quickies' campaign designed to impose a quota of British-made films (which, in fact, no one wanted to watch). Instead, audiences were reminded about the Duce's achievements in compulsory newsreels which had to be shown alongside the star attractions.[9] By the late 1930s, Italians were becoming decidedly bored by the sight of an increasingly flabby, supposedly athletic Duce prancing about on their cinema screens.

CORPORATIVISM AND THE GREAT DEPRESSION

The strength of Mussolini's position during the early 1930s was underlined by the emergence of Fascist movements elsewhere in Europe (such as Mosley's British Union of Fascists). The success of National Socialism in Germany in particular (Hitler was the leader of the largest political party by 1932) seemed to support the Duce's claim that Europe, like Italy, could be 'Fascistised'. And Mussolini's seniority in the Europe-wide Fascist movement allowed him to sponsor the International Conference of Fascist Parties at Volta in 1932. This marked an attempt to set up a Fascist International as some sort of rival to the Soviet-inspired Comintern. Mussolini must have been gratified by the appearance of the Romanian fascist Iron Guard movement so close to the heartland of his major ideological foe.

The early 1930s also presented the Fascist régime with the major crisis occasioned by the global depression. This in turn put the so-called 'Corporate State' under renewed scrutiny as an instrument for dealing with such a profound economic crisis, and posed the question of whether Fascism did present a 'Third Way' between liberal capitalism, which had been gravely shaken by the Depression, and Soviet Communism.

Bottai had become Minister for Corporations by 1930, and he was precisely the sort of Fascist intellectual and technocrat whom employers feared as an interventionist. Superficially the Corporate State did seem to increase its powers during the decade; in 1934 a new law created no fewer than twenty-two corporations which were supposed to cover all areas of industry, agriculture and services, and control prices for goods and services. In theory, the corporations were supposed to regulate economic relations between employers and employees, but in practice the tentacles of the Fascist dictatorship made this impossible. Mussolini, in fact, remained at the very centre of the decision-making process, which weakened the autonomy of the corporations. All discussions in the National Council of Corporations had to be approved by him, and corporation regulations could only be made effective by decrees from the Duce, which were rarely forthcoming.

Mussolini was supposed to be enthusiastic about the Corporate State, but the corporations remained ultimately toothless because whereas the employers were fully represented, the workforce was not. Representatives of the working class in the corporations were usually Fascist Party bureaucrats or Ministry of Corporations officials who had no real contact with the shop floor or village farm. In similar fashion Bottai's 'Charter of Labour', which was supposed to focus on labour relations and social issues, proved to be a sad disappointment for those syndicalists of the Rossoni era who had seen the Corporate State as a means of eradicating class tensions and regulating capitalism.

Employers in Confindustria were gratified that the corporations did not involve them in any kind of centralised Soviet-style planning mechanism. Neither were the Fascist syndicates represented at shop-floor level in the way that free trade unions were represented by shop stewards. In fact, the syndicates continued to be an instrument for the coercion of a working class which was penalised if it dared to strike, and which suffered severe wage cuts between 1930 and 1934.

What is striking about the Depression years is the way in which the corporations were excluded from the policy-making process needed to solve the problem. It was the government itself that imposed a forty-hour week in 1934 to alleviate unemployment, partly at the request of the syndicates. And it was the government that adhered rigorously to a misguided policy of refusing to devalue the lira (by contrast, both the pound sterling [1931] and the US dollar [1933] were devalued). This strategy ran down Italy's gold and dollar reserves and created an increasing balance of payments deficit.

The most radical government measure to deal with the Depression, however, was the setting up of the Institute of Industrial Reconstruction (IRI) in 1933. This was a reaction to the collapse during the Depression years of Italian banks which, under the unusual Italian system, also held industrial shares as collateral. The IRI was set up completely outside the corporative system, thus the State could own majority holdings in firms which would otherwise have collapsed (especially in the most vulnerable areas of shipbuilding and iron and steel production). Government holdings in this instance were compensation for paying off the vast debts the failing companies owed to the Bank of Italy. The IRI also strengthened the system whereby industrialists dominated, because they now sat on the boards of the new state-funded companies alongside PNF functionaries.

Nevertheless, the IRI was a significant innovation which survived into the post-Fascist era. Neither was it the only one. In practice, however, the government ignored the corporations (presumably thought to be too bureaucratic in the state of emergency that was the 1930s) in favour of other public bodies. This provides an important example of how Mussolini's statism overrode ideology, despite the fact that the Corporate State played a central part in Fascist propaganda.

If it was nothing else, the Corporate State was a massive propaganda success. Government critics such as Salvemini noted how waves of foreign economists and sociologists headed for Italy to study how the Corporate State had saved the country from the ravages of the Depression. They failed to detect that it was Mussolini's use of direct state power which alleviated such effects (albeit at a price).

Nevertheless, despite the fact that the Corporate State itself offered little more than a veneer of economic activity, the syndicates did have an impact. Some have argued that the coming of conveyor belts and so-called Fordism may have made authoritarianism inevitable on the Italian shop floor (this seems unlikely given that only big firms like Fiat employed such methods) and that there were discernible social benefits. The syndicates lobbied for the family allowances which were conceded in 1934, and were active in collecting funds for the unemployed. Paid holidays and Christmas bonuses came in under the auspices of the syndicates in the late 1930s, and it is true that under Fascism there were few industrial disputes. But the price paid for such apparent stability was the emasculation of workers' democratic rights, and this needs to be remembered. The Corporate State was a sharp demonstration of this fact. Employers had a hot-line to the Duce through their representatives. The workers did not, because the corporations which were supposed to represent them could not do so. In theory, the 1934 law enshrined an elective principle. In practice, worker representatives were just PNF or Ministry of Corporations nominees. Thus, corporations could not provide a forum for a genuine dialogue between employers and employees. By contrast, employers were happy enough to negotiate with the syndicates knowing that they were deprived of the weapon of strikes, and it was generally not necessary to use the tribunals set up in 1926 by Rocco to adjudicate in industrial disputes.

The creation of so-called 'mixed' corporations in 1934 changed little. Of the twenty-two approved, only the one representing artists and their

Plate 1 Mussolini in Tripoli
Source: AKG London

Plate 2 Allied representatives at the Lausanne Conference in Switzerland
Source: Mary Evans Picture Library

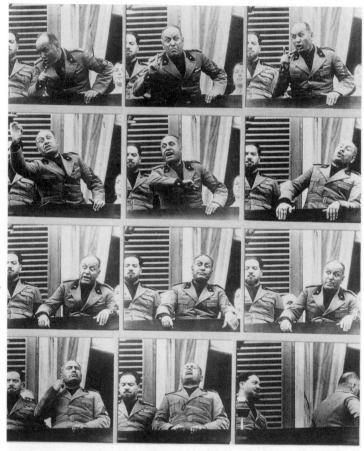

Plate 3 Benito Mussolini
Source: Hulton Archive, Getty Images

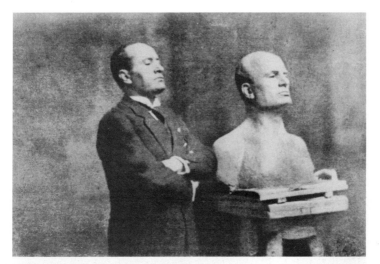

Plate 4 Mussolini with a bust of himself

Plate 5 Chamberlain talks to Mussolini during the Munich Conference
Source: Hulton Archive, Getty Images

Plate 6 Mussolini meeting Hitler at Brennero station in 1940
Source: Mary Evans Picture Library

employers was genuine. Corporativism, most historians have concluded, was a sham. It is a judgement that is difficult to refute. Mussolini himself deemed it wiser to leave his ideological showpiece out of the hard economic decisions which the 1930s demanded.

THE *DOPOLAVORO*

Mussolini had laid claim to the sporting arena as the prerogative of the Fascist Party. But he extended the Party's claims to the whole area of leisure through the so-called *Dopolavoro* (After Work) which was one of the wings of the Fascist movement that was most successful in the 1930s. By 1939 the OND (*Opera Nazionale Dopolavoro*) had almost four million members in Italy and owned football pitches, bars, billiard halls and libraries. Not only was the *Dopolavoro* fun, it was also cheap, putting on plays and concerts, and providing free summer holidays for children. Poor areas received welfare assistance from the *Dopolavoro* as well as holidays, and Mussolini's populist instincts were completely correct in this instance. He, as has been pointed out, also holidayed at the seaside resort of Riccione where the masses went, albeit not in the same accommodation, and had none of the snobbery which caused the middle and upper classes to sneer at the facilities provided by the *Dopolavoro*.[10] Fascism did not provide anything as exotic as the Nazi package holidays to the Canaries or Norway, but the *Dopolavoro* supplied ordinary people in Italy with cheap or free amenities that they had never had before.

OPPOSITION IN FASCIST ITALY

Given that Mussolini's hard-core support in Italy was probably quite small, it might have been expected that, as the years went by, fiercer internal opposition to his régime would manifest itself. That this was not the case, certainly before 1938, shows that the fragmentation of the opposition – a feature of the 1922–24 period – was still in evidence. This was partly a consequence of Bocchini's secret police apparatus and his army of informers, but it was also a result of the almost suicidal tendency of the Left to split. Even the merger of the reformist and maximalist wings of the PSI in 1930 did little to help here as it merely worsened the antagonism between Socialists and Communists. Political

Catholicism had, of course, been fatally weakened by the Lateran Pacts of 1929, although Catholic Action did provide some sort of a cover for those former members of the *Popolari* with political ambitions who rejected collaboration with Mussolini. Otherwise, the only real clandestine underground opposition was provided by the PCI, small in numbers though it was. Attempts to create a kind of super party through the GL (*Giustitizia e Libertà*) which would subsume socialists, republicans and other democrats achieved little. The leafleting exploit of de Bosis in 1931 was spectacular, but did little to dent the prevailing apathy of the population towards the régime.

Neither did Fascism arouse open opposition from intellectuals, even if it failed to create a distinctive intelligentsia of its own. In fact, until the latter stages of the régime in the Second World War, the most potent opposition came from the non-Italian races inside Mussolini's jurisdiction, in particular the sizeable Slovene and Croat minorities (amounting to over 400,000 people in all) who had been left inside Italy's borders by the post-war treaties and who bitterly resented not being part of the new Yugoslavia. Draconian Italian measures, such as enforcing the use of Italian in the law courts and schools to create a unitary state, only made matters worse. Both ethnic groups were overwhelmingly Catholic and resistance to Italianisation was often led by local priests. In 1936, and despite the collaboration between Mussolini and the Vatican, the Catholic bishop of Trieste was even forced out of his position for siding with the separatists. Bombings and assassinations of Italian officials followed in a struggle which received little attention outside Italy itself.

Matters were more peaceful in the South Tyrol, where 228,000 ethnic Germans lived, surprisingly so when the agitation in the largely German-speaking Czech Sudetenland during the same period is considered. But Italian rule was much resented nonetheless, especially when thousands of Italians were deliberately settled in the region in 1939 in a blatant attempt to create ethnic purity. By contrast, the attitude of most Italians to Fascism has been fairly assessed as 'acceptance, but not devotion'.[11]

ANTI-SEMITISM

Was this action in 1939 a straw in the wind or just part of an increasingly racist inclination on the part of Mussolini and his régime? It followed the introduction into Italy in 1938 of anti-Jewish legislation, which can certainly be compared with the infamous 1935 Nuremberg Laws in Germany. Yet, puzzlingly, there is no real evidence to justify the claim that Mussolini himself was a genetic racist of the Hitler or Himmler type. Indeed, Mussolini's latest distinguished biographer has gone as far as to say that to see the Duce as a 'philosophically convinced anti-Semite is absurd'.[12]

On a personal level, Mussolini showed none of the animus towards Jews of his erstwhile ally, Adolf Hitler. His most famous mistress, Margherita Sarfatti, was Jewish and he cared enough about her to ensure that, when the wave of anti-Semitic laws came in 1938, she was smuggled out of Italy to the United States. Mussolini had Jewish friends and is on record as saying that the small Jewish community (only 45,000 by 1938) had behaved loyally during the war and been good citizens generally. True, there were genuine anti-Semites in the Fascist Party, for example Farinacci, but he had been exiled from the centre of power in 1926 and no one believed his crudities, such as suggesting that the Pope's mother was Jewish, a gambit designed presumably both to embarrass the Supreme Pontiff and whip up anti-Semitism amongst radical Fascist anti-clericals.[13] Neither is there any evidence that, after Mussolini and Hitler became allies in 1936, there was any real German pressure on the Fascist government to follow the German route to biological Fascism.

Nevertheless, it does seem more than coincidental that anti-Jewish legislation was put into place in the year 1938, the year after Mussolini visited his German allies and was apparently mesmerised by the military potency of the Nazis. Foreign Jews (only 10,000 in the existing Jewish population) were deported on Mussolini's fiats, and, following the Nuremberg precedent, Italians, now described as Aryans, were banned from marrying Jews. Neither could Jews join the Fascist Party or (again following the German model) have Aryan servants. Only in the treatment of war veterans was any discernible difference evident between Italy and Germany, where the 12,000 Jewish dead in the First World War did nothing to save war veterans from Hitler's crazed racism. In Italy at least, war service could exempt Jews from the legislation, as would previous good service to Fascism (for example, that of former Under-Secretary Finzi).

As it turned out, the anti-Semitic policy was one of the worst mistakes Mussolini ever made, and he began to back away from it as early as 1939. The Pope, who was no particular friend of the Jews, was infuriated by the

Duce's behaviour, especially as even Jews who had converted to Catholicism were still deemed to be covered by the laws and 'mixed' marriages between Catholics and Jews were prohibited. Thousands of valuable Jewish citizens left the country and their businesses were closed down. Given the absence of any obvious pressure from Berlin to introduce such a policy, it is hard to account for Mussolini's change of direction. This was the same man after all who had said that Hitler's racism resembled that of 'a quack or market-square philosopher'.[14]

One suggestion is that Mussolini, apparently determined to mould a tougher Italian character by leading the country into war, doubted the loyalty of the Jews in wartime because they were not true Italians, but the earlier comments he made about their loyalty make this a dubious explanation.[15] We are left, therefore, with the explanation of political opportunism, the one provided indeed by Farinacci, that Mussolini was trying to ingratiate himself with his new German allies and that the anti-Jewish policy was purely pragmatic.

Mussolini did make disparaging remarks about Jews as he grew older, but another explanation for this hanging on to German coat-tails is that he never really understood the nature of German racism itself.[16] Anti-Semitism for Hitler was not a matter of political opportunism or expediency, but was at the very core of his beliefs. Clearly this was never the case with Mussolini. He did nevertheless condone overt racism by Italian forces in the Italy's East African empire.

WAS THERE A FASCIST CONSENSUS?

Mussolini made immense efforts to portray an image of Italian greatness, and the memory of Ancient Rome was constantly traded on in the régime's propaganda. Thus the normal handshake (deemed by Mussolini to be unhygienic) was replaced by the 'Roman Salute' and the Mediterranean became 'our sea'. Italians were also sold nonsense about the 'eight million bayonets' Fascist Italy was supposed to have. Some streams in Fascism demanded spiritual revival based on the concept of a 'New Rome'.

Symbols were also very important during the heyday of the régime, and again the link with imperial Rome was highlighted. Mussolini himself took his title of Duce from the Latin *Dux*, and Fascist organisations such as the MSVN had Roman formations such as legions and cohorts, as well as Roman officials such as centurions. Much of this symbolism seemed grotesquely inappropriate to critics of the régime, but it was part of an attempt to mobilise the people to Fascism's cause. Just as Napoleon had recognised the importance of baubles and decorations, Mussolini saw the potential in florid uniforms (a feature of Fascism) and high-sounding titles. It was a strange characteristic of Fascism that some of its leaders, including the Duce's own son-in-law, Ciano, were prepared to take the distinctly old-fashioned title of 'Count'.

But did it work? Certainly Mussolini won the loyalty of Fascist careerists and hangers on, and he was adept at playing off the various Fascist factions such as the syndicalists and the ex-Nationalists against each other. An army of bureaucrats also went along with the Fascist ethic, if only to keep their jobs. Otherwise, however, there is little evidence to support the Fascist claim that they achieved consensus with the Italian people. Mussolini himself remained popular, certainly until the end of the Ethiopian War in 1936, but his Fascist cronies, if 'heroic' figures like Balbo are discounted, were often regarded as corrupt acolytes of the Duce who owed their positions to his favour rather than their own abilities.

It was Turati who coined the phrase 'Mussolini is always right', but Starace was the high priest of the personality cult which 'assumed ludicrous proportions'[17] druing the 1930s. Starace was a dim-witted, humourless, obedient bureaucrat who flattered Mussolini remorselessly, but on whom Mussolini became as dependent as Hitler did on the equally unattractive Martin Bormann. The fact that he did so is an indication of the extent to which Mussolini was becoming a victim of his own propaganda by 1939. Starace was even known to stand to attention when speaking to his Duce on the telephone, and he was responsible for the 'rent a mob' characteristic of 1930s Fascism when large crowds of supposed enthusiasts chanting 'Duce! Duce!' appeared out of nowhere on demand.

Starace was also responsible for the pathetic manipulation of statistics which both exaggerated the number of Fascists who allegedly took part in the historic events of 1922, and allowed careerists to backdate their party membership to before October 1922 to demonstrate their seniority in the cause. The *gerarchi* or party bosses appointed by Starace during his eight-year reign as General Secretary were also famously incompetent, demonstrating only that it was as well that the Party was subservient to the State in the running of Italy.

Yet to a degree, until 1938–39, the Italians were deceived by the sound and fury of Fascist propaganda and its worship of Mussolini. The Duce's achievement in bringing stability to Italy after the chaos of the 'Red Two Years' was recognised by the middle classes, and some workers at least were seduced by the success of the *Dopolavoro*. It remains, of course, difficult to assess the popularity of a totalitarian régime in the absence of the usual electoral mechanisms which are available in a democracy. But historians have been able to agree that 'a mindless populism'[18] was a characteristic of Mussolini's régime during this period. Giuriati, who preceded Starace as General Secretary in 1930–31, was a man of a more independent cast of mind (which probably accounts for his short tenure of office), and he was troubled by Mussolini's growing isolation and megalomania at the beginning of the decade. As this isolation grew, Mussolini preferred the company of sycophants and time servers to people of ability, especially those daring enough to be critical of the régime. A Fascist diplomat, Cantalupo, who returned to Italy in 1936 after a three-year foreign tour, noted that Mussolini seemed to be living in a world of his own which had little to do with Italian reality.[19]

Had this not been the case, he would have shown more concern about the fact that Fascism had conspicuously failed to win over either Italian youth or the industrial working class in the decade under analysis. In 1937, the provincial secretary in the province of Turin even reported that young Fascists 'are deserting the meetings ... the young no longer go to groups',[20] while the hardened industrial workers recognised that 'Fascism had nothing to offer beyond the odd film or theatre production, generally of very low quality which the workers dismissed immediately as *roba dei fascisti* (Fascist rubbish)'.[21] Only in somewhere like Trieste, where the Fascists utilised Italian dislike for the local Slav population, could the régime claim to be popular. When, in adverse wartime conditions, Mussolini's own personal popularity began to decline, the weakness in Fascism's popular base was fully exposed.

6

THE ETHIOPIAN WAR, 1935–36

War was an implicit component of Fascism and was constantly referred to in slogans such as 'Believe, Obey, Fight'. It is easy to reject statements by Mussolini such as the one suggesting that the Italian people 'must be moulded by fighting' as mere rhetoric, but the record of the 1930s suggests that imperialism and militarism were intrinsic both to the Duce and to his movement. And it has been suggested that Mussolini did indeed have a programme of conquest which only the difficult circumstances of the 1920s prevented him from implementing. Following this analysis, it is possible to see that Mussolini realised quite quickly that to attain his objectives in Africa and the Balkans, he would need an alliance with an aggressive, revisionist Nazi Germany.[1] A common ideology, initially denied by the Fascists, made this increasingly likely as the 1930s drew on, and a full alliance was brought about in the Pact of Steel of May 1939.

The Ethiopian War of 1935–36 seems to have marked a clear watershed in Mussolini's foreign policy. He may well have miscalculated what British reaction to his attack on Ethiopia would be and thereby fatally damaged any chance of a permanent accord with the democracies, but thereafter the drift towards alliance with Germany became more tangible as each year passed between 1936 and 1939. The war itself was a predictable Fascist adventure in Africa, designed both to demonstrate Mussolini's military power and to right the perceived injustice of the 1919 settlement which denied Italy substantial colonial gains. The memory of Italy's humiliating defeat at Adowa at the hands of the Ethiopians in 1896 was also a strong motivating factor in Mussolini's desire to annex the backward African kingdom and please the national-ist wing of Fascism.

THE END OF THE OLD DIPLOMACY, 1932–35

A more traditional view of Mussolini's foreign policy is that he attempted in the period before the Ethiopian War to balance Italy between the Anglo-French bloc and Germany. The de Felice school of historians takes this view and highlights the importance of the abortive Four Power Pact (the four powers being Italy, Germany, France and Britain), known in Italy as 'Mussolini's pact' and the result of an Italian initiative in 1933.[2] Designed to achieve a general European settlement and a recognition of Italy's status as a great power, the Pact was never ratified. But 'there does seem to be much that is classically Italian'[3] about the Pact, as one of Mussolini's biographers has suggested. As the weakest of the European Great Powers, it was logical for Italy to press for a general settlement that would redress both German and Italian grievances without causing a major readjustment which would unduly strengthen any of these powers (Mussolini would certainly oppose any change in Austria's status). Whether it can be claimed, as de Felice does, that Mussolini continued to seek a policy of balance *after* the Ethiopian War is another matter entirely however.

THE AUSTRIAN CRISIS

The appointment of Adolf Hitler as German Chancellor in January 1933 carried with it the threat that Germany might seek to alter the status of Austria, which was forbidden by the Versailles Treaty from unifying with Germany. Mussolini regarded the quasi-Fascist Austrian dictator Dollfuss (who had ruthlessly crushed left-wing opposition) as his protégé and he vowed to protect Austrian independence.

It is now known that Hitler was intriguing with Austrian Nazis to bring about the overthrow of the Dollfuss régime.[4] He himself, after all, was an Austrian whose dearest wish was to secure *anschluss* between Germany and Austria (his Party had been banned in Austria in 1933).

But he was also a strong admirer of the Duce (there is a story that Hitler asked for a signed photograph of Mussolini in the 1920s but was refused), who at this stage was very much the senior dictator. A meeting between the two men was arranged in Venice in June 1934, but it was a disaster. For some reason Hitler was advised to wear civilian dress rather than a uniform (his raincoat concealed a black jacket and striped trousers, an outfit reminiscent of Mussolini in his early days in power). Mussolini, by contrast, was resplendent in a military uniform. It was also noticed that Hitler fidgeted continuously with his grey felt hat, prompting a French journalist to remark that he looked like 'a little plumber holding a troublesome tool in front of his belly'.[5] Mussolini was also made uncomfortable by the swarms of mosquitoes at the Villa Pisani near Padua, and had to move to the Grand Hotel in Venice where Hitler was staying. But there was little meeting of minds. Mussolini was bored by Hitler's long monologues and the German dictator was disgusted by the Duce's failure to stamp out degenerate modernist art in Italian galleries. More importantly, Mussolini flatly refused Hitler's demand that Austrian Nazis should be brought into the Dollfuss government. Mussolini, unlike Hitler, was able to speak the language of his fellow dictator, although he may have been puzzled by Hitler's accent which was a mixture of Austrian and Bavarian dialect. He was too vain to call on the services of Hitler's excellent translator, Paul Schmidt, who was to be present at many of the conversations between the two men. Mussolini himself had not bothered to provide a translator, an omission typical of slapdash Fascist diplomacy.[6]

At Venice Hitler promised to accept Austria's independence as he could not afford to provoke the Italians at a time of internal tension in Germany (two weeks after he met Mussolini, Hitler massacred the leading elements in his Brownshirt paramilitary movement, whose leader Röhm was deemed to be a threat). Neither was Germany in any position to start a full-scale war which might also bring in France on the side of Italy. Yet despite all this, Hitler appears to have believed an Austrian Nazi assurance that the army in Austria was planning a coup against Dollfuss, and agreed that the Austrian party should give their support. On 25 July 1934, therefore, Austrian Nazis stormed the office of Chancellor Dollfuss in Vienna, shot him down and left the tiny Austrian dictator to bleed to death on the carpet. The attempted coup was a fiasco, and the murderers of Dollfuss fled to Germany, but Mussolini was furious, not least because Frau Dollfuss and her family were staying with him in Rome at the time and he had to inform her of her husband's assassination (despite the complete volte-face in his foreign policy after 1934, Mussolini behaved honourably towards the dead man's wife and secured safe exile for her in Switzerland). Italian *Alpini* formations were ordered to the Austrian frontier on the Brenner Pass, and Mussolini called Hitler a 'horrible sexual degenerate, a dangerous fool'.[7] He went on to pour scorn in another speech on 'certain doctrines from the other side of the Alps which are espoused by the descendants of people who were illiterate at a time when Rome had Caesar, Vergil and Augustus'.[8] The Fascist propaganda machine enjoyed itself denouncing the mechanistic racism of the Nazis. Hitler's humiliation was complete when he was obliged to hand over the murderers of Chancellor Dollfuss to the new Austrian government headed by Kurt von Schuschnigg.

This was Mussolini in his role as protector of the status quo in 1934. But this image is misleading, for on 9 October 1934 the Yugoslav King Alexander and the French Foreign Minister, Louis Barthou, were assassinated during a royal visit to Marseilles. Barthou's death was an accident, a result in part at least of lamentable French security, but the assassin was an Italian-trained Croat terrorist who was a member of the Fascist *Ustacha* movement which Mussolini had funded for years. The Duce subsequently refused to extradite the *Ustacha* leader Pavelic (who was later to be guilty of monstrous war crimes in Yugoslavia in the Second World War) and his associates. Thus Mussolini supported the status quo only when it suited him, and this far from isolated example of state terrorism undermines the de Felice thesis that he was operating a classic balance of power foreign policy. In his zeal to destabilise Yugoslavia, Mussolini had endangered the chance of a better relationship with France, which supposedly he was working towards in 1934–35. Ideological factors were still a preoccupation with the Duce, and if (as has been suggested) Mussolini longed for an alliance with France in the same way that Hitler dreamed of one with Britain, the Barthou assassination was a piece of singular incompetence. Nonetheless Mussolini continued to be the paymaster of foreign extreme Rightists such as the Englishman Mosley.

In the short term, however, and despite Barthou's death, the Austrian crisis did push Italy and France closer together. Mussolini had a sympathetic collaborator in the French Foreign Minister, Pierre Laval, who was anxious to keep Italy in play as a counterweight to the Nazis who might threaten the European balance in the West. A Franco-Italian accord was signed to protect Austrian independence, and staff conversations took place between the Italian and French military about possible co-operation should Hitler dare to attack independent Austria. As late as May 1935, Mussolini was still talking of destroying Hitler.[9]

The high point of Mussolini's anti-German stance, however, was the Stresa Conference of 11–14 April 1935. British, French and Italian representatives came together in the Italian town to discuss two matters: Austrian independence and the threat posed by German rearmament. The discussions showed that Britain, actually in the process of secretly negotiating a naval agreement with Hitler, was more sympathetic to German aspirations than were the French and Italians. The final communiqué stated the intention of the three powers to consult together should the threat of German aggression reappear in the future. Stresa seemed to offer a model of how collective security could stop Hitler in his tracks.

THE ETHIOPIAN QUESTION

Stresa flattered to deceive, not least because of what was not discussed there rather than what was. Much has been written about what could, and should, have been said at Stresa about the Ethiopia question, and whether, had it in fact been dealt with, Mussolini could have been prevented from attacking in October 1935. To understand the issues involved, some analysis is needed of Italo-Ethiopian relations in the years that followed the 1928 arbitration treaty.

Mussolini's interest in the acquisition of Ethiopia (then known in Europe as Abyssinia) was obvious and clearly stated. At the very best, he would only have conceded satellite status to Ethiopia, which was portrayed by the Italians as a lawless, anarchic country in need of white civilisation. That it was anarchic is beyond dispute. Local tribes were a law unto themselves and over seventy languages were spoken. But in 1930, Ras Tafari, better known as Emperor Haile Selassie I, was crowned, and made real efforts to modernise his country. Railways were built, radio stations constructed, aeroplanes acquired (just ten) and efforts made to eradicate the plague of slavery. This was not at all what Mussolini wanted. His case for annexation depended on the premise that the country was ungovernable, and also a regional menace. Haile Selassie said that his country was 'the Palace of the Sleeping Beauty' which had stood still for 2,000 years. He knew that his people faced a possible attack, and sent out for machine guns and rifles from abroad (some were sent by an Adolf Hitler still smarting from his Austrian humiliation).

Then in December 1934 the 'provocation' that Mussolini was looking for seemed to come, at an obscure post called Wal Wal in the Ogaden desert on the disputed border between Italian Somaliland and Ethiopia. Fighting broke out between Italian and Ethiopian troops and Mussolini demanded compensation. There were red faces in Rome when it turned out that the group of wells at Wal Wal were actually sixty miles inside Ethiopian territory, but Mussolini still regarded the incident as provocation.[10]

He was now apparently determined to invade Ethiopia, and on 30 December 1934 a directive was sent to Marshal Badoglio, Chief of the General Staff of the Italian army. In the directive, Mussolini said that:

> The problem of Italo-Ethiopian relations has very recently shifted from a diplomatic plane to one which can be solved by force only. The Negus [Haile Selassie] has aimed at centralising the Imperial Authority and reducing to a normal level, through continuous violence, intrigue and bribery, the power of the *Rases* (Chieftains) living in the peripheral areas.[11]

The memorandum went on to suggest, quite falsely, that Ethiopia was equipped with 'really modern arms' and that, because of this, 'time is against us'. But the key passage shows Mussolini's anxiety about the process of centralisation which was taking place under Haile Selassie, together with his spurious concern for the authority of the local chieftains who had been keeping Ethiopia in a state of anarchy which was grist to the Italian mill.

Mussolini wanted to keep Ethiopia off the agenda at Stresa. Laval's visit to Rome in January 1935 had left Mussolini with the impression that France would accept de facto Italian control of Ethiopia even if he were unimpressed by the minute territorial concessions which the French were prepared to make in North Africa along the

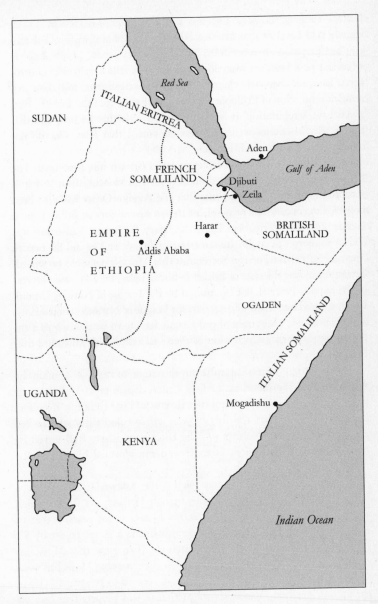

Map 2 Abyssinia in 1935

Libyan–Tunisian border. 'I'm not a collector of deserts,' Mussolini angrily told Laval. 'I sent Marshal Balbo to take photographs of the area you are prepared to concede ... They are lunar landscapes.'[12] Exactly what did pass between Mussolini and Laval is still a matter of controversy. Laval subsequently claimed that he had only agreed to Italian economic domination of Ethiopia, and this is what he told the British. But, given Laval's reputation, it is more than possible that he lied, and that this is why Mussolini went to Stresa convinced that France would not object to the invasion of Ethiopia.

The position was more complex as far as Britain was concerned. The British had been prepared to concede Jubaland to Mussolini, and it is clear from the British documents that the Foreign Office had also been prepared to concede the principle of Italian sovereignty in Ethiopia for a decade. The then Permanent Under-Secretary, Sir Robert Vansittart, was a keen supporter of Anglo-Italian rapprochement, and he did his best to convince successive Foreign Secretaries that Mussolini should be wooed. The problem was the state of British public opinion, for 1935 was the year of the famous Peace Ballot (sponsored by the League of Nations Union), which showed overwhelming support for League of Nations action against aggressor states. This strain of pro-League feeling in Britain worried the British government, which was not averse to a deal with Mussolini over Ethiopia.

For his part, Mussolini misread the state of British opinion by assuming that the notorious Oxford Union debate of 1933 (when the students passed a motion saying that they would not fight for 'King and Country') showed that the British were effete colonialists who lacked the stomach for war. Neither was the Duce particularly well served by his Ambassador in London, Grandi, who misinformed him about the true state of British opinion.

Nevertheless, Mussolini may well have known (thanks to the lamentable level of security at the British Embassy in Rome which allowed an Italian employee easy access to secrets for years)[13] that in 1934 the British government had commissioned a secret report by Sir John Maffey which endorsed the Foreign Office view that Mussolini should be allowed to colonise Ethiopia. At the time that Mussolini went to Stresa, therefore, official British opinion seemed to be sympathetic to the Italian position. Vansittart in particular was prepared to buy off Mussolini by ceding British Somaliland to him.[14]

Yet at Stresa there was no reference to Ethiopia during the conversations between Mussolini, Flandin and the British Prime Minister, Ramsay MacDonald, whom Mussolini reportedly called an 'old dotard'. There may have been references to it during the specialist committees involved during the Conference, but we have the testimony of the head of the Ethiopia department in the Foreign Office that he only had a five-minute conversation about Ethiopia with the British Foreign Secretary, Sir John Simon, even though he had written four long memoranda about Mussolini's threatening behaviour.[15] It has been suggested that Mussolini asked the British to exclude the subject of Ethiopia from the agenda at Stresa, and if this was the case, it was a serious error on the part of the British to agree, but their attitude may well have been affected by the parallel secret talks with Germany about naval disarmament, which were likely to offend France when they became public (the Anglo-German Naval Treaty was signed on 18 June 1935). Mussolini's acquiescence in this breach of Versailles was thus doubly important. Whatever the British motive, Mussolini was able to pretend that their silence effectively gave him the green light to launch an operation against Ethiopia. His biographer, Denis Mack Smith, believes that this 'was Mussolini at his cleverest and most brazen'.[16] Brazen because there is clear evidence that the British government did privately warn Mussolini that it would oppose an Italian resolution of the problem by force, that Ethiopia was a member of the League and that this would mean that Italian aggression would involve the rest of the international community. The British may also have hoped that Mussolini would be content with extracting concessions from Ethiopia short of outright annexation of the country. But the absence of a public statement about Ethiopia at Stresa allowed Mussolini to maintain that neither Britain nor France would oppose an invasion. He also chose to misinterpret any likely reaction to such aggression on the part of the British public.

Doubts remain, nonetheless, about how wholehearted Mussolini was in his resolve to attack Ethiopia. In May, the League of Nations set up a Committee of Five to try and achieve a compromise. Rumanian and Soviet objections to the cession of any Ethiopian territory meant that progress was slow, but on 18 September a report was produced which recommended League supervision of Ethiopia and effectively made Ethiopia an Italian mandate. Haile Selassie was prepared to accept this arrangement, and Mussolini was apparently on the brink of doing so (his representative in Geneva, Aloisi, begged him to do so, as did Grandi and officials in the Colonial Ministry). It was obvious that a fig leaf was needed to preserve the illusion of Ethiopian sovereignty if Britain were to be brought on board. Yet, maddeningly, in the manner that was sometimes the despair of his diplomats, Mussolini changed his mind, even though the Committee of Five was prepared to recognise 'a special Italian interest' in Ethiopia and Aloisi pointed out that the proposals could be revised in five years, giving Italy full control over Ethiopia by the back door.[17]

Did Mussolini rush madly into war as some historians have felt? His generals were certainly anxious at the prospect of an Ethiopian War (Badoglio referred to it as 'a troublesome burden') and his admirals well knew that British intervention in the Mediterranean would be a disaster despite the Duce's boasting. Italian air power was also more impressive on paper than it was in reality. The evidence suggests that the military were amazed at Mussolini's confidence that he could deal with British intervention (France might be reluctantly dragged in too, and the French had a powerful Mediterranean fleet based at Toulon).

The suggestion is then that to a considerable degree Mussolini was bluffing over Ethiopia, and that his bluff was not called by Britain or France. Pique also played its part, for in June 1935 Mussolini was affronted by a British offer to exchange territory which only involved giving Italy land in the Ogaden desert, while Ethiopia was compensated with an outlet to the sea at Zeila in British Somaliland. Worse still, Mussolini's rough language offended the British messenger, the young, highly strung Minister for League of Nations Affairs, Anthony Eden (although Eden subsequently denied that offence had been taken).[18] He became passionately anti-Italian and this did Mussolini little good when Eden became Foreign Secretary in December.

In the short term, however, Mussolini backed his instinct that Britain and France were desperate to avoid a conflict over Ethiopia and his instinct proved to be right. The mixture of unimpressive territorial concessions on the part of Britain and France combined with private warnings from London did not deter the Duce. He would naturally have accepted Ethiopia as a gift to appease Italian appetites but, unlike the others, he was also prepared to face the prospect of war while ignoring its likely consequences.[19]

THE INVASION OF ETHIOPIA

There was no official Italian declaration of war on Ethiopia. On 2 October 1935, Italians were summoned to their town and city squares to hear announcements that their Duce had authorised an invasion of Ethiopia, which was accused of aggressive provocations against their country. At that very moment, people were told, a fleet of Italian aircraft were flying to bomb Adowa, the site of the humiliating Italian defeat of 1896. The régime trumpeted the fact that Bruno and Vittorio Mussolini and the Duce's son-in-law, Count Ciano (who had married Edda), were flying with the airborne avengers.

On 3 October, a force of 100,000 Italian troops crossed the river Mares which marked the border between Italian Eritrea and Mussolini's intended victim. It was the vanguard of a huge force of half a million men which Mussolini had been concentrating in the area and was a curious mixture of Blackshirts, regular troops and native levies transported around by American trucks, Fiat cars and strings of mules.[20] The Italians, of course, ruled the skies as Ethiopia only had ten unarmed aircraft at its disposal. In charge of the whole operation was the Minister of Colonies, Emilio de Bono, a veteran Fascist whose appointment turned out to be a disaster. In sending his army into Ethiopia, Mussolini had ignored the opinions of both the king and the generals alike, and he was risking a hostile response from the British which his admirals knew could bring catastrophe for Italy's Mediterranean fleet. Realising, therefore, that he had adopted a high-risk strategy, Mussolini was a man in a hurry. The wretched de Bono, who failed to capture Adowa in the time scale envisaged by the Duce, was bombarded with telegrams from Rome. But the Italians were undoubtedly assisted by the refusal of the Ethiopian Chieftains to adopt the guerrilla tactics which their Emperor wanted. Instead, the Ethiopian tribesmen used heroic but unavailing frontal assault tactics which resulted in terrible losses. Haile Selassie's army had almost no artillery or tanks yet its desperate bravery still managed to unnerve de Bono, who was sacked in November and replaced by the portly, ruthless, former Piedmontese peasant, Pietro Badoglio, who had wanted to turn the regular army loose on the Fascists in 1922, and who was to desert Mussolini in an hour of need in 1943.

The question which exercised the Italian diplomatic and military establishment in the autumn of 1935 was what the reaction of Britain,

France and the League of Nations would be to the aggression against Ethiopia. Mussolini's attack on Ethiopia had already made him deeply unpopular in Britain, where within a week of the invasion the *Manchester Guardian* noted that he was being booed when he appeared on cinema screens in newsreels.[21] The British government was more circumspect, but public opinion was strongly pro-League and anti-Italian.

Fifty members of the League condemned Mussolini's aggression, but the question remained as to what action was to be taken against the Italians, particularly as the League of Nations Covenant made no provision for the raising of an armed force to be sent to aid Ethiopia. Following Britain's initiative (the French were more reluctant), sanctions were imposed on Mussolini in November, but these did not include oil or even the lorries and cars which the Italians needed to transport their armies around Ethiopia's difficult terrain. Britain did not even close the Suez Canal to Italian shipping, an action which Mussolini was to claim would have ended Italy's war within a week. As it was, Mussolini could always obtain oil from the United States, which was not a member of the League, or the Soviet Union (showing how Mussolini's pragmatic policy towards Moscow could pay dividends).

British policy seemed to be ambiguous. On the one hand, the British publicly deplored Mussolini's aggression, but on the other they entered into secret talks with him designed to reach an accommodation about Ethiopia.

THE HOARE–LAVAL PACT

The result was the ill-fated Hoare–Laval Pact of 8 December 1935, which followed a visit to Paris by the new British Foreign Secretary, Sir Samuel Hoare, during which he had secret talks with his French counterpart, Laval. The plan envisaged the ceding of about two-thirds of Ethiopia to Mussolini, leaving a rump Ethiopian state with a corridor of land giving Haile Selassie access to the sea. Mussolini seemed to be prepared to consider the plan favourably, telling Grandi in London that he might back away from his maximum demand that the whole of Ethiopia be ceded to him (it was quite possible that the rump Ethiopian state would prove to be unviable and could be swallowed up by Italy at some future date).[22] Another possibility was that an Italian mandate might be imposed on the Ethiopians.

Such possibilities were exploded by the leaking of the proposals to the French press, probably by an official at the Quai d'Orsay (the French Foreign Office) which was notoriously insecure in the 1930s. This caused uproar when the news of the Hoare–Laval plan became known in Britain, where it was perceived to be a sell-out to Mussolini. Hoare was deserted by his Prime Minister, Baldwin, and subsequently obliged to resign. To add insult to injury, the unfortunate Hoare, who had been en route to Switzerland for a holiday, fell and broke his nose while out ice-skating.

The die was now cast as far as Mussolini and Ethiopia were concerned. He may have still been open to negotiation over the issue, but after the tawdry collapse of the Hoare–Laval plan agreement with Britain and France became impossible.[23] On 18 December Mussolini told his people, '[t]he war which we have begun in Africa is a war of civilisation, and liberation. It is a war of the people.'[24]

Just what 'civilisation' meant to the Fascists was shown by the brutality with which the war was waged against people who were regarded as savages. Impatient for victory, Mussolini and Badoglio authorised the use of mustard gas against the Ethiopians despite the fact that this was banned under international law. The consequences were ghastly as a British observer of the war noted: the victims of this aerial terrorism (mustard bombs were dropped by Italian aircraft) had 'sores ... caked with thick brown scabs, men and women alike, all horribly disfigured and little children too'.[25] Vittorio Mussolini was disappointed that the bombs he dropped caused such small explosions amongst the rickety huts of the Ethiopian tribesmen, when he expected to see the dramatic ones he was used to in Hollywood movies. Yet even with such overwhelming air power, the Italians still made hard work of achieving victory. The decisive Italian victory came at Amba Aradam, where the cream of Haile Selassie's army was destroyed, but some front-line resistance continued until March 1936.

Half a million Ethiopians died in the war and probably a thousand Italians (Mussolini put the figure as high as three thousand)[26] before Badoglio entered Addis Ababa in triumph on 5 May 1936. He was rewarded with the absurdly pompous title of 'Duke of Addis Ababa' and King Victor Emmanuel wept with joy upon hearing the news that he was to become Emperor of Ethiopia. Mussolini was greeted everywhere by crowds chanting 'Duce! Duce!'

At the outset of the war, the Italians were unenthusiastic about Ethiopia and it was really the action of the League of Nations which swung public opinion behind Mussolini. Few Italians could stomach the condemnation of Mussolini's behaviour when Britain and France already had such large colonial empires and were obvious beneficiaries of the League mandates system while Italy was not. Twenty million Italians listened to the Duce's radio broadcast of 18 December 1935, and hundreds of thousands of women supported Queen Elena's campaign by giving up their wedding rings to be melted down for the war effort. Even members of the clergy brought in crosses to be melted down, and Pius XI made sympathetic noises. Easy conquests (albeit not as quick as Mussolini would have liked) made for cheap popularity, and historians have generally agreed that the Ethiopian War marked the high-point of Mussolini's domestic popularity. Even his old adversary D'Annunzio said that, as a result of the Ethiopian War, Mussolini had created his own legend. The king made the victorious Duce a Knight of the Order of Savoy, and if Mussolini was uninterested in such awards for himself, he understood their significance for others.

In fact, Mussolini had been lucky. Had the British challenged him, he knew that Italian aircraft lacked the range to attack Britain's naval base at Alexandria or the armour-piercing bombs needed to sink their capital ships. Bravado and bluster had paid off.

THE CONSEQUENCES OF THE WAR

The proclamation of Mussolini's new East African empire concealed uncomfortable realities. Mussolini had not bothered to cost the war, which ran to some twelve billion lire, the equivalent of almost a year's national income or three years of military expenditure. Neither could he tempt many Italian settlers to try their fortunes in the arid terrain of Ethiopia. Few were deceived by the régime's claims that Ethiopia would be an Italian gold-mine. In fact, it proved to be a drain on Italian resources before being lost in humiliating circumstances in 1941.

The Ethiopian War has been described by de Felice as 'Mussolini's masterpiece',[27] but its glory proved to be short-lived. The events set in train by Mussolini in October 1935 brought about a real 'diplomatic revolution' which saw Italy forsake the Anglo-French bloc in favour of alliance with Nazi Germany. Mussolini told Europe that Italy was now a satisfied power, but he had lost the trust of the democracies even though British and French statesmen still tried to woo him to deter Germany.

In fact, there is evidence to show that Mussolini was contemplating a rapprochement with Hitler even *before* he attacked Ethiopia. Increasingly under the influence of Count Ciano, his brash new Foreign Minister, Mussolini had already told the Germans in May 1935 that he was considering pro-German foreign policy alignment, and this was only a month after Stresa. And on 6 January 1936, Mussolini told the German Ambassador in Rome, Ulrich von Hassell, that he would not object to Austria becoming a German satellite as long as its independence was preserved. Hitler was also given every encouragement to send his troops into the demilitarised Rhineland on 7 March 1936 when on 22 February the Duce told von Hassell that should Germany make such a move, Italy would not honour its obligations under the Locarno Treaty of 1925.[28] In this sense, Hitler, rather than Mussolini, was the ultimate beneficiary of the Ethiopian War. The Stresa bloc was fatally sundered and the prestige of the League as an instrument against aggression fatally compromised, while Germany's isolation as a rogue European power was ended. In exchange for this, Mussolini had been able to pose as the conqueror of Ethiopia and had gained domestic plaudits, but he was to rue taking supper with the devil in the years to come. Ideological bedfellows though they might be, Italian and German interests were not always identical, and now Mussolini had left himself little option but to choose a German alliance.

Even in Ethiopia the military victory of 1935–36 was tarnished by what followed, for, belatedly, the Chieftains followed Haile Selassie's advice and adopted a guerrilla warfare strategy. The Italians were only able thereafter to hold on to the centres of population while the guerrillas operated outside.

Fatally though, Mussolini had drawn the wrong conclusions from the war, which deluded him into thinking that Italy could embark on new and even more ruinous, military adventures. There were now no limits to the new Caesar's ambitions, buoyed up as he was by a wave of domestic adulation.

7

INTO THE ABYSS: FOREIGN
AND DEFENCE POLICY, 1936–40

In the years between the end of the Ethiopian War in May 1936 and
Italy's entry into the Second World War in June 1940, Mussolini
seemed to slide relentlessly into alliance with Hitler and Nazi Germany.
His son-in-law, Count Ciano, declared that: 'In Italy, the most Fascist
ministry is that of foreign affairs',[1] and it is true that during this period
the ideological imperative in Italian Fascism seemed to become dominant. Mussolini fought a war in Spain to ensure the victory of the right-
wing authoritarian movement of General Franco which, if not overtly
Fascist, was at least a potential ally for both the Duce and his German
friends. By 1938 also, Mussolini had so altered his Austrian policy that
he offered no objection when Hitler occupied the country in March of
that year. Mussolini acted as a 'mediator', but in reality was in collusion
with Germany when Czechoslovakia was forced to cede the Sudetenland
to Hitler in September 1938. And so it went on, with Mussolini himself
aping German aggression by seizing Albania in April 1939. More and
more mesmerised by German power, it seemed, Mussolini threw in his
lot with Hitler until he committed Italy to a full-scale military pact
with Germany in May 1939. But then when Hitler attacked Poland in
September 1939, Mussolini hesitated and did not give Germany the
backing he had promised.

Why was this? Did Mussolini revert to the pattern of hesitancy
which had been a feature of his policy at the time of the Ethiopian
War, or was the decision to stay out of the war a result of a realistic

appraisal of Italy's military deficiencies? It is important to try to discern whether in fact Italy was or was not veering away at this point from the alliance with Germany towards a more traditional policy of trying to balance between the rival Great Powers. Only the sequel is certain. In June 1940 Mussolini seized the chance to attack a crippled France and took Italy into a war which was to lead to the ruin of both himself and his régime.

MUSSOLINI AND CIANO

Mussolini's growing megalomania could have been restrained, it has been argued, if he had had a man of stature and integrity as Foreign Minister during those years. In June 1936, he appointed his son-in-law, Count Galeazzo Ciano, to the position. Ciano, if not the best of the Fascists, had some claim to being the brightest. Certainly he was well informed enough to have advised his father-in-law about the dangers of the policy he was pursuing. The consensus view has been, however, that Ciano failed to do so until European war was looming.

Galeazzo Ciano was born in 1903, the son of a naval hero, Constanzo, who was made Minister of Communications in Mussolini's government in 1924. Constanzo Ciano was a very wealthy man, a newspaper owner, and the Fascist Party boss in Livorno. It was rumoured that the elder Ciano had been earmarked by the Duce as a possible successor. All this meant that the younger man had great advantages in the battle for preferment in Mussolini's régime.

The traditional view of Ciano has been that he was a lightweight libertine, more interested in lovemaking than diplomacy, who outdid Mussolini as a philanderer. Even as Foreign Minister, it has been suggested, Galeazzo Ciano preferred the company of film starlets and the golf course to working in the Palazzo Chigi. Ciano was loathed by veteran Fascists such as Balbo and Grandi as a parvenu who had been too young to fight in the war, and he owed his position to the fact that he had married Edda Mussolini on 24 April 1930 after a whirlwind romance. The distaste of the Old Guard was expressed in Ciano's nickname 'Ducellino'. And Rachele Mussolini, the most down to earth of the Duce's family, thoroughly disliked her son-in-law whom she regarded as a spoilt brat. Mussolini's latest biographer has described Ciano as 'a yuppy of his time'.[2]

Yet there is a real danger that just as the father-in-law has been written off as a posturing buffoon, the son-in-law has also been too easily dismissed by historians. To begin with, Ciano was no fool. He had come out second in the whole of Italy when he graduated from high school in 1921, and when he came to take the exams for the diplomatic service in 1924 (which were demanding), Ciano was 25th out of 37 candidates. This educational background gave Ciano the intellectual tools to become an excellent foreign minister, and if it is argued that he was far too young to be foreign minister at age 33, it needs to be recalled that the starchy British made Eden Foreign Secretary at just age 38. But like many very intelligent men, Ciano did not suffer fools gladly, especially fellow members of the Fascist hierarchy. Frequently they were witheringly dismissed; Dino Grandi, for example, was described to the Spanish Foreign Minister, Suñer, as 'quite uninteresting' and with 'the intelligence of a mosquito'.[3]

More serious is the accusation that, after he became Foreign Minister in 1936, Ciano ignored the advice of the long-service professional diplomats and ran the Palazzo Chigi through the Gabinetto, or Cabinet, which in the past had merely been the personal secretariat of the Minister. It was certainly true that Ciano liked to bypass the professionals whom he despised in favour of personal envoys such as Farinacci and Anfuso (a personal friend who happened also to be a member of the Gabinetto). Yet, unlike his German counterpart the odious von Ribbentrop (whom both Ciano and Mussolini disliked), Ciano did have the appropriate pedigree as a diplomat. He served in Italian embassies in Argentina and China before becoming Mussolini's Minister of Press and Propaganda, and therefore knew about the workings of the Palazzo Chigi before he became Foreign Minister. But he did see himself as the first real Fascist (apart, of course, from his father-in-law) to run the Foreign Ministry, and acted accordingly. In a sense, this was true: when Mussolini took over the foreign affairs portfolio after he dismissed Grandi in 1932, he had little to do with the day-to-day running of the Ministry because of his other duties as Prime Minister. After Ciano took over in 1936, there were an increasing number of complaints that diplomats were excluded from the decision-making process, and that the Gabinetto controlled information gathering. Ciano was also blamed for the pro-German stance adopted by the Fascist government.

In the light of events between 1936 and 1939, it is hard to refute this accusation, but it seems more likely that Ciano was merely following his father-in-law's lead when it came to the making of Italian foreign policy. As his *Diary* (a very important source for the period) shows, Ciano was sometimes a slavish admirer of the Duce, adept at unctuous flattery. It is difficult to detect any real evidence that Ciano fought hard against the Duce's growing obsession with Nazi Germany until the summer of 1939 when some signs of doubt emerged. But at least Ciano had the good sense to keep seasoned career diplomats in the top embassies, including Grandi, who had been sent to London by Mussolini in 1932 for not being radical enough and who had become part of the diplomatic machine (he was the only really senior diplomat with a Fascist background).

What of the personal relationship between Ciano and Mussolini? Both men were sexual adventurers and the Duce's reputation as a philanderer left him little ground for complaint about the Cianos' 'open marriage' (both Edda and Galeazzo took lovers), but the younger man was a member of the bourgeoisie whereas Mussolini cherished his working-class roots. Ciano purported to be a practising Catholic yet he was involved in the brutal killing of the leftist Carlo Rosselli, just as his father-in-law was implicated in the murder of Matteotti. Mussolini seems to have relied on Ciano, much in the same way that he relied on his old sparring partner, Farinacci, for an insight into the real outer world at a time when he was becoming more and more isolated on his pedestal of supreme power. But his position was that of a sympathetic sounding-board rather than an independent adviser, and Ciano made himself look increasingly ridiculous by aping the Duce's mannerisms. He copied Mussolini's aggressive postures and his abrupt responses to questions, as if seeking to turn himself into a model of the Duce.

For all that, however, Ciano was able to make a positive impression on important foreigners like Vansittart, who described him in 1934 as being

> a bounder. But bounding is no sin in the sun. He liked women and advancement; others have had the same tastes with less fulfilment. He enjoyed good looks with some good nature and an occasional sense of humour ... He was having too good a time to want trouble.[4]

Vansittart's description comes perhaps too early because Ciano clearly came to like 'trouble'. He flew as a pilot in the Ethiopian War, and was deeply implicated in Mussolini's wars in Spain, Albania, Greece and Yugoslavia. Others, like the noted US journalist William Shirer, found him to be a highly strung exhibitionist. Yet it must be to Ciano's credit that both von Ribbentrop (whose own period as a diplomat in London had been a catastrophic disaster) and Hitler came to hate him.

In the end, Ciano was to see through the propaganda mirage that surrounded Mussolini, but his betrayal of the Duce in 1943 was to have fatal consequences for himself. He realised too late that the German alliance was leading Italy to disaster, after being deceived into believing that putting on a black shirt and posturing on the European stage would make Italy a power on a level with Britain, France and Germany. Ciano was appointed by Mussolini in June 1936 to make the Foreign Ministry more Fascist, and at that stage he was strongly pro-German, making it extremely unlikely that he would wish to follow the traditional policy of balance that the de Felice school purport to still see in evidence after the Ethiopian War. It remains to examine the military context in which Italian diplomacy was obliged to operate.

THE MILITARY BALANCE

Mussolini was always boasting about Italy's military strength to the point where he swallowed his own propaganda about the 'eight million bayonets' available to Italy, and making the Mediterranean an Italian sea. Plainly, military strength was an essential factor in Fascism's expansionist ambitions, but Italy's real capability has to be seen in comparison to that of the other Great Powers. An additional aspect of this military balance is the degree to which Italian strength was taken at face value by other powers, how this influenced their own policies towards Mussolini's régime and how in the last analysis Italian foreign policy was affected by any presumptions the régime made about the country's military strength.

There is no doubt that Mussolini wildly exaggerated the strength of his armed forces. At the same time, for example, that Mussolini was talking about eight million bayonets in 1936, the fully mobilised strength of the Italian army was only 1.6 million men. Mussolini had boasted in the 1920s that the 'Regia Aeronautica' (the Italian airforce) would have so many aircraft that they would blot out the sun, and in 1939 it was claimed that Italy had 8,500 front-line aircraft. The real figure was probably less than a thousand. As late as 1940, 150 aircraft in the Italian airforce were obsolete biplanes, this despite all the glamorous exploits of Balbo and others which had suggested that Italy was at the cutting edge of aviation development. Much vaunted Italian aircraft, such as the Savio Marchettie (SM81) long-range bombers, were not the potent weapons that Mussolini claimed (the SM81 was usable only when close protection was offered by fighters). Italy's fighter aircraft were also unable to reach Britain's main Mediterranean naval base at Alexandria should war come because their bases in Libya were too far away. Technical deficiency then was combined with bloated propaganda, and the Italians were fortunate that the British tended to believe Fascist myths about the SM81 when it first went into service. Later, when their intelligence improved, the British refused to believe that the information they had about Italian aircraft having refuelling difficulties was accurate when in fact it was.

On the face of it, the Italian navy was better prepared. At the point where Italy entered the Second World War in June 1940, it had 4 battleships, 6 cruisers, 16 destroyers and 64 submarines (although the Naval Staff had refused to build any aircraft carriers). This meant that in purely numerical terms, Italian naval forces compared well with those of France and Britain in the Mediterranean. Here, though, lack of proper strategic planning undermined potential. There was no proper plan for using the large submarine fleet, and no strategy for fighting an Anglo-French naval coalition because the assumption seemed to be, despite the evidence of the Ethiopian War, that France would be the main enemy in the Mediterranean.

A lack of co-ordination between the armed forces was the main characteristic of defence policy under the Fascists.[5] And yet again Mussolini's personal tendency to overload himself with too much responsibility was evident. Between 1925 and 1929 the Duce was Minister for the Army, the Navy and the Airforce, and he held all three portfolios again after 1933. Marshal Badoglio was supposed to offer Mussolini advice on all military matters, but he was far more cautious than the Army Chief of Staff Pariani (in post from 1937), who formulated ambitious plans for Italian attacks on British Egypt with

Mussolini's encouragement. This was an example of the Ethiopian victory going to the Duce's head, and others also allowed themselves to be intoxicated. Marshal Balbo, the Governor of Libya, and the Duke of Aosta, then Governor of Ethiopia, formulated grandiose plans for 'lightning war' against Egypt and the Sudan with an army of 170,000 men. Yet, as events were to show in 1940–41, the Italian army had only the haziest notions of how to fight a desert war against opponents with strong tank formations. Neither did Italy have any tanks which were properly adapted for desert warfare. When Badoglio reported in 1939 that Italian forces in Africa should remain on the defensive, his report (based on an on-the-spot assessment) was ignored by Mussolini and other military leaders.

Despite Fascism's striving for consensus, the army's officer corps in particular was a caste apart from the Italian people. Ordinary Italian soldiers from the peasantry and the industrial working class spoke dialects which the officers could not understand. There was also resentment because middle-class university students were exempt from military service, and influence could be used to obtain exemption for others.[6] Professionally inept Fascists could also be given important roles in military leadership. Badoglio at least was a professional soldier; de Bono was not, with consequences which were only too obvious in the early stages of the Ethiopian War. Mussolini himself had served in the Great War, but he lacked Hitler's obsessive eye for military details. By contrast, detail bored him, and his interventions into the sphere of military planning were spasmodic and also ill-timed. He dreamt ambitious dreams but there was little indication of how his ambitious plans were to be carried out. Some of the technical deficiencies in the Italian armed services, therefore, bordered on the absurd. As there were no aircraft carriers in the Italian navy, it relied entirely on the Regia Aeronautica for air support, yet there was no means of radio contact available between the navy and airforce fighters and bombers.

Some of the military problems facing the Italians were a direct consequence of Mussolini's failure to put the Italian economy on a proper war footing. Italy was heavily dependent on foreign raw materials because she lacked any native supplies of coal, oil and iron ore. Mussolini tried to counter this weakness by stockpiling materials through a policy of so-called 'autarchia' (autarky), which was announced in 1936 and designed to achieve 'maximum economic self-sufficiency in the shortest possible time'.[7] By 1939, the Italian State owned some 80 per cent of the country's arms production capacity.

Yet the State failed to deliver. By 1942 the USA, then in its first year of war, could produce more planes in a week than Italy could produce in a year. And although firms such as Fiat had the expertise to produce adequate tanks and armoured vehicles, Fascist bungling and administrative malpractice prevented this. Consequently there were too many machine types, although, to be fair to Mussolini's régime, similar blunders were perpetrated in Germany which was far more industrially advanced.

Mussolini placed a massive financial burden on the backward Italian economy in his desperate attempts to make Italy a major military power. The Ethiopian War of 1935–36 obliged Italy to spend twice as much money on armaments as did Britain and France, and almost as much as National Socialist Germany which was a much richer country than Fascist Italy. Thereafter Mussolini introduced a huge new rearmament programme in July 1938 whereby five billion lire was to be spent on army modernisation. This followed an order for two new battleships for the navy in 1937, although this type of warship was to be made obsolete by air power in the Second World War. Rearmament, therefore, where it did occur, was the wrong kind of rearmament. This was combined with the strain of keeping 300,000 men in Ethiopia between 1935 and 1940 and 50,000 men in Spain between 1936 and 1939. All this meant that there was a fatal disparity between Italy's actual resources and Mussolini's desire for territorial gains in Africa and the Balkans. His foreign policy goals were operating in a different sphere from industrial and military reality. Attempts by moderates such as Bottai and Grandi to rein in Mussolini's excesses after 1935 were invariably unsuccessful.

It is important, nevertheless, not to accept ancient stereotypical views about Italian military performance under Fascism. The Italians were able to conquer Ethiopia more quickly than expected (despite de Bono's early blundering) and their performance in the Spanish Civil War was not as dire as has sometimes been suggested. In the period between 1936 and 1940, certainly, *perceptions* about Italian military strength were actually as important in the military balance as its reality. The British, for example, had to take the Regia Aeronautica seriously in the Mediterranean precisely because their own aerial strength there was so limited. This in turn allowed Mussolini to glory in the alleged prowess of his armed forces, making himself their formal head alongside Victor Emmanuel in March 1938. He was jealous of the king's role as head of the armed forces, and made both men 'First Marshals of the Empire'. If this reeks of absurd bombast, and Mussolini was not usually overly impressed by titles, it needs to be recalled that the Duce could praise his armed forces because foreigners took them seriously too. In the Fascist universe there could be no more important role than that of Commander-in-Chief of the Armed Forces.

Mussolini's problem lay in separating military fantasies from reality. Neither was he ever able to work out a proper system of military and economic priorities; instead he frittered away his time on bizarre projects like translating a novel on the *Risorgimento* into German. While he did so, Badoglio, Balbo, Aosta and Pariani bickered amongst themselves, lacking any firm direction from the Duce about how the Italian high command was to organise the triumphs he demanded. Mussolini may not have had Hitler's chronic aversion to meetings and memoranda, but the meetings that he did have were exercises in obfuscation and meandering irrelevance. It was a central irony of Fascist military policy that the régime which prided itself on forceful decision making should fail so abjectly in giving a lead.

INTERVENTION IN SPAIN

Mussolini's growing intoxication with military glory was clearly demonstrated by his decision to intervene in the Spanish Civil War which broke out in July 1936. It followed the right-wing insurrection under General Francisco Franco against the Spanish Republican government which was a coalition of Socialists, Communists and Liberals. Franco immediately requested assistance from both Hitler and Mussolini, but it was the Duce who was to make much the heavier commitment to the war. Ideology played its part too, for Franco's forces included the Fascist Falange Party and the authoritarian general was a much more comfortable bedfellow for Fascist Italy than the left-wing Republic (even though Mussolini had not got on particularly well with Spain's previous dictator, Primo de Rivera, who had ruled Spain before the Republic was established in 1931).

Inside Italy, Ciano was enthusiastic about intervention, but King Victor Emmanuel was not. He argued not unreasonably that Italy needed time to recover from the Ethiopian War, and that there were diplomatic dangers in provoking the other Great Powers with another display of military muscle. Mussolini himself appears to have thought the war would soon be over, and that an easy victory for Franco would help Italy to dominate the Mediterranean. He was wrong on every count save one. The war dragged on until 1939 and put even greater pressure on the Italian economy, while Franco proved to be too cunning an operator ever to fully commit himself to an alliance with Italy and Germany. Hitler was later to remark, after an interview with Franco, that rather than repeat the experience, he would prefer to have several teeth extracted. Only in his instinctive feeling that Britain and France would not fight to save Spanish democracy was the Duce proven to be correct. Indeed the Anglo-French went to extreme lengths to ignore provocations by Italian submarines in the Mediterranean during the war.

While Hitler lied in saying that he would support Franco to the hilt, Mussolini kept his word at considerable cost. In all, 50,000 Italians were sent to Spain, a mixture of Blackshirt militia and regular army units. Seven hundred Italian aircraft also flew on Franco's side in the war, giving the rebels a decisive superiority in the air (only the USSR provided the Republic with planes). People like Badoglio saw the dangers of such a level of intervention, and even Mussolini himself had to concede that the Spanish war had 'bled Italy white'. But he was fully committed to Franco's cause, not least because prominent anti-Fascist Italian leftists were on the other side amongst the famous pro-Republican International Brigades. It was they who won an embarrassing victory over Mussolini's Blackshirts at Guadalajara in 1937, but the Italian performance in Spain improved thereafter, with significant successes being won around Bilbao (it has also been suggested that Republican propaganda overstated the importance of the Italian reverse at Guadalajara).[8] Their contribution was far more important than that of Franco's German allies. The aerial Condor Legion infamously devastated the Basque town of Guernica, but the Germans contributed no significant ground force.

THE ROME–BERLIN AXIS

Few historians have disputed the fact that the Spanish Civil War pushed Fascist Italy and Nazi Germany closer together. This had begun to happen even at a personal level when in June 1936 Hitler received Edda Ciano in Berlin while she was spending a month's holiday in the city. The Führer deigned to take Edda around the network of lakes between Berlin and the suburb of Potsdam in his personal motor boat, but personal communication was difficult because Hitler spoke no Italian and Edda, whose husband had just been made Foreign Minister, spoke no German. Nevertheless Edda's visit was more than just a straw in the wind.

It is easy to jump to the conclusion that an ideological and military alliance between Fascism and Nazism was inevitable, but this was not the case. Hitler had continued to supply Haile Selassie with arms even after Mussolini invaded Ethiopia, and although Germany did not co-operate with the League sanctions campaign, it did not increase its trade with Italy either. The Dollfuss affair had not been forgotten in either Rome or Berlin, and the issue of Austria continued to be the major stumbling block to better Italo-German relations. Mussolini's overtures to Germany in January 1936 have already been referred to, and these marked a significant turning point at a time when Mussolini had been angered by Anglo-French attitudes. The Duce was also annoyed when Haile Selassie was invited to the coronation of King George VI in 1937. Against this, however, was Mussolini's irritation with continued evidence of German nationalism in Italy's own South Tyrol (*Alto Adige*). There had been protests when Italian Germans had been called up for the Ethiopian War, and dislike of the Italians was widespread in both Austria and southern Germany because of the problem of the South Tyrol.

This background of Italian–German tension makes the approval given by Mussolini to the so-called 'Gentleman's Agreement' between Austria and Germany on 11 July 1936 even more significant (it was oddly named as Adolf Hitler was no gentleman). Under the agreement, Nazi Germany recognised Austrian sovereignty and undertook not to interfere in its neighbour's internal affairs, but a crucial third clause obliged Austria to follow a foreign policy 'based on principles which correspond to the fact that Austria has acknowledged herself to be a German state'. This agreement could plainly not have been signed without Mussolini's sanction, and was the most important indicator yet (along with the appointment of Ciano the previous month) that Fascist Italy was moving towards an accommodation with Germany. Mussolini was now convinced, along Social Darwinian lines, that Britain and

France were decadent nations in decline, while Fascist Italy and National Socialist Germany were virile rising powers. Fascism above all was about being on the winning side, and Mussolini had become tired of his role as Austria's protector. His volte-face on Austria made union between it and Germany almost inevitable, as the Western democracies had no intention of defending Austria's independence by force. Hitler also showed his interest in making an agreement with Italy by offering to recognise the Italian conquest of Ethiopia without conditions on 29 June, two weeks before the Gentleman's Agreement over Austria was signed.

Further overtures followed. The odious Nazi Hans Frank, later the Butcher of Poland, was sent to Rome in September to invite the Duce to Germany, and in late October Ciano set out to meet Hitler at his mountain house in Berchtesgaden in Bavaria.

The meeting took place on 24 October after Ciano had already spoken to the German Foreign Minister, von Neurath, and Hitler was frank in his admiration for the Duce. 'Mussolini,' the Führer told Ciano, 'is the first statesman of the world with whom no one else had the right even remotely to compare himself.'[9] In return, Ciano was able to provide the Germans with interesting titbits which Grandi had obtained about British attitudes to Germany. Ciano returned to Rome convinced that he had the measure of the Germans, and that Hitler was a lightweight who could easily be manipulated by the Duce. The thrust of the talks was anti-Communist and anti-British, as Hitler was enraged by the unflattering remarks made about Germany in the captured British documents.

Doubtless gratified by such fulsome flattery, the Duce was now ready to take the plunge where Germany was concerned. On 1 November he made a speech in Milan in which he described Italy's new friendship with Germany as 'not a diaphragm, but rather an axis around which all European states, animated by a desire for collaboration and peace, can revolve'.[10] Thus was coined the term 'axis', which came to be commonly used to describe the Italian–German relationship, but it is important to note that a binding military alliance between Italy and Germany was still nearly three years away. Nevertheless, despite the nervousness of Victor Emmanuel and a revival of traditional Anglophilia in the Italian upper classes, Mussolini had made his choice. Subsequent flirtations with the British and French did not at any stage suggest that they were serious alternatives to a German alliance as far as Mussolini was concerned. Indeed, while Mussolini maintained his belief that the Mediterranean was 'mare nostrum' (our sea) a collision with the two Western powers was almost inevitable.

The love affair deepened in 1937 when the Duce took up Hitler's invitation to visit Germany. Mussolini took Ciano and Party Secretary Starace with him together with an entourage of about a hundred people. The climax of the visit was on 28 September when both dictators addressed a huge open-air meeting in Berlin attended by 800,000 people. Observers noted, however, that Mussolini's rather eccentric German made his speech difficult to understand, and halfway through it there was a tremendous thunderstorm. For once German organisation broke down, and there was complete chaos which left a soaked Duce to fend for himself. Ciano's diary entry for the day was laconic. 'Beautifully choreographed', he wrote of the phalanxes of Nazis who had paraded before the Duce, 'much emotion and a lot of rain'.[11]

Even so, the damage seems to have been done as far as Mussolini was concerned. He was mesmerised by what he saw in Germany in 1937 (the *passo romano* or Italian version of the goose-step was imposed because he was so impressed by an SS parade in Munich) and particularly by the vast production of armaments at the Krupp factories in Essen. Even an upsurge of his ulcer trouble did not lessen the impression made by Germany's military and industrial power.

THE FALL OF AUSTRIA

Mussolini's growing obsession with Nazi Germany was combined with the knowledge that his commitment in Spain was increasing his dependence on the Germans. At the same time he railed against the Italians' lack of martial spirit, telling Ciano that '[A]s long as he was alive he would keep them on the move "to the tune of kicks on the shin. When Spain is finished, I will think of something else"'.[12] But in the short term, the Duce was in no real position to prevent Hitler's ambition of incorporating his homeland Austria into the Reich from coming to pass. Yet to achieve this, Hitler had to ensure that there was no repetition of the Dollfuss fiasco in 1934, and Mussolini's approval for the move against Austria was zealously sought.

Before this though Mussolini had demonstrated his commitment to the anti-Communist cause by joining Germany and Japan in the 'Anti-Comintern Pact', which was aimed in particular against the Soviet Union and put an end to a period of relatively good relations with Stalin's government. Thus was the Axis pact of 1936 further strengthened, although Mussolini had still not gone the extra mile and concluded a binding military pact with the Nazis. The Anti-Comintern Pact was signed on 6 November 1937.

As far as Austria was concerned, however, the evidence suggests that Mussolini wanted the Anschluss to be delayed, although he conceded that it was probably inevitable. It seems to have been a case of hoping that if he ignored the problem, it would somehow go away. Given Hitler's mindset, there could be no question of this.

In February 1938, the Führer summoned the unfortunate Austrian Chancellor, von Schuschnigg, to Berchtesgaden and berated him for hours about Austria's unwillingness to recognise its 'German destiny'. Hitler's language was threatening and von Schuschnigg naturally looked to Rome, Austria's traditional protector, for reassurance.

The noises being made by Mussolini were not reassuring for the Austrian leader. He told Ciano that he was pleased by the wholesale changes made in the Nazi government on 5 February 1938, which included the placing of the incompetent von Ribbentrop at the Foreign Ministry (at this stage, the Duce and his son-in-law did not know von Ribbentrop well). He was deemed to be hostile to the British (which was true) but he was certainly no friend of independent Austria either. Yet Ciano and Mussolini purported to see in von Ribbentrop's appointment a strengthening of the Axis and the Anti-Comintern Pact. They also rejoiced in the removal of the German Ambassador, von Hassell, a career diplomat with anti-Nazi leanings who was to die in 1944 as a result of an attempt to overthrow Hitler.

Mussolini was not prepared to extend a helping hand to assist his supposed protégé von Schuschnigg. When von Schuschnigg told him that he was going to hold a plebiscite on the issue of Austrian independence from Germany (the official announcement was made on 7 March), Mussolini disapproved, telling Ciano that he thought 'this policy very dangerous'.[13] Mussolini's reasoning was that if a plebiscite gave a majority against Anschluss, the Germans would say it was faked, while if the verdict was inconclusive, the plebiscite would have been pointlessly provocative.

Plainly Hitler could not take the risk of allowing the Austrian people the opportunity of airing an opinion, because a vote in favour of von Schuschnigg's free, independent Austria was a distinct possibility despite Austrian Nazi thuggery. He may not have wanted outright annexation of Austria from the outset, but any change in Austria's status required the Duce's agreement.

So it was that Prince Philip of Hesse was sent to see Mussolini on Hitler's behalf on 11 March, at the very moment when German troops were massing prior to crossing the Austro–German border. Hesse told Hitler that his new friend had been very understanding. Austria was a German problem, Mussolini told Hesse, and he personally had warned von Schuschnigg against the dangers of a plebiscite. Hitler was overjoyed, telling Hesse four times on the telephone that he would never forget the Duce's understanding. If ever, Hitler said, Mussolini should 'be in any need or danger, he could be certain that I will protect him to the uttermost ... even if the world should rise against him'. This was one promise that Hitler would actually honour, for Mussolini's assurances about Italian non-intervention were decisive. Von Schuschnigg was on his own, and within hours he would be arrested by the Gestapo and imprisoned at the Hotel Metropole in Vienna. Mussolini had never held the man in much regard, unlike his predecessor.

On 16 March, Mussolini appeared before the Fascist Chamber and defended his inaction, which must have puzzled those loyal Fascists who remembered July 1934. Austria was now part of Germany, he told the assembled deputies, and if anyone asked why Italy had failed to intervene, the answer was that she had never undertaken any obligation to do so. The enthusiasm of the Austrian people for the Anschluss was obvious, Mussolini argued (conveniently ignoring the likely Nazi intimidation which followed in the rigged plebiscite on 10 April). Neither did Fascist Italy have anything to fear from a German Reich of eighty million. After all, the other Stresa powers, Britain and France, had done nothing other than issue diplomatic protests about the destruction of Austrian democracy. The implications of the Duce's actions for the balance of power in Europe seemed to have escaped both him and his Foreign Minister, although colleagues found Mussolini in bad humour at the time (as he tended to be when Hitler staged his glamorous coups in the period after 1936). The Italian public did not react well to the Anschluss, which was rightly seen to be a blow to Italy's independence and integrity.

No sooner had Mussolini swallowed the disappearance of independent Austria than he had to tolerate its executioner as a house guest. In May 1938, Adolf Hitler came to Italy despite the fact that Pope Pius XI was unhappy about the anti-Catholic thrust of Nazi domestic policy (the Anschluss had also predictably sparked off disturbances in the largely German South Tyrol). Indeed, Pope Pius ostentatiously retired to his summer residence when Hitler was due in Rome. Mussolini himself was irritated by the fact that constitutional protocol obliged the German dictator to stay with King Victor Emmanuel, who bored Hitler by asking pedantic questions about the number of stitches in German military boots. The king, for his part, dismissed Hitler as a psychopath with very poor table manners. Neither did the Roman population receive Hitler with any show of warmth, much to the irritation of their leader. Mussolini was grateful, nonetheless, for Hitler's references to him as a new Roman, even if the Germans laughed at Fascist Italy's military pretensions. Hitler, for his part, was delighted with Rome's historic monuments, and his host tried to impress him with the laboured Italian version of the goose-step. This decidedly odd couple were now in a close embrace for good or ill. Hitler spent a rushed half-day in Florence's art galleries where Mussolini, who disliked Italy's inevitable association with the visual arts rather than martial virtues, was a reluctant guide. Hitler's visit was not, of course, just about social pleasantries. There appear to have been German attempts to get Mussolini to sign a military pact but Ciano in particular was reluctant lest Britain be antagonised only weeks after Italy had signed an agreement with her. The British premier, Chamberlain, was on the point of recognising Italy's East African empire at a League of Nations meeting in Geneva, and Ciano did not want to make difficulties for him. But both he and Mussolini wanted a German alliance when the moment was appropriate.

Another possible irritant during the Hitler visit was the Jewish issue. Italian police were ordered to lock up local Jews or expel them from towns which Hitler was visiting. The Anschluss in Austria had been followed by attacks on the Jewish population in Vienna, but there is no evidence that the Germans exerted pressure on Mussolini in this respect (see also Chapter 5 for comment on Mussolini's Jewish policy).

THE CZECH CRISIS

Shrewd observers of the international scene in the spring of 1938 expected that Hitler's next target would be Czechoslovakia with its three-million-strong German minority, which resided in the frontier areas known as the Sudetenland. This was despite reassurances from Hitler's deputy, Göring, to the Czech President Beneš about German intentions at the time of the Anschluss.

Mussolini had little love for the Czechs. Czechoslovakia was the only real democracy in Central and Eastern Europe, and it was allied both to France and the Soviet Union. In addition, the Czechs were part of the so-called Little Entente with Yugoslavia and Romania, and Italian relations with the former state had been tense since 1919. It was not to be expected, therefore, that Mussolini would react unfavourably if Hitler wished to dismember the Czechoslovak State, especially as he had good relations with Hungary, like Italy a revisionist power with its own large Magyar ethnic minority in Slovakia. Poland was in a similar position, and when the Polish and Hungarian Foreign Ministers visited Rome in July 1938, Mussolini told them that he would support German policy towards the Czechs which was designed to detach the Sudetenland and unite it with the Reich. But at this stage, Mussolini apparently did not expect a European crisis over Czechoslovakia.

There has been a good deal of speculation amongst historians about Mussolini's motives during the Czech crisis, which dragged on through May 1938 (when Hitler was wrongly accused of being about to attack the Czechs over the weekend of 20–21 May) until the end of September. De Felice believed that throughout the crisis, Mussolini wanted to avoid 'any real commitment', but Professor MacGregor Knox has argued that Mussolini did make some preparations for war and had assured Hitler that Italy would support him, should the French and Russians decide to stand by Czechoslovakia.[14] Certainly Mussolini did provide Germany with committed diplomatic support, and conspired with the German Foreign Office to produce an agreement for the detachment of the Sudetenland.

Thus, when Mussolini arrived at the Munich Conference of September 1938, he was not the impartial mediator he claimed to be. This could hardly be the case given his known detestation of the Czechs and Italy's poor relations with France. Czechoslovakia in his eyes was a

French puppet-state which represented the Western power's interests in the Balkans. The Munich Conference broke up the Czech State, and gave the Sudetenland to Hitler without a shot being fired because the Western democracies feared war and the USSR would not assist Czechoslovakia alone.

Mussolini's role at the conference was far less important than he pretended, although he was the only one of the four leaders involved who could speak foreign languages (though his English was limited). This allowed him to be the centre of attention at the conference, and to claim that the meeting, from 29–30 September, was a triumph for Italian diplomacy. This was the way the conference was presented to the Italian public, and Mussolini's popularity did rise because he had seemingly saved Europe from war. Ciano was as usual exultant about the Duce's genius, but in reality Munich merely confirmed Mussolini's dependence on the German alliance. Had Mussolini opposed Hitler's Czech policy, he could hardly have prevailed. There is no evidence though that during the Czech crisis, Mussolini ever seriously considered a policy realignment with France and Britain which would have circumvented Hitler in the way the Stresa Front briefly did in 1934. Had he allowed Italy to be dragged into a war in 1938, the military consequences could have been catastrophic. Mussolini was therefore happy to use British Prime Minister Chamberlain's request to intervene to head off a conflict which Italy was not ready for (as Mussolini well knew). But this intervention was only on terms which had been worked out with the German Foreign Office.

MUSSOLINI'S POLICY TOWARDS THE DEMOCRACIES

Although he regarded Britain as a degenerate failing power, Mussolini could still see advantages in reaching agreement with her. Most of his enmity was reserved for the French, who stood in the way of Italian ambitions in the Balkans and North Africa. Between 1936 and 1938 Mussolini worked to detach Britain from its French alliance, a policy which seemed to have reached some sort of fruition in the so-called 'Gentleman's Agreement' of January 1937 which was supposed to put constraints on Italian intervention in Spain but which was largely ignored by Mussolini. This was followed by the accord of 16 April 1938 which recognised the Italian conquests in East Africa. As Ciano noted at the time, the French were discomfited by this agreement, as Mussolini had intended. French overtures for an agreement, apart from a period of brief flirtation in April and May 1938, were rebuffed. Italian policy was to reject British suggestions for a multilateral pact to cover the Mediterranean in favour of a bilateral treaty between Italy and Britain. Both the agreements referred to above deliberately excluded the French.

Mussolini was undoubtedly assisted in his policy by the disposition of Chamberlain and his government (apart from Anthony Eden who resigned as Foreign Secretary in February 1938 because of differences over policy towards Italy) to see Italy as a potential counterweight to Germany. This policy was a delusion, but the British were to persist with it into 1939. In the meantime Mussolini increased pressure on France to make concessions in North Africa, which was resolutely resisted. This resolution was probably assisted by the failure of a much publicised visit by Neville Chamberlain and his Foreign Secretary, Halifax, to Rome in January 1939 to achieve anything of substance. There were real differences between the British and French attitudes towards Italy in 1938–39, but they were not severe enough to endanger the traditional accord between these two nations. And given the Duce's overarching ambition in the Mediterranean, which threatened both powers, his attempts to divide Britain and France were doomed to fail in the long run.

THE ALBANIAN ADVENTURE

All the evidence available to us suggests that, although Mussolini wanted a German alliance, this would only be on the clear understanding that a major war in Europe must be postponed for at least five or six years. He was annoyed by the response of Italian public opinion to the Munich Agreement because it underlined his people's deep yearning for peace, but knew that his armed forces were in no condition to take on the British or the French even with Nazi Germany as an ally.

This did not, however, prevent Mussolini trying to extract concessions from the Western democracies, hopeful that their fear of war with Germany might make them more amenable. It was a dangerous policy, especially as Hitler was an unreliable ally motivated purely by self-interest. Just how unreliable was to be forcibly demonstrated on 15 March 1939.

At Munich Hitler had promised that he wanted no more territorial gains in Europe. But by mid-March he had bullied the new Czech President Hácha into allowing German troops into the rump state of Bohemia and Moravia, allegedly to restore law and order. At the same time, Slovakia, whose envy of the better-educated and more industrialised Czechs had been encouraged in Berlin, became a separate German client-state. Czechoslovakia had therefore disappeared from the map of Europe, and all this had happened without the Italians being consulted.

Both Mussolini and Ciano were infuriated by this cavalier behaviour which also had the effect of precipitating the British into a new policy of collective security as Hitler could obviously not be trusted. But the essential helplessness of Mussolini's position was demonstrated by his well-known remark to Ciano that 'the Italians will laugh at me. Every time Hitler grabs a country, he sends me a message.'[15] Mussolini's response was to grab a country himself, an act of aggression which placed him even more firmly in the German camp.

The victim was tiny Albania which had virtually been an Italian protectorate since the 1920s. Its king, Zog, had supposedly become too independent for Mussolini, and on Good Friday (7 April) 1939 he sent in his army, ignoring the sacredness of the day in the Italian Catholic calendar. Italian troops landed at Durazzo but the operation was chaotic, and had the Albanians been less divided themselves, Mussolini could have been embarrassed. As it was, the Albanians proved to be strongly resistant to Italian propaganda about their country's liberation, and Mussolini's militarism had the effect of scaring off foreign tourists on whom the Italian economy was heavily reliant. Albania proved to be a paper triumph, although Mussolini could point to Franco's victory in Spain as a positive development which ended the costly Italian intervention there.

THE PACT OF STEEL

Mussolini's blatant aggression against Albania could not be rubber stamped by the British and French in the manner of his Ethiopian conquest. Hitler's Prague coup on 15 March, together with Italy's aggression, had changed the atmosphere in Europe as the two Western powers made belated overtures to the Soviet Union for a military agreement to deter the Fascist powers.

From time to time Mussolini complained about German bad faith, but he was much more concerned about his country's military image, remembering Italy's treacherous turnabout in 1914–15. This, together with his infatuation with Nazism, made the conclusion of a definitive military agreement with Germany only a matter of time, although Mussolini prevaricated, aware that such an alliance aimed against his country's traditional friends would not be popular in Italy. In the end, it was Mussolini's belief in Nazi Germany's brute strength that carried the day. There was a preliminary meeting between Ciano and von Ribbentrop in Milan, and on 7 May 1939 the so-called 'Pact of Steel' was announced. Mussolini had already insisted on the need for the alliance before the Fascist Grand Council.

Ciano had told von Ribbentrop that, despite Italy's undertaking in the Pact to give military support to Germany, the Italians would not be in a position to go to war until 1942 at the earliest. Mussolini also succeeded in altering the open-ended commitment wanted by the Germans to one of ten years only. But it seems clear that von Ribbentrop lied to Ciano in Milan, because Hitler had already approved a plan to attack Poland as early as 11 April in pursuit of his desire to annex Danzig and the Polish Corridor (which had been taken from Germany by the Versailles Treaty).

The Pact of Steel was actually signed by Ciano in Berlin on 22 May. Article II of its text made the Italian commitment clear, for it stated that if one of the two powers should become

> involved in warlike complications with another Power or with other Powers, the other contracting party will come to its aid as an ally and will support it with all its military forces on land, on sea and in the air.[16]

Mussolini's problem was that Hitler was already involved in 'warlike complications', and on 23 August he pulled off an audacious coup by persuading Stalin to sign a non-aggression pact. This was a profound shock for Mussolini and Ciano and had the effect of freeing Hitler from the threat of Soviet intervention should he attack Poland. Parallel Anglo-French negotiations with the USSR to achieve a military alliance and safeguard Polish independence had failed.

By now the scales had fallen from Ciano's eyes. He had been disgusted by the revelation at a meeting with von Ribbentrop in Salzburg on 11 August that, despite the previous undertaking given in Milan, Germany intended to attack the Poles. Thereafter Ciano moved into the camp of those such as Bottai, Grandi and Balbo who can be described as anti-German.

Mussolini was as ever torn by his desire to maintain the German alliance, awareness of Italian military weakness and anger over the deceitful behaviour of the Germans. But it was the military factor which was to be decisive in the end (his vacillations are effectively traced in Ciano's diary entries between 14 August and 23 August). And for once, Mussolini trumped his domineering ally. On 26 August a list of Italian requirements was sent to Berlin without which Mussolini and Ciano said Italy would be unable to enter the war. It was a formidable list which included seven million tons of oil, two million tons of steel and seventeen thousand military vehicles. Ciano memorably said that it was enough 'to kill a bull, if a bull could read'.

Hitler knew, as did Mussolini, that Germany would be unable to meet these demands and in the short term the Führer was deterred. He called off the attack on Poland and reset the invasion date for 1 September. Mussolini's strategy was to try and convene another European conference after Neville Chamberlain had appealed to him to do so. But Mussolini's appeals to Hitler were ignored as the German dictator was determined to have his war with or without Italian help.

The German invasion of Poland duly went ahead on 1 September, and two days later Britain and France, both of whom had pledged to defend Poland, declared war on Germany when Hitler ignored their ultimata to withdraw his troops. The German blitzkrieg then rolled over Poland, and again Mussolini demonstrated his unease about Italian neutrality. When there were unfavourable references to it in the foreign press, Mussolini was heard to mutter 'nobody loves a neutral'. This was not the feeling of his people. Italians rejoiced over the fact that they were not going to war (even in Germany there was none of the war fever of 1914).

THE 'PHONEY WAR'

The period between the German conquest of Poland in September 1939 and the start of Hitler's offensives in the West in April 1940 was a bizarre one of military inaction and invasion scares. For Mussolini it was a period of frustration because his instinct was to join the War, but even he knew that Italy was not ready to do so. At first, he hoped for a peace initiative from Hitler who had obtained his objectives in Poland. When this did not happen, he hoped for a long drawn-out war of attrition like 1914–18 which would have left Italy in an advantageous position as a mediator between exhausted enemies. This policy would have made some sense for the weakest of the Great Powers, allowing Italy to follow a policy of balance, but it went against all Mussolini's instincts. His régime after all had bombarded the Italian people for seventeen years with slogans about the need to toughen up the Italian race. Fascism had lauded warriors and militarism; how therefore could Mussolini honourably remain neutral, especially as he remembered 1914–15 and the taunts about Italy being 'the whore of Europe' which changed sides in an instant?

In the short term, Mussolini had little option but to heed military warnings about Italy's lack of preparedness. In January 1940, Badoglio, the Army Chief of Staff, had to sharply remind him that the myth of the 'eight million bayonets' was just that, a myth. But Mussolini may have obtained some enjoyment from reminding Hitler that their main ideological enemy was the USSR, Germany's current ally under the 1939 non-aggression pact. Ciano even flirted with the idea of sending aid to Finland, which had been attacked by Stalin in November 1939 at the start of the so-called 'Winter War'. Bizarrely Britain and France, instead of concentrating on their German enemy, had the same idea (unfortunately implemented too late to save the Finns).

The picture of Mussolini that emerges from the winter of 1939–40 is that of a frustrated warmonger strangely anxious to postpone war for as long as possible, but fearful that a rapid German victory might prevent Italy from securing gains at any peace conference. He fretted because the Italians showed no enthusiasm for war, but also knew as did the Germans (whose enthusiasm for Italian intervention waned after September 1939) that his armed forces were in no condition to take on the allegedly cowardly and effete Anglo-French forces.

March 1940 was an important month for the Italo-German alliance. Mussolini met the irritating von Ribbentrop on 10–11 March and seemed to be enthusiastic about the prospect of war, but then lost his nerve again when the Foreign Minister went back to Berlin. A week later he met Adolf Hitler at the Brenner Pass. Their discussion followed a pattern which became increasingly common when the two dictators met. Hitler talked and, for the most part, Mussolini listened, although he made things harder for himself by insisting on conversing in his none too perfect German. Hitler assured him that Germany would win the war, but warned that Italian supremacy in the Mediterranean would be endangered if Italy's intervention in the war was put off much longer. Rather sheepishly, Mussolini told his ally that Italy would come into the conflict when it was clear that it would be a short one. He succeeded, however, in managing not to give a specific commitment about intervention.

In a minute written on 31 March, Mussolini underlined his doubts about Italy's readiness for war by saying that conflict must be postponed as long as possible. Plainly then the decision to enter the war had not yet been made, although Mussolini was worried that if he did not honour his commitment to Germany, there was a real risk that Hitler might attack him. He believed that Hitler might have an ambition to seize the Trentino, the South Tyrol and even Trieste. This is slightly surprising given the fact that Hitler had agreed to a transfer of ethnic Germans from the South Tyrol to the Reich and that thousands had already left, but it does help to explain the strange fact that, while he was wooing Hitler, the Duce was also constructing elaborate defences along the Italian–German frontier, a process which went on until 1942. Mussolini seems, therefore, to have shared some of Ciano's suspicions about the Germans.

Ultimately Mussolini allowed himself to be seduced by the sheer scale of Germany's victories in Western Europe between April and June 1940. Denmark and Norway were rapidly overrun in April, to be followed by Holland, Belgium and France in May and June. Observers such as Ciano noted how Mussolini sulked at the prospect of an overwhelming German victory, but he told his military commanders nothing about his intentions. Only on 28 May did Mussolini tell them that Italy would fight. When Badoglio told him that war would be suicide, Mussolini reportedly replied that the fighting would be over by September.

THE DECLARATION OF WAR

This was the nub of the matter as far as Mussolini was concerned. He could not afford to take heavy casualties, but neither could he stay out of the war now that France's defeat was almost certain (the British army was being evacuated from Dunkirk in late May). The best option was a short victorious war, and it seemed that by early June many of the other Fascist leaders agreed with this. And though Badoglio was cautious, another victor in Ethiopia, Marshal Graziani, urged the Duce to declare war. As did Edda Ciano, more belligerent than her husband, who told her father that not to fight would be dishonourable. Even the Catholic Church seemed prepared to stomach the coming of war, provided it was soon over. Ordinary Italians, brainwashed into passivity by the régime, showed no great enthusiasm for war but neither did they demonstrate against it. The correspondent for *The Times* noted that there were no national flags evident in Rome at the point when Italy was preparing for hostilities.

With France days away from an armistice, Mussolini declared war on it and Britain on 10 June. He made the announcement from the Palazzo Venezia to a hastily assembled crowd. 'We go into the field against the plutocratic and reactionary democracies of the West,'[17] Mussolini told the crowd, adding that the declaration of war was the logical development of the Fascist revolution. By coincidence, it was the sixteenth anniversary of the murder of Matteotti and, in the sense that violence was central to the Fascist message, Mussolini was right.

There may seem to be an inevitability about the way in which Fascist Italy was sucked into the Second World War. Alongside this suggestion is the presumption, often supported by historians after 1945, that the war was Mussolini's war. This is only a half-truth for it is clear that, with the fall of France in May–June 1940, there was a change in attitude amongst the civil leadership and the leading Fascists (Ciano and a few others apart). Even Victor Emmanuel was prepared to sublimate his anti-German stance in the interest of obtaining cheap military glory for Italy. Mussolini's decision thus had the support of those forces which had supported him in 1922, and which had sustained him in power since then. In this sense, the war was not just Mussolini's war but a war willed by the Italian establishment, even though it had shared the Duce's doubts about entering the struggle. He himself, it should be noted, tried to hedge his bets to the last, sharing secret talks with Britain and France before Hitler's offensive in the hope of making gains in territory which would be obtained without fighting (they were apparently on offer). And his continuing mistrust of the Germans, well justified as it turned out, has already been referred to.

In the end, Mussolini decided to intervene in the war because he could not see a viable alternative. Italian honour demanded it, while fear of German retribution alarmed Mussolini about the possible consequences should he not enter. He believed that he had seized the hour in June 1940, and was even prepared to put aside his Balkan ambitions (he frequently spoke about possible attacks on Yugoslavia or Greece) to please Hitler. The Führer advised Mussolini to embark on an African war with the British, for which the Italians were very poorly prepared (oddly, Mussolini had rejected a German offer of heavy tanks before the declaration of war). He himself simply could not resist the urge to be seen acting decisively and carrying Fascism to glory. It was a decision which was to cost him dearly, but it had its undoubted origins in the dynamic of Fascism.

8

THE SLIDE TO DISASTER, 1940–43

One of Mussolini's latest biographers has written of Italy's role as 'Germany's ignoble second'[1] between 1939 and 1941. The phrase could be equally well applied to the period between 1941 and 1943. Unlike his son-in-law Ciano, who admitted to sadness when Italy entered the war, Mussolini was jubilant, sweeping aside the opinions of the doubters in the expectation of victory.

At no stage, however, in the four years to be examined in this chapter, was Fascist Italy able to replicate the victories of its Nazi German ally between 1939 and 1942. On land, on sea and in the air, the story was the same as Italian forces were successively routed in Greece, North and East Africa, Russia and ultimately in Italy itself. And much of this military catastrophe was attributable to the Duce himself, who fragmented Italian effort and dissipated Italian manpower over as many as five different fronts. As a military leader, Mussolini was a failure, not least because his expectations were totally unrealistic. Frequently Italian troops fought bravely (contrary to post-war myth), but they were badly led, badly equipped and ultimately suffered poor morale when it became abundantly clear that Fascist rhetoric was no substitute for modern tanks, guns and aircraft. What equipment the Italians did possess was often more appropriate to the First World War than the Second. It remains to examine whether Mussolini, who was not unaware of these deficiencies, ever made a serious effort to detach his country from the rush towards disaster which was so clearly looming in 1942–43.

THE AFRICAN CAMPAIGNS

Fascist Italy should have been at an obvious advantage in June 1940, with France traumatised by the German blitzkrieg and Britain expecting an invasion at any moment and without the heavy equipment left on the beaches of Dunkirk. Yet those advantages were frittered away by Mussolini and his military leaders, especially in Africa.

The omens were poor from the start. Mussolini had entered the war against France and Britain to obtain cheap glory, but he was unable to deal adequately with the very small French forces along the common border. On the Alpine Front, thirty-two Italian divisions were unable to drive back three French ones, while on the Côte d'Azur the Italian forces were held at bay by just one French NCO and seven men.[2] Hitler was decidedly unamused by Mussolini's shoddy attempts to secure parity at the peace table with the defeated French. But oddly, Mussolini then withdrew his demand for Nice, Savoy, Corsica and Tunisia, contenting himself merely with a zone of occupation along the Franco-Italian border.

Early raids by the British into Italian Libya also found the Duce's forces unprepared, and Marshal Graziani was extremely reluctant to launch the offensive into Egypt which Mussolini wanted. Graziani had 300,000 men in Libya facing just 36,000 British in Egypt, yet he had somehow convinced himself that the British had as many men as he. On 15 July Mussolini ordered Graziani to attack Egypt but he did nothing, forcing the Duce to recall him to Rome. Then on 8 August the Marshal was given a dressing down by Ciano which was designed to stiffen his resolve. The interview failed to remove Graziani's doubts. He argued, not unreasonably, that Italy's preparations were incomplete, and it was certainly true that the army, without any authentic armoured divisions, was woefully unprepared to fight a desert campaign. But the delay in launching an offensive allowed the British, still under the threat of German invasion in July and August 1940, to supply their forces in Egypt with tanks and guns.

Meanwhile, Mussolini fretted. He rejoiced when the Italians defeated the British forces in British Somaliland and overran the colony, ignoring the fact that the Italians had a five-to-one advantage in numbers. This paper victory made Mussolini even more belligerent in his attitude towards the unfortunate Graziani. On 29 August he ordered the

Marshal to attack by 10 September, and when he still procrastinated, threatened him with dismissal. Ultimately, in mid-September, the offensive was launched, although Ciano noted in his diary that 'never has a military operation been undertaken so much against the will of the commander'.

Graziani advanced sixty miles without meeting any substantial opposition as the British were pulling back to their defence line at Mersa Matruk. Mistaking this advance for a decisive victory, Mussolini, reported Ciano, was 'radiant with joy'.[3] He was soon disillusioned for, bizarrely, having made his advance, Graziani dug in and constructed a series of fortified camps before staying put. This allowed the British, under Wavell, to send in more armoured units which they were to use to deadly effect. Even then, they did not launch a counter-strike until early December, making Graziani's inertia seem even more extraordinary. When the British did eventually strike, their advantage in tanks was decisive as they swept through the gaps between Graziani's fortified camps and captured them one by one. Soon the British armoured pincers were driving into Libya; Tobruk fell in January 1941, and the Italians were forced to evacuate Benghazi. They were only saved from utter disaster by developments in the Balkans.

THE GREEK CAMPAIGN

Ironically, events in the Balkans were precipitated by arguably Mussolini's worst military decision of the war, when he sent his army against Greece on 28 October 1940. This was an extraordinary act as Italy had no territorial claims against Greece, and the authoritarian régime of General Metaxas was as much an ideological bedfellow of Fascism as Franco could claim to be in Spain. Adolf Hitler was also infuriated by an act which got the Axis Powers bogged down in a potential Balkans quagmire. And it was typical of the ramshackle Fascist decision-making process that Graziani only heard about the Greek invasion on the radio news in Egypt.

Why did Mussolini embark on this reckless adventure? First, because he had convinced himself that the Greeks were an inferior race who would easily succumb to Fascist military prowess. And second, it seems, because he wanted to show the Germans that Italy too could launch a blitzkrieg, even though Berlin had tried to direct Mussolini's ambitions towards Africa. Italian strength had been further dissipated by sending aircraft to participate in the Battle of Britain (they proved in the event to be quite useless), which the Germans did not want, and which could have been used more profitably in either Greece or Africa.

The Italian campaign in Greece was supposed to be short and sweet. This was far from being the case, and it rapidly turned into a severe set-back for the Duce and his régime. Elementary precautions, such as the issue of winter clothing, had been neglected, and the Italians were rapidly driven out of Greece back to their starting point in Albania. The millions of lire which Mussolini had spent bribing Greek generals not to fight had been wasted, and any element of surprise had been surren-dered by Ciano's verbal indiscretions in the days before 28 October.[4] The morale of the Italian forces sank rapidly, and even a three-week visit by Mussolini himself failed to restore spirits. The only positive aspect of the campaign from Mussolini's point of view was that the British, fore-seeing German involvement and anxious to support the Greeks (who were reluctant recipients of such aid), transferred some badly needed armoured forces from Libya to Greece, inadvertently saving Mussolini's fortunes in Africa. Otherwise, the Italians found themselves engaged in a desperate battle in Albania, one-quarter of which had fallen into Greek hands. Mussolini's own popularity waned in the aftermath of the Greek defeat, and there were stories that his appearance on newsreels in cinemas was greeted with stony silence.

The defeats in Greece and North Africa were the result of over-stretching Italian resources, but also of the military deficiencies that had been obvious before June 1940. The Italians were afflicted by poor intel-ligence, there was no coherent strategy and Mussolini failed (for example) to authorise attacks on the crucial Mediterranean island of Malta until it was too late. His army looked strong on paper until it was remembered that he had reduced the number of troops in a division by half. It was also top heavy with generals (no less than 600 in 1939), and there was no real mechanism for co-operation between the army and the other two ser-vices. The Italian army was organised to re-fight the Alpine campaign of 1915–18, not campaigns in Africa and Greece, while the navy lacked air-craft carriers, and the airforce's two best fighters, the Macchi 200 and the Fiat CR42, were both slower than the British Spitfire.[5] Italy also lacked radar, and its woeful lack of anti-aircraft guns was vividly demonstrated when Anglo-French forces bombed Milan and Genoa shortly after

Mussolini's declaration of war. Such deficiencies became even more glaringly obvious when Mussolini opened a war on far too many fronts, making Fascist Italy heavily dependent on an increasingly contemptuous Nazi Germany. Even then, as has been seen, Mussolini unwisely declined the offer of German heavy tanks in May 1940. Colleagues noticed that, under the strain of successive defeats, their Duce looked increasingly pallid and elderly. He was shaken, especially by the disaster in Greece, and fell back in characteristic fashion on berating the Italian people for their lack of soldierly qualities.

Catastrophe on land went hand in hand with disaster at sea. In 1940 the navy appeared to be the strongest of the Italian forces, with 155 surface ships (most of which were new) and 115 submarines; it had 4 battleships, 6 cruisers, 16 destroyers and 64 submarines ready for service. Yet it lacked a proper fleet air arm and was therefore increasingly dependent on shore-based aircraft for defence in the absence of carrier-based ones. In this instance, it was the admirals, who refused to recognise that air power rendered battleships obsolete, who were to blame rather than Mussolini himself.

Italian propaganda pumped out nonsense about how the British Fleet in the Mediterranean had lost half its strength as a result of Italian attacks. Nothing could have been further from the truth as first the Italian airforce bombed its own ships at Punta Silo in July 1940, and then an inadequately defended anchorage at Taranto allowed the British to mount a carrier-based attack which put the Italian battle fleet out of action in November.

Worse was to follow. In March 1941, at Cape Matapan, three cruisers and two destroyers were lost when air support arrived too late, and thereafter Italy's biggest warships were obliged to stay within a hundred miles of the coastline to ensure adequate air cover could be provided. In effect, the navy, supposedly the most efficient of the Fascist forces, had been neutralised. By contrast, Germany, with its much smaller surface fleet, caused the British far more difficulties with its submarines. The Italian navy in the Mediterranean conspicuously failed to take advantage of Britain's preoccupations elsewhere in 1940–41.

GERMAN INTERVENTION

Seeing his ally floundering from one disaster to another, Hitler felt obliged to intervene in March 1941. Mussolini was reluctant to accept

German help, especially against the Greeks (in Africa, at least, he could pretend that he was worsted by another great power), but he had little real option.

Germany destroyed the Greek army in just two weeks, but Mussolini refused to assist the Germans by taking the offensive in Albania, instead waiting for the Greek army to fragment before attacking. Simultaneously the Germans had invaded Yugoslavia, devastating Belgrade from the air because the Yugoslavs had impertinently installed a pro-British government under King Peter. The Italian army was not involved in the Yugoslav campaign, but Mussolini was further humiliated when the Greeks declined to surrender to an enemy that had totally failed to hold an inch of their territory. The Duce insisted on his pound of flesh however: Italian forces were to be involved in the occupation of both Greece and Yugoslavia and in the latter particularly were guilty of serious atrocities. It is difficult to be certain whether such killings were entirely at Mussolini's behest or whether the Italian army was following its own path. As ever, Mussolini's rhetoric was ferocious, saying, for example, that hostages should be shot and villages burnt to the ground, but, as Ciano noted, his father-in-law often failed to implement such orders. Nevertheless, it is difficult to entirely disentangle the militaristic, anti-Slav rhetoric of Mussolini's Fascism from the behaviour of occupying Italian forces in Greece and Yugoslavia. This contrasted with the humane behaviour of the Italians in their French zone of occupation, which became a refuge for persecuted French Jews.

In Africa, the pattern was the same from the moment when General Erwin Rommel, one of the stars of the German triumph in 1940, arrived with elements of the so-called Afrika Korps. Rommel soon drove the British out of Libya, but there were command disputes with Mussolini who demanded that the *comando supremo* should have authority over the General. In theory it did, but in practice Rommel did as he pleased, and had field control of the Italian forces. Attempts by Mussolini to claim the credit for Rommel's victories fooled no one: Rommel had a coherent strategy for fighting in the desert which Graziani and the Italian commanders never did.

The weakness of the Italian forces when they were left to their own devices was demonstrated again when Mussolini's East African empire collapsed in April 1941. Eritrea, Somalia and Ethiopia were all lost to the British as the Duke of Aosta surrendered with 250,000 men, all this taking place far more quickly than the Italian conquest of Ethiopia in 1935–36. Even with the Axis satellites like Croatia, Mussolini seemed to have no luck. Ostensibly the Italians had an administrative role there alongside the Fascist Pavelic and his *Ustacha* militia but Ciano described them as 'cut throats' (accurately as it turned out).

As far as relations with Hitler were concerned, Mussolini was by now indisputably the junior partner. The two men met at Hitler's headquarters in Rastenburg in East Prussia in August 1941, two months after Nazi Germany had attacked the Soviet Union. Although he was initially anxious about the conflict, this came to please the Duce because war with the USSR had a clear ideological edge which was supported by both Victor Emmanuel and the Vatican. But Mussolini made the fatal error of volunteering to send as many as ten divisions to Russia, and two months later in October he wanted to send another ten. Hitler, who had a low opinion of the Italian forces by now, was unimpressed. Mussolini's divisions lacked guns and trucks, which the Wehrmacht was expected to provide. Yet again, Mussolini was allowing Italy's limited resources to be fragmented. In peacetime, he had gone to some trouble to cultivate reasonable relations with the USSR; now he was opening up another unnecessary front for his beleaguered forces.

Mussolini's argument over Russia, as it had been over France in 1940, was that the more casualties Italy sustained in Russia, the bigger its role in a victorious peace conference. It included the dangerous assumption that the Germans would win in Russia, a preconception that was challenged as early as December 1941 when they were flung back by a counter-offensive in front of Moscow. All Mussolini achieved in the long term was to put his already demoralised troops under greater strain in yet another remote theatre of war instead of providing ideological support and letting Hitler get on with his ultimately catastrophic war in the East.

This blunder was compounded by Mussolini's decision to declare war on the United States after Imperial Japan attacked Pearl Harbour on 7 December 1941. Mussolini, like Hitler, absurdly underestimated the Americans' industrial strength and had also been guilty of ridiculing President Roosevelt because he was in a wheelchair as a result of the polio he contracted in the 1920s. He was soon made to rue his arrogance and regret following Germany's lead yet again. In the 1914–18 war, Italy had never been at war with Germany because it was not in her interest to be so. By contrast, as the weakest of the major belligerents, instead of husbanding his resources, Mussolini plunged recklessly into every available conflict. He would have done much better to have imitated Franco's wily pragmatism; the Spanish dictator could never be lured into a world war on Hitler's side.

THE WAR ECONOMY

Underlying all Mussolini's military problems between 1940 and 1943 was chronic economic weakness and disorganisation. Italy never had the economic base needed to fight a war against powers like Britain and the United States. This weakness was compounded by Mussolini's assumption that the struggle would be a short one which would allow him to paper over the cracks. As it was, Fascist Italy was only able to survive three years of conflict before its chronic economic and military weakness caused it to implode.

An unwillingness to face unpleasant economic realities was a feature from the outset. Initially, Mussolini was reluctant to impose food rationing, and even boasted about how he had avoided this when Britain and Germany had been obliged to resort to it. Again, he was betrayed by his belief in a short war which would render such emergency measures unnecessary.

Reality then intervened. Rationing did have to be imposed, and food consumption was actually cut by a quarter between 1939 and 1943.[6] Thereafter, basic commodities such as soap and coffee became luxuries, cats were being eaten in Rome and by 1943 bread was being sold for eight times its official price on a flourishing black market. Mussolini himself was well aware of how peasants were enriching themselves by selling most of their produce, especially grain, on the black market rather than handing it over to the Fascist authorities.

These were symptoms of a war economy which was not working. Italy's problem was that it had no indigenous oil supply, and was heavily dependent on German coal which became scarcer as the war drew on. Steel production actually fell during the war years and arms production was only adequate for a few months in 1942. Then, as the British and Americans stepped up their bombing of Italian cities, industry was disrupted and production levels fell off again. And, unlike Germany, the Italians did not have an armaments minister of the calibre of Albert

Speer to repair the damage. One result was that workers in the anti-Fascist factories of Turin went on strike in protest at having to work as many as forty-eight hours a week. Attempts by the régime to counteract demoralisation by allowing the syndicates into engineering factories to address grievances and smother unrest invariably failed. The Duce was now linked with the unpopularity of Fascism. As he himself admitted, by 1943 Mussolini had become 'the most hated man in Italy'.

It was ironic, therefore, that at this point Mussolini seemed to be reverting to the Socialism of his youth. He alarmed Ciano and Grandi by talking of nationalising electricity and blaming all Italy's woes on the middle classes.[7] But this was just a variation on his usual theme – that the Italians lacked fighting qualities and 'moral courage'.[8]

German assistance did stem the tide in the short term in North Africa, and Rommel even managed to recapture Tobruk and threaten Egypt. But Mussolini's command structure remained chaotic, generals were shuffled and reshuffled (Cavellero replaced Badoglio as Chief of Army Staff), while the Duce demanded that Italian soldiers should die at their posts.

None of this could counteract the irrefutable logic of Anglo-American superiority in North Africa. In November 1942 the Afrika Korps was defeated at El Alamein (Rommel was sick and only intermittently present on the battlefield). Tripoli fell to the British in January 1943, and American forces had already landed in French North Africa. On 13 May the remaining Axis forces in North Africa surrendered, and the way was open for the Allies to invade Sicily and then the Italian mainland.

Mussolini struck those around him at this time as being a man in physical and mental decline. His ulcer problem had become severe; on one occasion he was found writhing on the floor and a servant thought he was dying. Balbo even suggested that Mussolini was dying of the syphilis he had contracted in his youth. Whatever the truth of the matter, Mussolini was undoubtedly subject to violent mood swings which made decision making a hazardous and erratic process.

Matters were not assisted by the growing influence of his young mistress, Claretta Petacci, who used her position to secure favours for her family. This was a subject of continual gossip among Mussolini's entourage. Their relationship was a tempestuous one. On one occasion, Mussolini hit Petacci so hard that she fell against a wall and was rendered unconscious.[9] Yet she maintained her influence to the end, although it mired Mussolini in sleaze and worsened the already poor image of the régime.

THE COLLAPSE OF THE DICTATORSHIP

As the war drew on, evidence of the Italian people's disillusionment became sharper. People had ceased to believe Mussolini's propaganda and, as early as 1940, the police were reporting that many were secretly listening to the BBC. Years of lies had taken their toll. Slogans such as 'Death to the Duce' appeared on walls. The German alliance was widely unpopular, a sentiment strengthened by the series of Italian military reverses which flowed from it.

In a desperate attempt to shore up the régime, Mussolini had loosened the rules for joining the Fascist Party, allowing all servicemen to join in 1940, but this measure did nothing to strengthen a discredited and badly led organisation. Neither did Mussolini help the PNF's situation by making wretched appointments. In December 1941, for example, he appointed Aldo Vidussoni as Party Secretary, an incompetent young man of twenty-eight who owed his position to the fact that he was a friend of the Petacci family. The Fascist Old Guard hated Vidussoni as an upstart, just as they had loathed Ciano. Ironically, some leading Fascists then approached Ciano about securing Vidussoni's removal, but he dared not raise the subject with Mussolini. It was an extraordinary lapse of judgement on Mussolini's part to make such an appointment and demonstrated the degree to which he had lost touch with reality. Vidussoni was a figure of fun. So increasingly was the PNF and, by extension, Mussolini himself.

As the grip of Fascism weakened on Italian life, so opposition to the régime began to appear. Underground Catholic, Communist and Socialist newspapers circulated by 1942, and the Communists particularly were involved in inciting strike action in the North. It is important to keep these developments in proportion however. As late as March 1943 there were still only eighty Communist Party members out of 21,000 workers in the main Fiat factories in Turin. Ultimately it would be the Italian establishment which would have to take responsibility for Mussolini's removal.

THE CONSPIRACY AGAINST MUSSOLINI

Opposition to Mussolini was beginning to emerge within the Fascist movement before the end of 1942. In September Bottai visited Ciano and told him of his disillusionment with Mussolini and the war. This was an obvious gambit by Bottai, Grandi and other moderate Fascists to draw Ciano out and see whether he might join an attempt to remove Mussolini. The approach was premature for Ciano was genuinely attached to his father-in-law, and he dismissed Bottai's justification for opposition, namely that Mussolini had declared war in 1940 without consulting the Grand Council, as a technicality.

The second major opposition grouping in the Italian establishment was in the military, led by Badoglio, who had been put out to grass when Mussolini sacked him as Army Chief of Staff. Between the two manoeuvred King Victor Emmanuel, indecisive as ever but a key figure if the loyalty of the army were to be secured. But behind Victor Emmanuel was the more pro-active figure of the Minister of the Royal Household, Duke of Acquarone, who had good lines of communication to all the factions. By January 1943, Acquarone had persuaded the king that Mussolini had to go.

Somehow Mussolini seems to have found out about the plotting against him and confronted Ciano about it, plainly suspecting him of involvement. At this stage Ciano had not committed himself but, perhaps hurt by the accusation of treachery, he did throw in his lot with Grandi and Bottai in mid-January. Ciano gave Mussolini one last chance to detach himself from the German alliance when the two men met on 20 January. Ciano suggested that, as the war was lost, Italy should approach the Allies to seek peace. He was also subtle enough to throw in a reference about the need for a common front against Bolshevism. The response was disappointing. Mussolini still fantasised about German strength, telling his Foreign Minister on 21 January that 'five hundred Tiger tanks, five hundred thousand men in reserve, and the new German gun can still reverse the situation'.[10]

This interview was only days away from the devastating surrender of the German Sixth Army at Stalingrad, which is generally regarded as the decisive turning point on the Eastern Front. Mussolini can only be defended in the knowledge that it was not until May 1943, after the failure of the last German offensive at Kursk, that the Red Army was able to go on to the offensive. As it was, he confused Ciano by saying on 22 January that the German military bulletin for that day was the worst of the war, and that Rommel was ignoring the plight of Italian forces in his withdrawal westwards in North Africa. Plainly though, Mussolini, despite his persistent complaints about the Germans, would not sever the link with Hitler.

Victor Emmanuel seems to have thought that a watered-down Fascist régime under someone like Grandi might have been able to continue, but Grandi was unacceptable to the Allied powers with whom Ciano and others were in contact. By mid-January, as has been seen, Ciano was firmly in the conspirators' camp, and Mussolini made things worse for himself by striking out at his moderate Fascist opponents in a cabinet reshuffle on 5 February. Ciano was sacked as Foreign Minister, Bottai was removed as Minister of Education and Grandi himself lost his position as Minister of Justice. This move may have been an attempt by Mussolini to protect his power base, but if it were, it misfired. Unlike Hitler's coup against his moderate opponents inside the German régime exactly five years before, Mussolini's action was a consequence of weakness rather than strength. It merely drove the moderates into outright revolt. The dismissal of the absurd Vidussoni as Party Secretary in April 1943 and his replacement by Scorza, a member of the Fascist Old Guard, did little to redress the balance in Mussolini's favour.

Worst of all was Mussolini's disinclination to withdraw from the alliance with Germany during those months. It can reasonably be argued that Mussolini feared a drastic German military response if he did so, but he lacked the courage even to denounce the vile policy of mass murder in the East which he knew about in 1942. On 11 October 1942,[11] he had met Himmler, who tried to cover up the worst Nazi excesses against the Jews, but a visit to the Eastern Front by Vidussoni confirmed that the Holocaust was well underway. When the Party Secretary reported back, Mussolini attempted to excuse the atrocities by saying that they were just an inevitable consequence of war. The accusation that Mussolini turned a blind eye to the Holocaust before he fell from power is therefore a just one. Faced with clear evidence of the moral depravity of his allies, the Duce lacked the courage to protest, let alone sever the relationship.

Military collapse merely hastened Mussolini's end. The British and Americans landed in Sicily on 9 July, and Mussolini failed in a meeting with Hitler at Feltre in mid-July to persuade the Führer to move troops from the East to the Mediterranean theatre. Faced with military catastrophe, Mussolini had little option but to agree to the convening of the Grand Council to discuss the war (it had never actually met during wartime).

Meanwhile, the Vatican too was involved in trying to despatch Italy's dictator. Ciano had approached the British Foreign Office in November 1942 but was distrusted, especially as it was run by his old sparring partner, the strongly anti-Fascist Eden. The Vatican was a much more satisfactory intermediary for the Anglo-American powers, who listened to its advice (naturally excluding the Italian Left) on the composition of an alternative Italian government. The gist of this was that the Italian people were still attached to the House of Savoy and that a military government under Badoglio would be the best option available. By late May the Americans, clearly by now the senior partner in the Western alliance, agreed to accept the principle of a separate peace between the Allies and a non-Fascist government, probably headed by Badoglio. If Mussolini feared his German ally, King Victor Emmanuel and the opponents of Mussolini feared that Italy's cities could be devastated if peace were not agreed (the process was after all well underway in German cities such as Hamburg). The lesson was sharply forced home on 19 July when Allied aircraft bombed Rome, killing more than a thousand people. This raid probably sealed Mussolini's fate. The meeting of the Fascist Grand Council was set for 24 July.

MUSSOLINI'S DEPOSITION

The meeting began at 5.15pm and lasted, with a half-hour interval, until 3.00am. But it is clear that much of the preliminary spadework had already been done, for Grandi, Ciano, Bottai and other members of the Council had already agreed that Mussolini should be replaced as head of the Armed Forces by the king. Grandi put forward a resolution at the meeting which demanded that Mussolini's one-man dictatorship should end. Mussolini himself gave a meandering, incoherent two-hour explanation of Italy's war situation. He also tried to inspire his old comrades by saying that it was time 'to tighten the reins and to assume the necessary responsibility'. The strategy failed and, after Marshal de Bono had defended the army against criticism, Grandi rose to speak on his motion. It was, according to Mussolini, a speech 'giving vent to a long-cherished rancour'.[12] Grandi called for the restoration of Victor Emmanuel as head of the Armed Forces and criticised the Fascist Party General Secretary Scorza. He was supported by Ciano, before other members of the Grand Council such as Farinacci and de Marsico (the new Minister of Justice) had their say. Scorza and Farinacci tried to introduce their own resolutions, thus dragging out the discussion until midnight, at which point Scorza wanted to adjourn matters until the next day.

Grandi violently objected to this ploy, shouting: 'We have started this business and we must finish it tonight!' In his own account, Mussolini claims that he agreed with Grandi's viewpoint, and accepted a short adjournment (this sounds odd as he must have realised that the mood of the meeting was against him). On the resumption of the discussion, Bottai and Scorza also spoke before Grandi's motion was put to the vote. Nineteen voted in favour of the motion, seven against, with two abstentions (one was Farinacci). Mussolini, according to his own account, told his colleagues that 'You have provoked a crisis of the régime'.[13] Mussolini left the Palazzo Venezia at 3.00am. He was due to have his usual fortnightly meeting with King Victor Emmanuel the next evening.

Did Mussolini foresee his end at this juncture? He must surely have done so, even if the occasion of his outright dismissal might have surprised him. For it was to be the man who Mussolini had contemptuously dismissed as 'the little sardine' who was to finally remove him from power, just as he had been instrumental in securing Mussolini's appointment as prime minister in 1922.

According to his own account, Mussolini spent the early afternoon of 25 July in the Tiburtino area of Rome which had been heavily bombed during the Allied raid on 19 July. He claims to have been cheered by the victims (this smacks of dishonesty – Mussolini was a propagandist to the last), before returning to his residence at the Via Torlonia. He then went to meet King Victor Emmanuel at the Villa Savoia.

The king was resplendent in a marshal's uniform but apparently in an agitated state. He told the Duce that 'it's no longer any good. Italy has gone to bits ... At this moment you are the most hated man in Italy.' Victor Emmanuel gave Mussolini assurances about his own personal safety, but told him that Italy's situation demanded the creation of a new government under Marshal Badoglio. Mussolini told the king (in his own version of events) that he had taken 'a grave decision' and left the royal palace.[14] As he and his Secretary, de Cesare, were about to get into their car, they were intercepted by a *carabinieri* captain called Vigneri accompanied by a group of men and ordered to get into a motor-ambulance standing nearby. Mussolini may have thought that this measure was being taken for his safety, but in reality he was under arrest. So ended the eighteen years of Mussolini's personal dictatorship in Italy.

The fallen leader was taken to a military hospital and then, on 27 July, he was escorted by Admiral Franco Mangeri to his first prison on the island of Ponza. There he was kept in a shabby, old house well away from the main settlement which had ironically been used to imprison anti-Fascists. Mussolini was now to suffer the very same *confino* that he had inflicted on others after 1922.[15]

The authorities were obviously nervous about Mussolini's security, fearing a possible rescue attempt. So they moved him first to a naval base off Sardinia on 7 August, and then to the Campo Imperatore (Imperial Camp), a ski resort on the Gran Sasso some 2,000 metres above sea level. This was on 26 August. The threat of a rescue attempt by Mussolini's German friends remained in the background. Bizarrely, while at the naval base at La Maddalena Mussolini had received a late sixtieth birthday present from the most important of those friends. Predictably perhaps, Adolf Hitler's gift was a complete, twenty-four-volume set of the works of Nietzsche.

Mussolini's period of captivity is of interest to historians because it confirms the patterns of Mussolini's earlier life, particularly during times of adversity. For a time, when he was on Ponza, Mussolini seemed almost relieved to be without responsibilities, but by the time he was transferred to La Maddalena he was starting to reassess his career. There were comparisons between himself, Napoleon, and even Jesus Christ, both of whom, the fallen Duce observed, had been the victims of betrayal. Napoleon, he noted, had then become a symbol of French greatness and this is what he expected to happen in his own case as well, once the Italians had come to their senses. There were the familiar complaints too about the Italians' lack of backbone and military virtues, mixed in with a degree of fatalism about his own fall, which he came to regard as in some way predetermined. While on La

Maddalena, Mussolini wrote in his diary: 'To redeem oneself, one must suffer. Many millions of Italians of today and tomorrow will have to experience in their own bodies and souls what defeat and dishonour means.'[16]

It would not have been immediately evident to the Italian people that their Duce was suffering, even in his hour of personal defeat (save perhaps that he continued to be racked with stomach pains). At Gran Sasso, in particular, Mussolini had a pleasant enough lifestyle and even had to reprove the staff for treating him like a guest rather than a prisoner. The entire hotel had been emptied to accommodate Mussolini, and he was allowed to go for walks (accompanied by a *carabinieri* sergeant) and listen to British, German and Italian radio broadcasts. He also spent a good deal of time playing cards with his jailers, who appear to have treated him throughout in a humane and friendly manner. Their position as the guardians of the Duce was not eased by a series of confusing orders from Badoglio about what to do in the event of an attempted rescue. First of all, Mussolini was to be shot if the Germans tried to rescue him, and then the guards were to use their own discretion. Some appear to have considered handing him over to the Germans to ingratiate themselves with Italy's frightening former ally.

While Mussolini was at Campo Imperatore, he knew exactly what the Italian people were going through. Allied air raids took an increasing toll of Italian lives, and many other Italians were turned into refugees by the Allied landing in Sicily. Mussolini showed not the remotest interest in the fate of such individuals, and neither did he admit that the German alliance was a mistake, insisting (apart from a brief period of wavering) that Italy must stay in the war on Hitler's side.

Instead, he took a childish delight in being incarcerated in 'the highest prison in the world', while also giving vent to his hypochondria. He may well have been suffering from pain associated with his ulcer but this, as the hotel manageress noted, was probably his own fault as he ate far too many grapes. Otherwise his diet was bland. Rice, eggs and milk (not easily obtained at the time) were combined with a little meat, while Mussolini bored hotel staff with endless complaints about his eighteen years of suffering as a result of his ulcer. Nevertheless, he showed his misanthropic side by insisting on eating alone in his room throughout his time on the Gran Sasso. This was the man, after all, who referred to ordinary people as 'the herd'.

THE RESCUE

The Germans had little difficulty in finding out where Mussolini was being imprisoned, not least because Italian security was so poor. Hitler appointed an SS Officer, Otto Skorzeny, to organise the rescue, and the Germans did plan to mount a naval operation to free Mussolini when he was at La Maddalena on 27 August. But this operation had to be aborted because Mussolini was moved up to the Gran Sasso the day before.

Skorzeny was then able, by using a German surgeon who was quite innocently attempting to explore the possibility of using the hotel as a malaria hospital, to find out that quite unusual precautions were being taken to guard an important prisoner in the Campo Imperatore. A frontal assault was rejected as requiring too many troops, and a parachute landing was also ruled out because of the climatic difficulties. Instead, it was decided to use gliders, even though the hotel had very limited landing space, and the operation was planned for 6 September, just three days after Mussolini learnt that Italy had agreed armistice terms with the Anglo-American forces. One of its terms was that Mussolini himself should be handed over to the Allies. Rather than submit to this humiliation, Mussolini told his captors that he would shoot himself. And he was found in possession of some razor blades which were promptly removed along with all other sharp objects. It was not, of course, the first time that Mussolini had threatened to commit suicide, and it is legitimate, therefore, to be sceptical about his intentions in this instance. As it was, events were to dramatically alter Mussolini's circumstances.

Skorzeny's rescue attempt on 6 September also had to be cancelled, however, as the required glider force had not yet arrived. But on 12 September the audacious attempt to free the Duce from his mountain fortress was launched. Mussolini was in his room that Sunday afternoon when at 2.00pm he saw a glider landing just a hundred yards away. Dismissing the idea that the khaki figures who emerged from the plane might be English, he then watched as other gliders landed nearby. The *carabinieri* sounded the alarm, but the Germans had subtly increased the confusion by including an Italian General (Soleti, at that time head of the Fascist 'Public Security Police') in their party. Mussolini seems to have increased the general chaos by shouting, 'There is an Italian general there. Don't fire! Everything is all right.'

In fact, no shots at all were fired during the entire operation. Skorzeny gave the *carabinieri* a minute to surrender and they duly did so, Mussolini reportedly telling him that he knew 'my friend Adolf Hitler would not desert me'. The Austrian SS Commander was shocked by Mussolini's shabby appearance and unhealthy pallor, having seen him years before in all his pomp on the balcony of the Palazzo Venetia.[17]

The sequel to these events was bizarre as the entire staff of the Campo Imperatore was solemnly paraded in front of Mussolini so that he could thank them personally. Mussolini was then put in a German Storch light plane for a perilous flight to the airfield at Practica di Mare. It was made even more dangerous by the insistence of Skorzeny in coming on board an aircraft which was only designed for two persons. As it was, the aircraft hit a rock before getting clear of the heights of the Gran Sasso and flying out.

Mussolini was flown from Practica di Mare to Vienna, where he was lodged in comfortable style in the Hotel Continental. Hitler called him on the telephone and Mussolini was gratified by his old friend's concern for his welfare. In his new affluent surroundings, Mussolini seemed to regain his confidence. From Vienna, he went on to Munich on 13 September where he met his wife and younger children (Vittorio was already in Germany and was helping to draft a Fascist appeal to the Italian people at Hitler's headquarters). Rachele was alarmed by her husband's state of health, but in her usual practical way she also noted that he badly needed a bath.

The next day, Mussolini had a meeting with his daughter Edda. This was difficult because the Duce naturally regarded his son-in-law Ciano as a traitor, and Edda pleaded for him. Ciano had fallen into German hands but wanted to go to South America which they would only allow if he travelled via Munich (he had been removed from Rome on Himmler's orders on 27 August, well before the declaration of the Armistice). There is some confusion about whether Mussolini actually agreed to see Ciano.[18] Rachele's attitude towards Ciano was unforgiving – she is reported as saying that she would have liked to have killed Ciano. Mussolini's main animosity was reserved for King Victor Emmanuel – he was heard to remark that his greatest enemy was the House of Savoy and that he should have made Italy a republic (this would never have been practical in Italy). It may be, however, that Mussolini allowed Rachele's hatred of Ciano to sway him into refusing an interview.

The family obviously played second fiddle to what was now the crucial relationship of Mussolini's life, that with Adolf Hitler. Mussolini was flown to meet Hitler at his wartime headquarters in East Prussia. Hitler seemed to be glad to see his fellow dictator, but this changed when the two men had a formal meeting on 15 September where the atmosphere was frosty. Hitler appeared disillusioned with Mussolini, and he was implacable on the subject of how Ciano should be treated. His betrayal of Mussolini, according to the Führer, was made even more perverse by the blood tie between the two men. According to Goebbels, who had spoken to Hitler a few days before on the subject, Ciano was 'a poisonous mushroom'[19] who might pour odium on the Axis cause in the memoirs he was planning to write. Goebbels had little time for Mussolini either, and in speaking in such terms on 15 September, Hitler may well have been influenced by his Propaganda Minister's hostility.

The interview was one between a master and a servant. When Mussolini suggested that he should retire from public life to avoid a bloody civil war in Italy, Hitler flatly rejected such a suggestion as nonsense. He also told Mussolini that a new Fascist régime in Northern Italy could not contain men such as Farinacci and Pavolini (or even his own son, Vittorio) because they were unacceptable to the Germans. Nevertheless, it was Mussolini's task to go back to Italy and deal with the traitors of 25 July.

The diatribe went on for an hour, with Mussolini hardly able to interject. The weakness of his position was underlined by the fact that he was forced to agree to the German annexation of the South Tyrol, Trieste and the Trentino. The loss of Trieste, with all its associations with Mussolini's successful struggle against the Yugoslavs, was especially painful, but Mussolini later claimed that he made these concessions to prevent greater punishment at German hands, much as the collaborationist Vichy régime had claimed in France.

In fact, the Germans had already turned on their former ally before the Hitler–Mussolini interview. All of Italy behind the German lines (their forces having rushed southwards well before the Italian surrender to the Allies was announced) had already been declared a war zone. Worse still was the German insistence that more Italian workers be sent to Germany to work in war industries, where they frequently endured worse treatment than Allied prisoners of war.

When Mussolini was finally allowed to speak by his new master, his rather strange suggestion that the Germans should seek a separate peace with Stalin in order to break up the Allied bloc was impatiently dismissed. It did, of course, ignore the fact that Nazi behaviour on the Eastern Front made a positive response unlikely in Moscow. Insult was added to injury when Hitler, noting Mussolini's pallor and unhealthy appearance, suggested that he be examined by his own doctor, Professor Morrell, a notorious quack who took advantage of the Führer's credulity on health matters to prescribe useless potions and injections for his patient. Morrell found nothing seriously wrong, other than the underlying ulcer condition. Mussolini got off lightly, with just one session with this medical charlatan, but the episode demonstrated how pathetic a figure he had now become in the eyes of the Germans. Hitler complained that, though no traitor, Mussolini lacked his own superhuman qualities.

The Duce was instructed to speak to his people via the radio, and this he duly did, from Munich on 17 September. Rachele went with him to the broadcasting studio and noted that his performance was shaky (apart from anything else, Mussolini rarely broadcast live, previously his public speeches had merely been relayed via radio). He appealed to the Italians to support him against the traitors in the Badoglio government, but his words carried little conviction. Neither he, still less Hitler or Goebbels, expected the Italian people to rally around a lost cause. When he did return to Italy, any power that Mussolini retained would rely on German bayonets.

9

THE LAST PHASE, 1943–45

The last two years of Mussolini's life were a humiliating sequel to the events that brought about his downfall in July 1943. The so-called Republic of Salò over which Mussolini presided until his death in April 1945 had an illusory independence because it depended entirely on German goodwill and on German military support. All the decisions taken by Mussolini during this period had to be filtered through the representatives of the German Reich at Salò. In this sense, the Duce was recognising his real position when he told Hitler, before returning to Northern Italy, 'I have come to receive my orders'.[1] His role as a German puppet strengthened the hatred of the Italian people for him, a fact which was vividly demonstrated when the executed dictator's corpse was suspended upside down in Milan to be abused by the population.

The chief interest, therefore, in this last phase of Mussolini's life, is not in the endless self-justification in which he indulged, but in the apparent lurch towards radicalism in the Verona Manifesto of February 1944, and the degree to which the measures advocated in it represented a real change in the economic and social policies propounded by Mussolini since the mid-1920s. Was the Republic of Salò a real rejection of the compromises Mussolini had had to make with the monarchy, the Church and the capitalists after 1922, or merely a cynical attempt on his part to obtain (belatedly) genuine popular support by widening the base of his régime? As always with Mussolini, the evidence can often seem contradictory, but the issue remains important in the attempt to resolve the question of the degree to which Mussolini had genuine political beliefs or was driven by naked ambition.

THE FOUNDATION OF THE ITALIAN SOCIAL REPUBLIC

After his rescue by Skorzeny, and the meetings with Hitler in September 1943, Mussolini wanted to return to Rome but the Germans would not allow this, probably fearing that his nearness to the front line might provoke an Allied version of the Skorzeny rescue. Instead, Mussolini was sent to the town of Gargnano on Lake Garda, which had the advantage of being much nearer to Germany. There, he was surrounded by German guards and, more pertinently, cut adrift from the government departments of the new rump Italian Social Republic (*Repubblica Sociale Italiano*) which had been established at Salò, hence the common title given to the régime of the Republic of Salò.

Two themes can be identified during the short life of the Social Republic. One was its desire for vengeance on the traitors of 25 July, and the other was the attempt to transform or reform the Fascist movement. Now, after all, Mussolini was freed from the constitutional constraint represented by King Victor Emmanuel, and the physical closeness of the Vatican.

Mussolini was less vengeful than the hard-line Fascists who surrounded him in the new régime (and within the family, Rachele was much more unforgiving about Ciano's treachery than was her husband). Nevertheless, and in the absence of the king whom he regarded as his greatest enemy, Mussolini came to see the punishment of the traitors as essential. The problem was that amongst all those who had participated in Mussolini's deposition in July 1943, only two were in the hands of the reconstituted Fascist régime. One was Ciano, who had carelessly allowed himself to fall into German hands, as has been seen, the other, the octogenarian veteran of the Ethiopian war, Marshal de Bono.

As far as Mussolini was concerned, the die was cast for his son-in-law, and he ignored pleas for mercy both from Ciano and his daughter Edda. A show trial was held in Verona in January 1944 and Ciano and de Bono were condemned to death alongside three lesser Fascist figures (Gottardi, Marinelli and Pareschi) who had deserted Mussolini after the meeting of the Grand Council. Ciano accepted his fate calmly, writing from his prison cell that his sentence had already been decided beforehand by 'a sham tribunal' influenced by 'that circle of whores and pimps which for some years has plagued Italian political life'.[2] Ciano and the other four condemned were shot outside the gates of Verona early in the morning of 11 January 1944. Even if Mussolini's resolve had weakened over the execution of Ciano, the Germans, who were well aware of Ciano's opposition to the Italo-German alliance after 1939, would undoubtedly have forced his hand. As it was, Mussolini declined even to reprieve the aged de Bono, one of his oldest Fascist comrades. His satisfaction at the blood purge was muted only by the knowledge that Grandi, the inspiration behind the coup d'état of 25 July 1943, had escaped.

According to some accounts Mussolini had seen Ciano in Munich after he returned from his visit to see Hitler, much to Rachele's annoyance. But he had put on the façade of the implacable dictator, barely speaking to his son-in-law and refusing to say goodbye to him at this, their last meeting. Desperate pleas by Edda had been equally unsuccessful. Mussolini was upset by a letter she wrote to him and by her threats to make embarrassing revelations (as late as 1980 she was providing an editorial note to a new edition of her husband's *Diary*), but at their last meeting before Ciano's execution, he was implacable. Edda left the room in tears after her father had told her that, like a Roman father, he would stand by his decision.[3] She never forgave Mussolini for his refusal to reprieve her husband who had, in fact, committed no real offence other than to support the constitutional mechanisms of the Fascist Grand Council and the monarchy. Edda was Mussolini's favourite child, but their relationship was sundered forever. Ciano had gone to his death crying 'Long Live Italy'. The firing squad initially had bungled the execution, forcing the commanding officer to put a bullet through his head. As a final humiliation, Ciano and his fellow victims had been tied up to chairs with their backs to the squad, but the former Foreign Minister had managed to break his bonds to face his executioners. For a man frequently described as frivolous, Ciano showed considerable courage at the end.

A DICTATOR'S TWILIGHT

Mussolini frittered away the hours in this last phase of his life. On the surface, he seemed to be the hard-working dictator of the past, who sometimes left for the office before 8.00am, and did not return until 8.00

or 9.00pm. But much of the fallen dictator's time was spent reading newspapers and cutting out personal references to himself. And the reason that Mussolini left for work so early was that he could not endure the domestic atmosphere in the Villa Feltrinelli where the Germans had installed him at Gargnano. His son Vittorio and his wife, the widow of his son Bruno, his teenage son Romano and his youngest daughter Anna Maria all lived in the Villa together with Rachele and some of the grandchildren. There were the inevitable domestic rows and noise, but most serious was Rachele's hostility about Mussolini's affair with Claretta Petacci (amazingly she had only found out about it during the night of 25 July 1943 when a servant had told her). Petacci had in fact been imprisoned in Novara in the wake of her lover's overthrow, but the Germans had located her and put her (ironically) in a house inside the grounds of D'Annunzio's villa near the Mussolinis. The evidence suggests that Claretta was expected to show due gratitude for her release by supplying the Gestapo with information about the Duce. She may even have been supplying them with copies of his letters.[4]

As it was, Mussolini saw little of his mistress as Rachele's jealousy had become so intense that 'Ben', as Petacci had nicknamed him, dared see her only on rare nightly visits. On one occasion Rachele stormed around to the house to see Petacci, roundly abused her in front of the resident German SS officer, and then burst into tears. Mussolini tried to break off the relationship on a couple of occasions, but lacked the will to do so. During the last months of his life, therefore, he was in the middle of a noisy dispute between these two strong-willed women.

As with everything else at this time, the hand of the Germans could be seen everywhere in Mussolini's life. Everywhere he went, Mussolini was followed by a lorry full of German soldiers, German officers were installed in his house and Himmler had provided him with a German doctor, Professor Zachariae. Unlike the quack Morell, Zachariae, who became a great admirer of the Duce, was a genuine physician who brought about a transformation in Mussolini's health. He succeeded in getting Mussolini away from his fixation with milk-based diets, and his entourage thought the Duce looked younger than he had done for years. He played some tennis (although his opponents still let him win – old habits died hard!), rode a bicycle around the shores of Lake Garda and walked in the woods. He also began to read from a wide selection of literature and history. Books on Frederick the Great (his critic Goebbels was also an admirer) and Christ were mixed with works by Sorel, Plato, Tolstoy and Ernest Hemingway.

An interesting feature of the Salò period was the way in which Mussolini avoided personal relations with the ministers of the Social Republic. These men, notably Pavolini, the fanatical Party Secretary, Buffarini-Guidi, the intriguing Minister of the Interior, and the youthful but more able Mezzosomma as Minister of Popular Culture, were selected because they had stood by Mussolini after 25 July. But Mussolini preferred to spend his time with the journalists Carlo Silvestri and Nicola Bombacci. Bombacci, in particular, was an interesting confidant. He had been a member of the Italian Communist Party since it was founded in 1921, but had also been a long-standing acquaintance of Mussolini's who had been a schoolmaster with him at Gualtieri. It was to Mussolini's credit, and highlights his inconsistency, that when Bombacci was out of work because of his political attitudes in the 1930s, Mussolini went out of his way to help him and his family. The journalist was so grateful that he chose, rather perilously, to attach himself to Mussolini in this last phase of his political life. Mussolini's motives, as was so often the case, remain a mystery, and while he befriended Bombacci, he also tried to deny his involvement in the murder of Matteotti.

Mussolini went to visit his protector, Adolf Hitler, in Germany in April 1944. He was warmly greeted by the Führer, and even summoned up the courage to protest about the annexation of Trieste and the South Tyrol by the Germans. Encouraged, perhaps, by the presence of Marshal Graziani and the Italian Ambassador to Berlin, Anfuso, he went on to complain about the deplorable treatment of Italian workers in Germany. Hitler promised to look into these matters, but months passed and nothing further was heard from the German side.

Mussolini's next visit was on 20 July 1944, a momentous day in the history of the Third Reich. Hours before his arrival in Rastenburg, an attempt was made on Hitler's life by a group of dissident generals and army officers (with a degree of support from politicians of the German Left and Right). The actual assassin, Klaus von Stauffenberg, was selected not just because of his realisation that decisive action was needed, but also because as a one-eyed, one-armed veteran of the Eastern

Front, he was less likely to attract suspicion in the hyper-secure environment of the Führer's headquarters.

Mussolini arrived in the chaotic aftermath of the assassination attempt to find Hitler convinced that Providence had spared him to continue his mission. Wisely, in the circumstances, Mussolini agreed (although subsequently he could not fight off a degree of pleasure about what had happened – it showed that Germans too could be disloyal). But he was amazed and shocked by what followed. First of all, he was treated to a wholesale row involving Göring, von Ribbentrop and Keitel which culminated in Göring calling von Ribbentrop 'a dirty little champagne salesman' (the unpopular Foreign Minister had started his career selling wines). Then Hitler, who had been unusually quiet, not surprisingly under the circumstances, launched into a half-hour diatribe against the traitors behind the Bomb Plot and those who were not worthy of his leadership. Mussolini sat through all this, barely uttering a word. He dared not raise any of the issues from his April visit which had not yet been resolved.

The day, which was unusual even by the standards of National Socialist Germany, ended with Hitler gazing fervently into his old comrade's eyes at the railway station, saying that he depended on Mussolini's loyalty. But Mussolini returned to Italy empty-handed, his assurances in April that he fully believed in Germany's ultimate victory having secured nothing. Hitler only seemed interested in taking bloody revenge on the 20 July conspirators, their relatives and friends. This he duly did in a manner which made Mussolini's purge of the Italian plotters seem mild by comparison. Privately, Mussolini was scathing about the Germans, calling them brutal, uncouth barbarians, but his dependence on them was absolute. The decisions he had so recklessly made in 1936–37 had come back to haunt him.

Mussolini's dependence on the Germans was further underlined by the appointments he made to the Social Republic's government. Radicals like Farinacci and Preziosi, whom the Germans would have found unpalatable, were excluded from the administration. Instead, men like Buffarini-Guidi (Minister of the Interior) Mezzosomma (Minister of Popular Culture), alongside the fanatical Pavolini, another lamentable appointment as General Secretary of the reconstituted Republican Fascist Party, were included precisely because they were known to support the German alliance.

THE CONGRESS OF VERONA

Nevertheless, the new Republican Fascist Party did attempt to give Fascism a new direction in its one and only congress at Verona in November 1943. The programme which emerged from it swept away the monarchy, demanded a republican government elected on the basis of popular sovereignty, the categorisation of Jews as aliens and the continued status of Catholicism as Italy's official religion. Mussolini had his revenge on the monarchy, but he also seemed to be turning the clock back to 1919 in the call for the socialisation of industrial production, and the demand that uncultivated land should be handed over to agricultural labourers or farmers' co-operatives. State ownership of key industries was promised together with the establishment of management councils and the introduction of profit sharing in private industries. All these plans were encapsulated in the Social Republic decree of 12 February 1944.

The question at issue with the so-called Verona 'Manifesto' is the extent to which it represented a radical shift away from the state capitalism of Mussolini's heyday, to a genuinely progressive social and economic policy. Obviously Verona also showed that Mussolini's racism remained a crucial feature of his policies, albeit policies that existed under the watchful eye of the Germans. Nevertheless, there was also a nod towards elective democracy with a plan for a Constituent Assembly, a greater role for trade unions and an independent judiciary. There was even supposed to be a free press and a promise to investigate the notorious corruption which was such a feature of the Fascist hierarchy after 1922 (illicit fortunes were to be investigated). In many respects, the Verona Manifesto seemed to represent a repudiation of Fascist history since the acquisition of power.

Closer examination of the historical context, however, undermines the claim of the Congress that it had freed Fascism from the 'pluto-monarchical' compromises of 1922. The Constituent Assembly never met, the head of State was still unelected and, despite the promise of an independent judiciary, a Special Tribunal was set up with the specific task of taking revenge on Grandi, Ciano, de Bono and those other Fascists who had taken part in Mussolini's removal from power on 25 July. Neither did the promise to allow a free press ever see the light of day.

Crucially also, the Manifesto did not result in the adoption of a Fascist 'Third Way' between capitalism and communism which syndicalists and populists dreamed of. In key industries shareholders still played a central role, trade unions had no real power over management and neither were they to be involved in the degree of state planning which was possible in the shambolic rump state of Salò. Looming over all these aspirations in any case was the spectre of German military power. Mussolini's masters would not allow industrial reforms to interfere with their plans to exploit Italian industries. Mussolini must have known this only too well, which must create the suspicion that the Verona Manifesto was 'myth-making in the grand style'.[5] In retrospect, Mussolini's absence from the Verona Congress (a letter from him was merely read out when it met) was symbolic. The apparent concessions to a Third Way were mere window dressing, and only in its rejection of the House of Savoy could the Fascist movement be said to have really moved on. Mussolini's followers may have aspired to return to the heady days of 1919, but their aspirations were never to be implemented. Neither did Mussolini ever break away from the non-Fascist Old Guard which had sustained him in power for so many years. Marshal Graziani, for example, who remained as Army Chief of Staff, claimed to be merely a soldier obeying orders who had never been a member of the Fascist Party. Even in its own terms, the Verona Manifesto lacked coherence, as the creation of the Special Tribunal made nonsense of the claim that the State would not interfere with the judicial process. As Ciano fully recognised before his execution, the verdicts against himself, de Bono and the others had been pre-ordained.

Students of Mussolini's career are left, therefore, with one intriguing explanation for all the rhetoric in the Verona Manifesto. It is that Mussolini was seeking, quite deliberately, to sow the seeds of political mischief in a post-Mussolini Italy, that he was, in Professor Bosworth's words, 'leaving *mine sociali* (social mines)'[6] for his successors which would make the task of national recovery harder. Mussolini did not collapse into the desperate, anarchic desire of Adolf Hitler to pull Germany down about his ears in the last days of the Third Reich, but there was in him, nonetheless, a cynical misanthropy which would have rejoiced at the prospect that middle-class Catholics and Conservatives, or their Socialist counterparts, would be afflicted by the sins of Fascism in the post-war world. The debate about the future of the monarchy, for example, was bound to be divisive, and the forces of the Centre-Right might be expected to remain loyal to Victor Emmanuel III, just as the Left would demand his head. As it was, Mussolini's old enemies in the industrial proletariat were not deceived by the decree of 12 February 1944. The reaction of the workers in Northern Italy to Fascist promises was to take part in a massive wave of strikes on 1 March. Fascism's failure to win over Communist and Socialist supporters in the northern industrial cities was one of its greatest historic failures.

In one sense at least, the Social Republic was strongly reminiscent of the period between 1919 and 1922. For just as the PNF had relied on extra-parliamentary violence to intimidate its opponents before Mussolini came to power, the Social Republic was characterised by the existence of gangs of paramilitary thugs who were, if anything, even more out of control than the *squadristi* had been in the early 1920s. At the same time, familiar tensions existed between Ricci's party militia (*Guardia Nazionale Repubblicana*; GNR) and the Republic of Salò's regular army under Graziani who wanted a single national army. Eventually, in August 1944, the GNR was amalgamated with the army proper. But this amalgamation meant little while Party Secretary Pavolini had licence to encourage the so-called Black Brigades (*Brigate Nere*) to create even worse mayhem than the *squadristi*. The context, of course, was different as a bitter civil war raged in Italy in 1944–45 between these Fascist gangsters and Communist and other Leftist partisans. Atrocities were committed by both sides, none worse than those perpetrated by the *Decima Mas* of Prince Valerio Borghese, whose exploits tarnished a distinguished Italian name. Borghese, like the radical *squadristi* leaders twenty years before, even dared to question the Duce's authority and suggest that he had gone soft in his old age. So concerned indeed was Mussolini about Borghese's activities, and the danger of a coup d'état, that he tried to neutralise him early in 1945 by offering him the sinecure of Chief of Staff of the Salò Navy (it had no navy).[7] Other brutish groups included the so-called 'Italian SS'.

Mussolini's role in all this did him little credit. He was concerned about threats to his personal power base, as has been seen, but he also condoned the atrocities committed by the Black Brigades. These were committed under government auspices when villages were destroyed because their men evaded the draft, or simply because inhabitants were suspected of sympathising with the Partisans. In parallel with Fascist atrocities went German ones, one example being the killing of over 300 men in the Ardeantine Caves (including dozens of Jews) in response to a Partisan bombing in Rome in March 1944. Mussolini did remonstrate about some German excesses (such as the displaying of bodies in public in northern cities) but to no effect. The excesses of his own supporters weakened the impact of such protests, even supposing that the German commanders in Italy were disposed to listen to their enfeebled ally.

THE LAST DAYS

In April 1944 Mussolini paid his last visit to Milan, the city which had been so important at the start of his political career. He gave a characteristic apologia for his career to a Milanese audience, and even managed to arouse comparisons with the old days amongst the onlookers. But Mussolini was now a man who was increasingly going through the motions of leadership and finding it difficult to reach decisions on anything. This was no longer a health-related matter (Professor Zachariae believed that Mussolini's stomach trouble must have had a serious effect on his leadership between 1940 and 1944), but one of lassitude and inertia. It showed in small but significant ways, such as Mussolini's willingness to allow those who came to see him to sit rather than stand as before. Excessive deference before a man with such little power now seemed absurd, and perhaps the Duce recognised this.

Increasingly, he lived in a world which had less and less to do with reality, punctuated by delusional phases during which he convinced himself that Hitler still had secret weapons that could win the war. But then, in obvious contradiction, he sought out contacts with the Anti-Fascist opposition in Italy, in the deluded hope that he could come to some agreement with them. He chose as an intermediary, Schuster, the Cardinal Archbishop of Milan, and the two men met in Milan on 25 April 1945. Mussolini wanted Cardinal Schuster to arrange a meeting between himself and Cadorna, the Commander in Chief of all Partisan forces in Northern Italy. Marazzo, the Secretary of the new Christian Democratic Party, was also expected to attend.

Mussolini arrived first and the lengthy conversation that he then had with Schuster provides us with the last major account of Mussolini's attitude and thoughts in what was to be the last week of his life. Schuster warned him to prepare for the end and reminded him of

Napoleon's fall (doubtless Mussolini would have little appreciated the comparison), but also told him that the Church had not forgotten his work for the Lateran Pacts. For his part, Mussolini denied that he had ever encouraged anti-clericalism and claimed that he had 'always resisted when others tried to induce me to take measures against the Church'.[8]

Schuster let this inaccuracy pass as he saw that Mussolini seemed very depressed, then asked him (oddly) whether he had read a book about Saint Benedict which he, Schuster, had just written. The Duce had to confess that he had not but told Schuster that, when he had been a prisoner on the island of La Maddalena in 1943, he had considered renewing his life as a Catholic (this seems to have been part of Mussolini's desire at the time to be all things to all men). Schuster told him that he should appeal to the Vatican for help, and that Pope Pius XII would try to help him. It is unlikely that any such intervention would have saved Mussolini.

As the representatives of the anti-Fascist opposition had still not arrived at this point, the conversation dragged on with Mussolini strangely praising the English genius for avoiding heavy casualties in wartime, whereas Germany, he believed, would be in no position to wage a war for many years to come.

At this point, Cadorna and Marazzo arrived and the talk ended with Cardinal Schuster advising Mussolini to put his trust in God. The opposition leaders then demanded that the Fascist forces should surrender, promising that they would be protected as prisoners of war by the Hague Convention. The same protection would be given to the families of Fascists, and these reassurances, according to Schuster, seemed to satisfy Mussolini. He had to be reminded by Marshal Graziani, who was also present at the meeting, that the Italians could not negotiate a separate peace from the Germans without repeating the treachery of 8 September 1943 which had so infuriated Mussolini.

At this point, Schuster interjected to tell Mussolini that the German army in Italy was already using him as an intermediary for a cease-fire. Mussolini angrily retorted that the Germans were acting behind his back, a theme which was as old as the Duce's ill-fated alliance with the Nazis. He insisted on his own freedom of action regardless of what the Germans did, and demanded time to consider the terms offered to him by Cadorna, Marazzo and the so-called Liberation Committee. He then decided to leave Milan without first informing Cardinal Schuster. The Cardinal remained convinced that had Mussolini remained in Milan and allowed himself to be taken prisoner, he too would have been protected by the Hague Convention.[9]

This last portrait of Benito Mussolini is revealing. His capacity for self-delusion clearly remained (did he really believe that anyone would take his comments about Catholicism seriously?) as he had long lost the freedom of action to which he referred at the meeting. Mussolini swings from depression to open anger as he is confronted with the reality of his situation. He must, at the same time, have been a very frightened man, as the news that his German allies were seeking a cease-fire made it clear that his life was now in danger.

One option which Mussolini clearly considered was to immediately head for the Swiss frontier in the hope that he would be granted sanctuary (his arrival would hardly have been entirely welcome to the wary, traditionally neutral Swiss government). But he seems to have fatally hesitated and considered some sort of final heroic stand. The location chosen for this last ditch defiance was Valtellina near the Swiss frontier, but the military thought the proposal absurd and no preparations had been put in train for such a stand. Other options which Mussolini was supposed to have considered included flight to Spain, where presumably he could have expected the protection of his old ally Franco, or to Argentina, where the 'crypto-Fascist' Juan Peron was now in power (he was a long-time admirer of the Duce and a one-time Argentine military attaché in Rome).

In the event, Mussolini decided against all these options, although he had at times also fantasised about creating an Italian Stalingrad in Milan. He was now an ageing man of 61, racked by fear, unable to sleep and fast losing his appetite. But these were merely physical symptoms of the political and psychological vacuum in which he had been living since July 1943. He could not make up his mind about what were the best steps to take to save his life, but what became brutally clear in those last days was the unwillingness of his fellow Fascists to fight for him any more. Once he realised this on arriving at Lake Como, Mussolini, accompanied by the ever-present Bombacci, decided to make a dash for the Swiss frontier by driving up the west side of the lake. But by now it was too late, as the border guards had gone over to the Partisans and blocked the exit route. The other alternative on that day,

25 April 1945, was to await the arrival of US forces which were driving up from Bologna, but the Duce had vowed never to fall into the hands of the Allies. It is also likely that, contrary to the assurances given by the members of the Liberation Committee on 25 April, an order had been given that Mussolini was to be executed on capture and that he had become aware of this.[10]

A last possibility remained. Mussolini, along with Claretta Petacci and leading Fascists like Pavolini, could join a convoy of German trucks which was attempting to go through Partisan lines on its way to Austria. To create the illusion that he was in fact a German, Mussolini put on a Luftwaffe greatcoat and a German helmet. He was also given a machine gun and a pistol for his protection.

It was a desperate expedient because the countryside north of Milan was full of Partisans, but Mussolini had by now exhausted all other avenues. His hopes were soon to be dashed. At 6.30 on the morning of 27 April, the convoy was stopped by obstructions on the road at Dongo, and ragged firing burst out during which one innocent civilian was killed. The German lieutenant in charge of the convoy then opened talks with the leaders of the 52nd Garibaldi Brigade of Communist Partisans. The Partisans agreed to let the German convoy go on its way to Austria, providing that all Italians were handed over (they already had suspicions that Fascist Party members were hiding in the German trucks). Once this agreement had been made, Mussolini's fate had effectively been sealed, although the Germans tried to protect him by pretending that he was indeed a Luftwaffe member. Mussolini was forced out of his truck, disarmed and deprived of his greatcoat and helmet. He was immediately recognised by one of the Partisan leaders who shouted 'We've got Big-Head'.[11] Mussolini was then arrested and taken to the Town Hall in Dongo. He spent part of the last night of his life in a nearby military barracks. Pavolini was also brought in after a desperate, but fruitless, attempt at escape.

At 2.30 in the morning of 28 April, Claretta Petacci was also brought to Dongo by car. Mussolini greeted the 'Signora' formally and asked why she was there. It was a fair question, but Petacci had decided that if her beloved 'Ben' was to die, she would die with him. The two lovers were then put in two separate cars and driven through the night to a peasant farm near Bonzanigo which was thought to be safe. It was a perilous journey as fighting continued in the nearby hills. On arrival,

Mussolini and Petacci were placed under guard in a bedroom. The two guards could hear Mussolini's heavy breathing as he slept through what was left of the night.

Mussolini and Petacci remained in the house of the peasant family, named de Maria, until the late afternoon of 28 April. They were then taken to the nearby Villa Belmonte for summary execution, there having been no trial. The whole operation smacked of undue haste as, first of all, the executioner Audisio could not fire his machine gun and then found that his pistol would not fire either. In the end, Audisio had to borrow a French-made machine gun from a colleague. According to one version of events, Claretta Petacci had seized the barrel of the machine gun in a desperate attempt to stop the execution. According to another eyewitness, Mussolini's last words were 'Shoot me in the chest'. But it took two bullets to despatch him whereas one sufficed to kill Petacci. The bodies were left lying outside the Villa Belmonte before being collected later and transferred to a removal van which took them to Milan.[12]

Mussolini's public life ended, therefore, as it had begun, in Milan amidst tawdry scenes. His body was strung upside down alongside Petacci's in the Piazzale Loreto. The choice was symbolic, as in August 1944 the Germans had executed fifteen Partisans there as a reprisal. There are varying accounts of what followed. One version has it that the locals were shocked by the desecration of the bodies and strewed flowers over the corpses. Another has it that the bodies were beaten with sticks and that women urinated on Mussolini's corpse.[13] It may be that both versions of events have an element of truth. The Milanese had, after all, plenty of reason to be angry with Mussolini even if some may have been disturbed by the barbaric treatment of the corpses.

After a day on public display, Mussolini's body was taken down and removed to the hospital at the University of Milan for an autopsy. It was then taken to a cemetery outside the city and buried in an anonymous, unmarked plot bearing the number 384. A man who had set such store by recognition and importance was now seemingly to be consigned to oblivion. But he was not, in fact, to be forgotten in the way in which his enemies would have hoped. Just a year later in April 1946, Fascist sympathisers dug up the Duce's corpse and fled with it. It took three months before the remains were located by the police.

There was a certain symmetry about the ends of Benito Mussolini and his long-time ally, Adolf Hitler. Mussolini had been executed at about 4.10pm on the afternoon of 28 April, and Hitler seems to have learnt of his fellow dictator's fate the next day. Unlike Mussolini, Hitler had spent his last weeks in the claustrophobic atmosphere of the Führer bunker beneath the Reich Chancellery in Berlin, as the units of the Red Army drew nearer and nearer. Hitler, like Mussolini, had no desire to fall into the hands of the Allied powers and he determined to take his life rather than allow this to happen. Before this, Hitler wrote out a ranting, vindictive, last political testament (Mussolini had at least avoided this final indignity) and then shot himself just after 3.30pm on 30 April.[14] His long-standing mistress, Eva Braun, whom he married belatedly the day before, stayed with Hitler just as Claretta Petacci had remained faithful to Mussolini. But whereas Mussolini had a family (Edda apart) to mourn him, the misanthropic German dictator left no human legacy.

None of Mussolini's major biographers, with the exception of de Felice, have found much to sympathise with in the manner of his death. Mussolini had lived by the sword and he died by the sword, but in its last phase his life had largely become an irrelevance. In one sense, there-fore, it would have been better for Mussolini had he died in July 1943 at the point where real power was lost. It would certainly have been bet-ter for the Italian people, for many more lives were lost in the bitter civil war which followed the Duce's reincarnation under the Germans. As it was, Mussolini spent almost two years in a twilight world specu-lating about his place in world history and complaining about the unre-liability of his German allies.

With time on his hands in those last days, Mussolini talked endlessly of his admiration for Stalin, who had headed a coherent, disciplined movement where he had failed (he was impressed by the way in which the Communists had recovered their position in Italy via the Partisan movement). Churchill too elicited Mussolini's admiration, but he had little positive to say about Roosevelt, and speculated about whether the Anglo-American alliance might break up. Interspersed with meander-ings about how he would fight to the last Italian, these final days demonstrated the bankruptcy of Mussolini and the Republic of Salò. The apparent ideological volte face at Verona was an illusion because Mussolini's desire for personal power, however much it was constrained by his dependence on the Germans, remained paramount, even though his indecisiveness made it a pale shadow of earlier days. Only in his final rejection of King Victor Emmanuel and the House of Savoy, and the brutal revenge which he took on Ciano and de Bono, could Mussolini achieve much satisfaction, but even in the case of Ciano he wavered until an unrelenting Rachele strengthened his resolve. And the workers' strikes of 1 March 1944 demonstrated yet again Fascism's failure to create a consensus with the industrial proletariat of the northern cities.

Worst of all was Mussolini's obvious humiliation at the hands of Hitler when he had to agree to the loss of hard-won Italian territories and the virtual enslavement of a million Italian workers in Germany. The Duce was, therefore, absolutely right when he had ruefully told Hitler in 1943 that he had come to receive his orders, because the substance of power had finally disappeared and left him as little more than a German puppet. Even then, despite all evidence to the contrary, and in the teeth of the damage that the German alliance had done to his country, Mussolini continued to whistle in the dark, hoping for a German victory.

All the gloss that had surrounded Mussolini when he seemed to have created an East African empire and won the admiration of many Italians had long disappeared. His squalid end in the Piazzale Loreto represented an absolute failure which no past success could redeem, and who can argue that it was not well deserved? Mussolini's régime had survived on the threat of force and intimidation both at home and abroad, and if this terror could appear amateurish when contrasted with its Nazi and Stalinist cousins, the reality was bad enough. Fascism reflected Mussolini's personality, for it was boastful, intellectually trivial, brutal and hollow. The eccentric young tearaway who had grown up in the Romagna became a dictator who supped with the devil, and it was the Italian people who paid the price.

CONCLUSION

Mussolini's life span was some sixty years and embraced two World Wars, the defeat and devastation of his own country and the founding (according to his admirers) of the most influential of the twentieth century's political movements. Yet Mussolini was also a human being whose inglorious death in 1945 had profound consequences for his own large family.

The authorities allowed him to be reburied in Predappio in 1957 alongside his parents, his brother Arnaldo and his son Bruno in a family vault. Subsequently, the tomb became an object of veneration for those extreme Rightists who continued to haunt Italian politics after the war. But life for his surviving relatives did not prove easy. Donna Rachele returned to live in the Romagna and remained a figure who attracted respect until she died in 1979. The fates of her children varied. Edda reverted to the wild lifestyle which had infuriated her father during his lifetime, while the unfortunate Anna Maria, who had contracted polio, never married. To the day of her death in 1995, Edda never forgave Mussolini for his desertion of Ciano in 1943.

Mussolini had been disappointed by his sons, and none of them achieved much after the Duce's death. Bruno had died in an air accident in 1941, but the eldest son, Vittorio, flitted between Italy and South America before permanently returning to Italy in 1968. He first went to Argentina in 1946, where he received a warm welcome from Mussolini's admirer, Juan Peron, having used one of the notorious Vatican networks for smuggling Fascists and Nazis out of Europe. Visits to Italy before 1968 were spasmodic and coincided with attempts by Vittorio to defend the family name in a frequently hostile post-war climate.[1]

Romano had a career as a jazz pianist (his father would not have approved) and published a memoir of Mussolini, but his greatest claim to fame was that he married the sister of Italy's best-known post-war film star, Sophia Loren. His daughter Alessandra, after a somewhat sleazy youth, managed to get herself elected as a parliamentary deputy for the neo-Fascist *Alleanza Nazionale* (National Alliance) in 1992. She too was a tenacious defender of her grandfather's reputation but was unable to find a place in the party's leadership.

Edda Ciano had two sons, one of whom ran unsuccessfully as an MSI (Italian Social Movement) candidate for the Constituent Assembly. He then emigrated to South America, like his uncle Vittorio. Her other son, Marzio, died of alcoholism in the 1970s, destroyed perhaps by the ghosts of the past. That memories could still be long in Italy was vividly demonstrated in 1971 when an extremist bomb blew out the door of the family tomb in Predappio.

The sufferings of the Mussolini family were trivial in comparison with those of the Italian people however. Some 400,000 Italians died in Mussolini's various wars and as many as a million of other nationalities may have died in Ethiopia, Spain, Greece and Yugoslavia at Italian hands. The impact on Italy's infrastructure was just as devastating. Three million houses were destroyed in the war or badly damaged, and along with them thousands of bridges and roads. Industrial output was down catastrophically to only a quarter of the 1941 figure and the Gross National Product was the same as in 1911. Ordinary Italians were also taking in a thousand fewer calories per day in 1945 than they had done in June 1940, while inflation was more than twenty times higher than it had been in 1938.

Alongside the terrible human loss went the devastation of Italy's cultural heritage in the aftermath of 25 July 1943. Florence suffered most as the retreating Germans blew up all the bridges except the Ponte Vecchio, and destroyed Dante's old mediaeval city. This despite Hitler's declaration that Florence, which he had so admired on his visit to Italy before the war, should be an open city to save its artistic treasures. Further south the desperate fighting around the famous old Benedictine monastery of Monte Cassino ended only when the building was attacked by Allied bombers. And so the toll mounted as Italy's artistic treasures, which Mussolini had affected to despise, were damaged or destroyed. In Rimini the great church of San Francesco was damaged, while in Naples the church of Santa Chiara was burnt to the ground. When the Allies landed at Salerno in 1943, the Cathedral of Benvento was destroyed in the operation's aftermath.[2] For Mussolini's German allies, the cultural destruction wrought by the war was to be even more devastating.

The devastation that Mussolini's régime had left behind also produced a desire for revenge, especially in Northern Italy. This gave rise to the process of *epurazione* (purging) in which unofficial lynch law was followed by a systematic legal process aimed at those who had been identified as Fascists or who had collaborated with the German occupiers in the North. As many as 1,700 people may have perished as a result of random lynchings or sentences by Partisan tribunals, but few significant figures were brought to justice by the official courts. When they were, absurd legal technicalities allowed them to escape. Thus, in the case of Orano, Mussolini's former Chief of Staff and later Under Secretary at the Ministry of the Interior, the case was dropped because the court could not decide whether his behaviour contributed to the destruction of Italian democracy (this though Orano had been Chief of Staff at the time of the March on Rome in 1922). In similar fashion, Renato Ricci, the leader of the GNR in the Republic of Salò, was discharged because the tribunal determined that his force was merely an internal police one.[3] Stretching legal definitions also allowed those guilty of torture and the multiple rape of female Partisans to escape justice at the hands of the so-called 'Purges Commission' set up in 1945. Legal obscurantism was also combined with sheer incompetence. General Roatta was allowed to escape during the course of his trial. Neither was the net for Fascists cast particularly widely. When a judicial amnesty was introduced in October 1946, a mere 4,000 Fascists remained in custody.

In one sense, the incompleteness of the process, which mirrored the German experience, cannot come as a surprise, for widespread application of a purge would have made Italy virtually ungovernable in the immediate post-war period. All civil servants had to have a Fascist party card in the Mussolini period and no government in Italy had the stomach for a wholesale purge of 800,000 civil servants. Yet the superficial nature of the post-war purge in other areas remains remarkable. For as late as 1960, sixty-two of sixty-four Prefects in Italy had served under Mussolini, and all of the country's police chiefs had also been functionaries under Fascism. Neither was any real attempt made to purge the judiciary, which ensured that as many anti-Fascist cases as possible were dropped. Mussolini's shadow loomed large over much of the Italian bureaucracy in the years after 1945. That it did so was a consequence of the superficial nature of the *epurazione* in 1945–46.

That process, such as it was, was headed by Prime Minister Parri of the Action Party, which was very much the party of the northern resistance who had challenged both the Republic of Salò and the German occupiers. But the Purge Commission set up by Parri was resented by former Fascist civil servants who feared the threat of unemployment and disassociated themselves from the crimes of the Fascist régime. When the Parri government fell late in 1946, it was replaced by one dominated by the Christian Democrats under de Gasperi which speedily abolished the Commission and made the purging of Fascists a much lower priority. Yet it has to be recognised that the Left too seemed to want to bury the memory of Fascism, for it was the Communist leader Palmiro Togliatti who, as Minister of Justice, drafted the decree in June 1946 which ended the 'purging' in Italy. The suggestion by one historian that the most effective purge in post-war Italy was the Christian Democrat purge of former Partisans in the civil service and the police force seems, therefore, to be entirely justified.[4] As is the parallel suggestion that Mussolini deliberately left 'mines' in Italy's social fabric to afflict the country when he was gone. The way in which the civil service became associated with Fascism under the Duce made it virtually impossible to detach the central administration from the Fascist legacy after 1945.

In other respects also continuity between the Mussolini period and the new Italian Republic can be detected. A crucial line of continuity concerned Church–State relations which Mussolini had formalised in 1929 and which, given the emergence of a powerful Communist Party through the Partisan movement, might have been expected to have created severe tensions in the new Italian State.

In fact, this was not the case. The new Italian constitution which was drafted in 1946–47 did not penalise the Church for its association with Fascism but merely reiterated (in Article 7) the privileged position that Mussolini had conceded to the Church in the Lateran Pacts.[5] Article 7 further recognised that the State and Church were 'each in its own sphere, independent and sovereign'. Such a position could be expected from the Christian Democrats but the surprising element in the acceptance of Article 7 was that it was the PCI which went along with it, together with bourgeois parties like the Liberals and the Christian Democrats. Togliatti, like Mussolini in his day, was anxious to conciliate the Church, showing that once in office the Radical Left could be as conservative as the Radical Right. Togliatti also made the classic error of assuming that the Christian Democratic Party, like its predecessor the *Partito Populare Italiano*, was a progressive force in Italian politics when it was not. De Gasperi was determined to prevent the Vatican from trying to dominate his Party, but his main aim, especially at the onset of the Cold War, was to exclude the PCI from Italian governments, an aim which he shared with successive Popes. Nevertheless, Mussolini would doubtless have derived some wry satisfaction from the fact that his most doughty political opponents were apparently prepared to underwrite the Lateran Pacts.

He would have been pleased, too, by the final demise of the Italian monarchy in June 1946. The Resistance movement had agreed in 1944 that a referendum would be held to decide the fate of the House of Savoy, and Victor Emmanuel III abdicated in favour of his son, Umberto II, a month before the referendum was held. Yet, despite the clear links between the monarchy and Fascism since its earliest days, which could hardly have been exorcised by Victor Emmanuel's role in the events of 25 July 1943, only 54 per cent of the Italian people voted in favour of a republic. One and a half million voters either spoilt their ballot papers or were disqualified, showing that the pre-war political divide continued to exist. The result showed an Italy fragmented as before along geographical lines. The North and the Centre (the very regions where the Resistance had been active) voted for the Republic while the monarchist South supported the retention of King Umberto. Even in the post-Mussolini era, the country which he had superficially united under Fascism showed how deep its political fissures were. Parliamentary elections in 1946 made the Christian Democrats the largest party in parliament, but they received only 35 per cent of the total vote. The revised electoral process made it impossible for one party to dominate as it adopted proportional representation. The new post-Fascist Italy was to be run by coalition governments of the type Mussolini had so despised before 1922. In this sense, there was a clear break in continuity between the Fascist and post-war Republican eras.

This new political system co-existed with a legal framework which was undeniably Fascist. The laws by which Italy was governed in the years after 1945 were based on the Fascist Rocco's 1931 penal code and the parallel 1931 public security law, while the judiciary itself, as has been noted, was left unreformed both in respect of its serving judges and the way in which they were recruited. Italy, therefore, had 'a liberal Constitution, a Catholic government and Fascist laws'.[6] The failure to weed prominent Fascists out of the system was a consequence of this strange hybrid mechanism.

It would be dangerous, however, to exaggerate the extent to which Fascism continued to influence the post-war democracy. In vital areas, the Fascist past was clearly rejected. Mussolini had flirted with welfarism and statist economic intervention, and both were firmly rejected after 1945. Togliatti again showed his conservatism by stating that the PCI would accept the aid of private industry to assist Italy's post-war recovery. As it turned out, this recovery was much assisted by the Marshall Aid Programme set up by the US capitalists, aid which Stalin's satellites in Eastern Europe were forbidden to accept.

Importantly, too, Republican Italy was prepared to devolve authority to Italy's regions in a manner which would have been anathema to Mussolini. Where he had tried to 'Italianise' Venezia Giulio and the South Tyrol, the Republic was generous in allowing the French-speaking Valle d'Aosta and the Slav majority Venezia Giulio to have their own regional assemblies with protection of their languages and culture. It can, of course, be argued that this was pure pragmatism as the alternative was secessionist unrest in those regions, but the contrast with the Fascist era is sharp enough. Whether such concessions can be attributed to the fact that de Gasperi came from the Trentino must be a matter for conjecture, and he was still cautious in his treatment of the South Tyrolese. Mussolini would not make any concession to Hitler over this issue (at least while he had real power up to 1943) and de Gasperi merged the south Tyrol with the Trentino in an effort, which was not entirely successful, to keep the Germans in line.

One part of Mussolini's legacy was compulsory. Fascist Italy had gone to war with Britain and France in 1940 in a reckless adventure, and its republican successor paid the price in the post-war territorial settlement. The treaty between Italy and the Allied powers in 1947 stripped Italy of all its colonies save Somalia, and even its control here was limited to a ten-year UN trusteeship. Libya remained under British control until independence was ceded in 1952, Eritrea was given to Ethiopia, and in Europe, France gained some Alpine territory while Yugoslavia obtained Dalmatia, Istria and Fiume. Mussolini left Italy an even smaller territorial base than the one he had inherited in 1922, and its humiliation was worsened by the insistence of the Allied powers that reparations be paid to Greece, Yugoslavia and the USSR, all victims in varying ways of Fascist aggression. The treaty did not accept the principle that the overthrow of Mussolini in 1943 from within Italy absolved the Italian State from its responsibilities towards its victims. Where a fundamental difference *did* exist between Italy and its late ally Germany was in the absence of any international legal court to deal with Italian Fascism's crimes in the way that the Nuremberg Trials of 1945–46 dealt with the excesses of Nazism. Badoglio and Graziani were not put on trial for the crimes of Italian forces in Ethiopia as they should have been or brought to account in the way Generals Keitel and Jodl were in Germany. The failure of the Allied powers to grasp this nettle may have reflected their fear that such trials might provide an opportunity for the growing Communist threat which they (the USA in particular) thought they had identified in Italy. But Togliatti's own unwillingness to purge the Fascists in 1945–46 can only have strengthened Allied resolve not to bring the leading Fascists and their military collaborators to book. When Graziani was put on trial, it was for his role in the Republic of Salò rather than for condoning the massacres of hapless Ethiopian tribes-men. And this internal process did not wish to look closely at Italy's record in Ethiopia. The racism which had been a feature of Mussolini's colonial policies continued to cast its shadow over Italian politics.

Equally serious was the Italian record in occupied Yugoslavia, a sub-ject which has been neglected by historians in the light of the whole-sale barbarism of the Germans in Eastern Europe and elsewhere. In southern Slovenia, for example, Partisan officers reported that the Italian occupation had been 'every bit as cruel and violent as the subse-quent German occupation'.[7] Farms and villages were burnt to the ground, hostages shot and looting was commonplace in a policy which was orchestrated by the Italian High Command in Ljubljana in 1942.

A document which fell into the hands of the American Office of Strategic Services demanded that anyone found in possession of arms of any sort who aided the Partisans or who dealt in forged passports or papers should be shot out of hand by the Italian army. The category also included any male found to be behaving suspiciously within the zone of occupation, and the policy was linked to the wholesale destruction of any buildings deemed to be of use to the Partisans. An OSS report on the destroyed village of Ravnik in Slovenia stated that: 'The sight of Ravnik today is pitiful. You find no other living creatures among the debris but half-starved dogs and cats.'[8] And such atrocities were carried out in areas which in the eyes of the Fascist authorities were part of metropolitan Italy as a consequence of annexation. While it is possible to argue that such killings may have been a result of unilateral action by the Italian army, there can be no doubt that the overall responsibility for the killings lay with Mussolini. His rhetoric encouraged blood lust, however sceptical Ciano may have been about whether he had the will to implement such policies. The record clearly shows that such atrocities *were* carried out in Italian-occupied areas, and that they have been glossed over in the post-1945 era. This has been partly a result of the fact that, in the English-speaking world, the tendency to heighten the comic opera aspects of Fascism has caused its terrorist capacity to be underestimated.

Its heirs in the post-war world have continued to show a capacity for terror. The MSI (Italian Social Movement) had links, for example, with extreme Fascist groups, one of which was responsible for the outrage at Bologna in 1980 in which eighty people were killed. Despite such links, the MSI continued to poll heavily in the South, and had even greater support in Italian ex-patriot communities in Australia and Argentina (already noted as the refuge of Vittorio Mussolini for many years).

MUSSOLINI IN RETROSPECT

Mussolini's career ended in failure, but it is possible to see that it might have taken another path. Three turning points can – or so it seems to this writer – be identified when Mussolini made decisions which drastically altered his political career and ultimately the history of the Italian people.

One was his decision to abandon the Socialist Party in 1914 and support Italian intervention in the First World War. Up to this point, Mussolini had appeared to be a leftist revolutionary ideologue, even if there could have been doubts about the depth of his political convictions. Political radicalism was in his blood as the son of Alessandro, and Mussolini had a lengthy flirtation with revolutionary Marxism before swinging violently to the Nationalist Right. Yet it needs to be remembered that, as late as 1912, Mussolini, the future conqueror of Ethiopia, was denouncing Italy's war in Libya. Once he had resigned as editor of *Avanti!*, however, Mussolini severed his connections with the political Left forever. His near deathbed re-conversion to radicalism during the Salò period thirty years later fooled no one. We need though to be cautious about assertions that Mussolini's swing to the Right was inevitable because of the flaws in his character which made the dramatic and the violent attractive options for him. Equally unstable personalities have featured in the history of the Left. But what we can say, perhaps, is that Mussolini, who had arguably greater intellectual gifts than either Hitler or Stalin, was a man for whom consistency was an elusive virtue. While he personally despised the sedentary lifestyle of the academic, he possessed the intellectual's ability to see all sides of a question, albeit in his case frequently at a superficial level.

Once he became a nationalist and an anti-democrat, it is tempting to see Mussolini's creation of a personal dictatorship as inevitable. But was this actually the case? Mussolini behaved prudently in the years between 1919 and 1922, anxious not to alienate Italy's élites yet needing to balance their anxieties against the aspirations of his own radical Fascist followers. And once in power, Mussolini was careful to work in a coalition context, to marginalise the radicals of the *ras* and to reassure the Catholic Church about his intentions. Had it not been for the Matteotti murder in 1924 and the crisis that it provoked (the second major turning point), Mussolini might have run a régime of the Centre-Right which had authoritarian leanings but which stopped short of the personal dictatorship he felt obliged to unveil in January 1925. He had to do so because his personal authority in the Fascist movement was under assault from the Radical Right in much the same way that Hitler's was in Germany in 1934. Mussolini's problem was that he never had Hitler's electoral mandate and that he was constantly constrained by the influence of Church and monarchy. The disappointment which his radical followers such as Farinacci felt after 1925 meant that they tended to overlook the degree to which their Duce was inhibited by these traditional constraints. But the puzzle with Mussolini is the degree to which he was the unwilling prisoner of Victor Emmanuel III and Pius XI, both of whom approved of his anti-parliamentary, anti-Bolshevik credentials. These allowed them to go along with the attack on personal liberties in Italy after January 1925 and the prevalence of informers and internal exiles which were features of the Fascist régime. The price demanded was Mussolini's accommodation with the traditional power structure, most notably in the Lateran Pacts of 1929. Radicals were horrified by his church marriage to Rachele, but if Henry IV thought Paris was 'worth a mass' so evidently did Mussolini where Papal approval was concerned.

Mussolini was apparently anxious to achieve a national consensus, and the Fascist propaganda machine worked overtime to pretend that this had been attained. But the Duce, in his more realistic moments, was quite capable of seeing that this was not the case, and astute enough to realise that a coalition of interests was needed to keep his electorally fragile party in power. Arguments from cultural historians of Fascism that some sort of national consensus was achieved do not convince. What Mussolini did achieve was a consensus between the traditional power groups – the Church, the monarchy, the land-owners, the industrialists and the army – about the need to keep the Fascists in power. Such a coalition of interests did not need the curbs on individual freedom which were introduced in 1925. These were a sop to the Fascist radicals who were disappointed that their Duce was not living up to the rhetoric of the 1919 party programme. Mussolini, like many seeming radicals, found that the realities of power demanded compromises. His record before January 1925 does not suggest that he found the negotiation of compromises onerous. But it still leaves open a scenario where a more radical Mussolini could have operated had political conditions in Italy allowed this. Later on in his career, Mussolini often proved to be a ditherer, but in the period between 1919 and 1925 he showed considerable skill in both achieving power and consolidating it. Nevertheless Mussolini, like all political leaders, had to recognise that politics was the art of the possible. What he did was to try and create an aura of omnipotence around himself, which was to be brutally punctured in July 1943.

As a dictator, Mussolini needed to produce dramatic successes. The nature of the Fascist régime demanded that some of these should be in the sphere of military conquest. This necessity brought him to his last and fatal turning point in 1936–37. Up to that point, Mussolini could claim to have achieved a considerable degree of personal popularity, especially in the wake of his conquest of Ethiopia. Another leader perhaps would have cried halt at this point, recognising the fragility of Italy's economic resources and the dangers which were implicit in further adventures (recognised by his irritating co-ruler Victor Emmanuel III). Mussolini did not do so, despite the reservations of others like Grandi (and ultimately Ciano) in the Fascist leadership.

A complex mixture of motives seems to have been involved in Mussolini's decisions to abandon a policy of moderation, which might perhaps have allowed his survival as an Italian Franco or Salazar, for one of reckless adventurism. True he was antagonised by British policy over Ethiopia, but Germany too had showed barely concealed friendship for Haile Selassie. Much more significant then is Mussolini's belief, which was Social Darwinian in origin, that Britain and France were effete, played-out nations, whereas Fascist Italy and Nazi Germany represented the wave of the future. This made a coming together of Fascism and Nazism logical and the coincidence of the Spanish Civil War's outbreak in July 1936 accelerated this process. The formalisation of such a friendship through the Anti-Comintern Pact, with its anti-Soviet overtones, was another stage on the way to a formal Italian–German alliance. Mussolini abandoned the relative moderation of his domestic policies for the fatal flirtation with a Hitler who had spawned a Fascist movement with a biological imperative that was a long way from the motive force behind Italian Fascism. Mussolini's moonstruck behaviour in Germany in 1937 showed him at his worst. Judgement was thrown aside in his misguided adoration of the mechanised barbarism and racial intolerance characterised in National Socialism. At home, too, Mussolini now abandoned Italy's traditionally tolerant attitude towards the Jews in favour of a vicious and discreditable persecution campaign, even though there is no evidence that the Nazis ever put him under any pressure to introduce such a campaign.

Clearly, there was an ideological imperative behind Mussolini's decision to cement a friendship with Nazi Germany in 1936–37. Both powers disdained democracy and both harboured authoritarian regimes of the Far

Right. Mussolini also had clear points of tension with the French over Tunisia and with the British over Egypt and the Middle East. Mussolini's object of turning the Mediterranean into an Italian lake was hardly likely to inspire British approval either. But his anti-Communism was also shared by Hitler, even if inter-state relations with the USSR were cordial enough during the early 1930s.

Even so, when due allowance is made for the fact that Hitler and Mussolini were ideological bedfellows, the suspicion remains that much of Mussolini's behaviour in the period between 1936 and 1940 was dictated by a giant-sized inferiority complex. He was constantly quoted as referring to Italy's desertion of the Triple Alliance in 1915 as a national dishonour, while at the same time decrying Italy's lack of military virtues. Hitler's dramatic foreign policy successes between 1936 and 1939 seemed only to sharpen the Duce's insecurities, so vividly demonstrated in 1939 when he complained that the Führer merely sent him a message every time Germany occupied a country. Thus, while Italian intervention in the Second World War was not inevitable in June 1940, it was rendered almost so by the whole drift of Mussolini's foreign policy from 1936 onwards. Italy's lack of economic capacity and the glaring weaknesses in its armed forces, which were often brought to Mussolini's attention, were ignored as he became increasingly intoxicated at the prospect of war and the predicted easy victories over the British and French.

There were, of course, passages when Mussolini doubted, and seemed open to the influence of his son-in-law, Ciano, who came to be a critic of the German alliance in 1939, but the pattern of moaning about the Germans which persisted once war had come amounted to nothing more than the Duce talking aloud in sympathetic company. When he went to visit Hitler, the German dictator dominated the agenda, and in the end Mussolini was reduced, as has been seen, to a pathetic request for his 'orders'.

Yet while recognising the fatal change of direction which Mussolini made in 1936–37 and the role which 'the Brutal Friendship' played in his downfall, it also needs to be accepted that Mussolini's foreign policy goals were already unrealistic even if he had not thrown in his lot so irrevocably with the Nazis. For Italy to attempt to challenge Britain and France for control of the Mediterranean was a patent military absurdity, as were his dreams of challenging the democracies in Africa. While his blundering into the Balkans in 1940, against German advice, seems to have been primarily motivated by a desire to ape Hitler's victories in the West, Mussolini's invasion of Greece in 1940 made no military or political sense whatsoever, and his search for cheap glory resulted in a humiliating fiasco. This was particularly humiliating for a régime which placed such emphasis on military prowess and which sought zealously to inculcate martial virtues into Italian youth.

The last ten years of Mussolini's career were marked, therefore, by a dramatic downward spiral which ended with the bathos of the Republic of Salò, the last two years demonstrating, if any reminder were needed, how complete Mussolini's dependence on the Germans had become. This final constraint on Mussolini's power makes it doubly difficult, for historians and biographers alike, to judge whether the so-called Verona Manifesto marked a real return to the radicalism of Mussolini's youth. The view taken in this study, purely on the basis of the actual implementation of the Manifesto, is that by then Mussolini was too wedded to the concept of personal dictatorship to be able to make real concessions to democracy or the idea of a redistribution of economic resources in Italy.

If Mussolini had avoided the fatal entanglement with Nazi Germany, his régime could have survived into the post-war world, as that of Franco did in Spain (until 1975). For while there were anti-Fascist sentiments in the Western democracies after 1945, these rapidly lost impetus in the Cold War climate after 1948 when strong anti-Communist credentials were the best evidence of political respectability. Ultimately though, this decision would have rested with the Italian people, but the durability of the Franco régime in Spain and the Salazar régime in Portugal shows that authoritarian regimes of the Right could resist popular impulses for change. Neither dictator was faced by a popular uprising, although it is also true that neither Iberian leader had created a party structure which was perceived to be as corrupt and unpopular as Mussolini's.

Mussolini's Fascist régime has recently been described as a 'period piece'[9] whose xenophobia and nationalism are out of place in a world of globalisation and domination by immensely powerful US multinational corporations. These, it has been argued, and not without some validity, have rendered the whole concept of national sovereignty, and indeed the kinds of internal intervention in the economy advocated by

Mussolini, an irrelevance. It is hard to imagine an absurdity such as Mussolini's 'Quota 90' being tolerated by the market-driven world of the twenty-first century. But it is also hard to be so sanguine about the irrelevance of nationalism in the post-Cold War world, especially in Europe. For what the collapse of the USSR and its satellite system brought in the early 1990s was a reversion to a crude nationalism that Mussolini would certainly have recognised.

In Czechoslovakia, for example, a state which Mussolini had so disliked in his day, ancient tensions between Czechs and Slovaks led to a division of that state in the so-called 'velvet divorce'. Most spectacularly, his Yugoslav antagonist imploded in a series of civil wars which left Slovenia, Croatia and Bosnia and Herzegovina as independent entities, while Serbia was sundered by a final struggle to rid itself of Eastern Europe's last Stalinist dictator. Its death throes also involved a genocidal war in Kosovo, which had to be ended by external intervention, and which carried unmistakable Fascist overtones. The revival of ancient prejudices against Jews, gypsies and foreigners in general in some of the former republics of the USSR has also been a depressing reminder of the vicious racism which was a characteristic of inter-war Rumania, Poland and Hungary.

Mussolini, the revisionist, would also have recognised some of the old territorial disputes which plagued the new Europe, such as the ongoing Hungarian claim to Rumanian Transylvania, and would doubtless have seen the potential for exploiting the tensions caused by the surge of emigrants into Western Europe from the poorer East and the Third World. Neither can the emergence of figures such as Le Pen and Haider in France and Austria be taken lightly, despite their attempts to make Fascism of the generic sort respectable. Mussolini thrived on what was described as a crisis of post-war capitalism in Italy, and the threat of major economic disruption in European states is always going to offer opportunities to the Far Right. What protects them is the strength of their democratic institutions, so that in Britain, despite the economic uncertainties of the 1930s, Mosleyite Fascism, which aped that of Mussolini, never succeeded in securing one seat in parliament. To let the democratic guard slip is to see a possible revival of the Far Right such as the one briefly manifested in France's 2002 presidential election. Globalisation does not offer a secure defence against Fascism, unless democracy itself, which is not synonymous with globalisation, remains secure. Neither does the existence of the European Union, based on democratic principles, provide a fail-safe defence against Fascist upsurges.

When Joseph Stalin died in 1953, the famous Soviet poet Yevgeny Yevtushenko warned his fellow citizens to 'triple the guard beside his grave so that he will not rise again and with him the past'. He warned against a real danger in a context where Stalin still had many admirers and the succession was still in dispute. In Italy, by contrast, Mussolini seemed to leave no obvious legacy save a physical one of destruction and mayhem. This, as has been seen, was a superficial impression because Mussolini did leave an imprint on the political and legal structure of Italy. It might not have been necessary 'to triple the guard' around his grave but the willingness to allow his re-burial in Predappio in 1957 showed both an unwillingness to consign Mussolini to a well-deserved oblivion and a national reluctance to come to terms with his crimes. There was still a yearning, especially in the South, for the smack of firm government which Mussolini had allegedly provided, in an Italy where terrorism was still rampant and prime ministers could be discovered to be hand-in-glove with the Mafia. Under Fascism, a major achievement in the South was the 'battle against the Mafia' which was brutal but effective. Fascists understood gangsters, but it was demoralising for the Italian people to find politicians such as the former premier Andreotti being indicted for collusion with organised crime as late as 1993 (Andreotti had held the post of Prime Minister of Italy seven times).

Mussolini would probably have seen the Andreotti case as proof of the corruptness of the democratic process, a reality which justified his own appointment as prime minister in 1922. But in office, the Fascists proved to be just as corrupt as their democratic predecessors and, worse still, they were unaccountable. This was the obvious flaw with Italian Fascism and all its generic offspring. Mussolini was arrogant in his belief that he deserved power and that he did not need to consult the people. Losing touch, therefore, with his constituency, he was more out of touch with reality than the most corrupt republican politician in his era or in the years to come. He surrounded himself all too often with incompetent sycophants, which is a price often paid for supreme power, but one that was all too predictable, given the Duce's cynical distrust of his fellow man and awareness of how easily

people could be manipulated. That Mussolini had concrete achievements is undeniable, but those achievements were tarnished by his
ultimate contempt for his own people, whom he led into a catastrophic war which the ordinary man and woman in the street never
wanted. As his corpse swung upside down in the Piazzale Loreto in
1945, Italians could recall that this was the man upon whom they had
once wasted such adulation.

NOTES

INTRODUCTION

1 J. Pollard, *The Fascist Experience in Italy*, London (Routledge), 1998, p.1.
2 C. Seton Watson, *Italy from Liberalism to Fascism*, London (Methuen & Co.), 1967, p.25.
3 M. Clark, *Modern Italy 1871–1955*, London (Longman), 2nd edn, 1996, p.24.
4 *Ibid.*, p.137.
5 The work consists of the following volumes: *Mussolini il rivoluzionario 1883–1920*, Turin (Einaudi), 1965; *Mussolini il fascista, I: La Conquista del potere 1921–5*, Turin (Einaudi), 1966; *Mussolini il fascista, II: L'Organizzazione dello stato fascista 1925–9*, Turin (Einaudi), 1968; *Mussolini il duce, I: Gli anni del consenso 1929–36*, Turin (Einaudi), 1974; *Mussolini il duce, II: Lo stato totalitario 1936–1940*, Turin (Einaudi), 1981; *Mussolini l'alleato, II, 1/2: L'Italia in guerra 1940–43*, Turin (Einaudi), 1990.
6 R. Vivarelli, 'Benito Mussolini del socialismo al fascismo', *Rivasta Storice Italiana*, Vol.79, No.2, 1967, p.444.
7 D. Mack Smith, *Mussolini*, London (Weidenfeld & Nicolson), 1981, p.xiii.
8 R.J.B. Bosworth, *Mussolini*, London (Arnold), 2002, p.11.
9 *Ibid.*, pp.74–5.
10 M. Blinkhorn, *Mussolini and Fascist Italy*, London (Methuen), 1984, pp.26–8.
11 The title of G. Seldes's 1936 study (London, Arthur Barker).
12 R. Miller and G. Pugliese (eds), *Ciano's Diary*, London (Phoenix Press), 2002.

1 THE SHAPING OF A POLITICAL LEADER, 1883–1919

1 L. Fermi, *Mussolini*, Chicago (University of Chicago Press), 1967, p.9.
2 B. Mussolini, *My Autobiography*, London (Hutchinson), 1928, p.25. Like most of Mussolini's publications, it should be regarded with caution as a source, and was in fact largely written by his brother Arnaldo and Luigi Barzini. A grovelling foreword was provided by a former US ambassador to Rome, Richard Washburn Child, a slavish admirer of the dictator.
3 *Ibid.*, p.19. On the alcohol point, see Bosworth, p.41.
4 Mussolini, p.20; Bosworth, pp.42–4.

5 C. Hibbert, *Benito Mussolini*, London (Longmans), 1962, p.6. Bosworth suggests that the Salesian fathers were malicious in blaming the young Benito for the political sins of his father (Mussolini, p.51).

6 See R. Mack Smith, *Mussolini*, London (Weidenfeld & Nicholson), 1981, p.2; Fermi, p.17.

7 Mussolini, p.22.

8 *Avanti!*, 2 February 1901.

9 Hibbert, p.20.

10 B. Mussolini, *La Mia Vita*, Rome, 1947, pp.69–70.

11 Mack Smith, p.4.

12 Hibbert, p.7.

13 Mussolini, p.26.

14 Sir I. Kirkpatrick, *Mussolini. Study of a Demagogue*, London (Odhams), 1964, p.36; Mack Smith, p.6.

15 Mussolini, p.26.

16 M. Sarfatti, *The Life of Benito Mussolini*, London (Thornton Butterworth), 1925, p.84; as always with Mussolini, there are doubts about the genuineness of his proletarian experiences (Bosworth, p.60).

17 A. Balabanoff, *My Life as a Rebel*, London (Hamish Hamilton), 1938, p.60.

18 E. and D. Susmal (eds), BMOO, 6 February 1904.

19 Mussolini, p.28.

20 *Ibid*, p.29.

21 *Ibid*. The parallel with Hitler is again quite striking, the family doctor remarking of him that: 'In all my career, I never saw anyone so prostrate with grief' when he attended at the deathbed of Hitler's mother Klara in 1907. See J. Tolland, *Adolf Hitler*, New York (Doubleday), 1976, p.27.

22 Quoted in Hibbert, p.12.

23 N. O'Sullivan, *Fascism*, London (Dent), 1983, p.122.

24 B. Mussolini, *Fascism: Doctrine and Institutions*, Rome (Ardia), 1935, p.7.

25 Mussolini, *My Autobiography*, p.30.

26 L. Rafanelli, *Una Donna e Mussolini*, Milan (Rizzoli), 1946, pp.67–9.

27 Mussolini, p.46.

28 B. D'Agostini, *Colloqui con Rachele Mussolini*, Rome (OET), 1946, p.16.

29 *Guardian*, 1 September, 2001.

30 For further detail on their affair, see Bosworth, pp.91–5, Rafanelli, *ibid*.

31 Mack Smith, p.25; R. de Felice, *Mussolini il rivoluzionario 1883–1920*, Turin (Einaudi), 1965, p.277.

32 Kirkpatrick, p.64.

33 Mussolini, p.49.

34 M. Clark, *Modern Italy 1871–1945*, London (Longman), 2nd edn, 1996, p.183.
35 23 marzo, *Il Popolo d'Italia*, 18.3.1919.
36 Mussolini, p.51.
37 *Ibid.*, p.56.
38 008/285 16/6/1917; *Vita Italiana*, Nov. 1928, p.72.
39 Mussolini, p.57.
40 P. Brendon, *The Dark Valley. A Panorama of the 1930s*, London (Jonathan Cape), 2000, p.19.
41 Mussolini, p.82.
42 Clark, p.205.
43 Seton Watson, p.596.
44 Bosworth, p.135.

2 THE ACHIEVEMENT OF POWER, 1919–24

1 P. Morgan, *Italian Fascism 1919–45*, London (St Martin's Press), 1995, p.14.
2 *Ibid.*, p.13.
3 Mussolini, pp.73–4.
4 Clark, p.214.
5 Mack Smith, p.33.
6 I. De Bengnac, *Palazzo Venezia: Storia di un Regime*, Rome (La Rocca), 1955, p.158.
7 A. de Grand, *Italian Fascism: Its Origins and Development*, Nebraska (University of Nebraska Press), 1982, p.24.
8 Mussolini, p.116.
9 Morgan, p.35; Mussolini, pp.115–17.
10 Mussolini, p.122.
11 de Grand, p.31.
12 Blinkhorn, p.20.
13 Quoted in A. Lyttelton (ed.), *Italian Fascisms: From Pareto to Gentile*, London (Cape), 1973, pp.211–12.
14 Mack Smith, p.45; Bosworth, p.158.
15 de Grand, p.35.
16 The relevant chapter in Mussolini's autobiography is entitled 'Thus We Took Rome', pp.164–87.
17 For speculation on why Victor Emmanuel acted as he did, and the background to Mussolini's appointment, see Bosworth, pp.166–9; Mack Smith, pp.53–5; Morgan, pp.56–8; de Grand, pp.36–7; Blinkhorn, pp.21–3; G. Carocci, *Italian Fascism*, London (Penguin),

1975, pp.21–3. Mussolini's own inaccurate, exaggerated account can be found in *My Autobiography*, pp.173–83.

18 P. Morelli, *Mussolini: An Intimate Life*, Rome, 1957, p.93.

19 Z. Sternell, 'Fascism' in D. Miller (ed.), *The Blackwell Encyclopaedia of Political Thought*, Oxford, 1987, pp.148–50.

20 R. Griffin, *The Blackwell Dictionary of Social Thought*, Oxford, 1987, pp.223–4.

21 For a useful attempt to define the characteristics of generic Fascism, see D. Prowe, ' "Classic Fascism" and the New Radical Right in Western Europe: Comparisons and Contrasts', *Contemporary European History*, 3 (3), 1994, pp.289–313.

22 C.G. Segrè, *Italo Balbo. A Fascist Life*, Berkeley and London (University of California Press), 1987, p.114.

23 de Grand, p.41.

24 Mussolini, p.185.

25 J. Cornwall, *Hitler's Pope. The Secret History of Pius XII*, New York and London (Viking), 1999, p.98.

26 de Grand, p.51.

27 These distinctive groupings broadly follow those given in Blinkhorn, p.24 and Morgan, p.62.

3 CRISIS AND CONSOLIDATION, 1924–29

1 E. Riboldi, *Vicende socialiste: trent'anni di storia italiana nei ricordi di un deputato massimalista*, Milan, 1964, p.119; nevertheless, de Felice, in his massive and sympathetic biography of Mussolini, denies that he was responsible for his opponent's murder. See de Felice, *Mussolini il fascista, II*, pp.622–3; Mussolini's latest biographer in English, Professor R.J.B. Bosworth, deems the case against him 'not proven' (Bosworth, p.196). This usage of the Scottish legal judgement leaves open the possibility that Mussolini was indeed guilty.

2 Segrè, p.127.

3 Mack Smith, pp.77–8.

4 Segrè, pp.127–8.

5 Mussolini even tried to pretend that Marinelli and Rossi had not been close to him. See de Felice, *Mussolini il fascista: II*, p.778.

6 MacGregor Knox, 'Expansionist Zeal, Fighting Power and Staying Power in the Italian and German dictatorships' in R. Bessel (ed.), *Fascist Italy and Nazi Germany. Comparisons and Contrasts*, Cambridge (CUP), 1996, p.128.

7 Bosworth, p.197.

8 Mussolini, p.221.

9 *Ibid.*, p.222.

10 Mack Smith, p.144.

11 Martin Clark makes the point that OVRA was not really new at all. Italians assumed that it was but, in fact, the organisation was mostly made up of the old secret police branch of the Ministry of the Interior with a new, dramatic, but largely meaningless, name. See Clark, p.233.

12 de Felice, *Mussolini il duce, I,* p.83.

13 BMOO, Vol.XXI, Florence, 1952, p.362.

14 S. Payne, *A History of Fascism,* Wisconsin and London (University of Wisconsin and UCL), 1996, p.10.

15 Segrè, p.137.

16 E. Tannenbaum, *Fascism in Italy. Society and Culture 1922–1945,* London (Allen Lane), 1973, p.71.

17 Clark, p.233.

18 A. De' Stefani, *Una Riforma al Rogo,* Rome (Giovanni Volpe editore), 1963, p.12.

19 Clark, p.235.

20 *Ibid.*, p.238.

21 Mack Smith, p.101.

22 Bosworth, p.226.

23 Morgan, p.99.

24 R. Jenkins, *The Chancellors,* London (Macmillan), 1998, pp.307–10.

25 Carocci, p.60.

26 *Ibid.*, p.53.

27 Bosworth, p.223.

28 *Ibid.*, pp.224–5.

29 de Felice, *Mussolini il Duce: I* and L. Passerini, *Fascism in Popular Memory: The Cultural Experience of the Turin Working Class,* Cambridge (CUP), 1987; for critiques of this position, see P. Corner 'Italy' in S. Salter and J. Stevenson (eds), *The Working Class and Politics in Europe and America 1929–1945,* London and New York (Longman), 1990, pp.154–71 and A. Cento Bull, *Capitalismo e fascismo di fronte alla crisi. Industria e società bergamasca 1923–1937,* Bergamo, 1983, pp.142–66.

30 T. Abse, 'Italian Workers and Italian Fascism' in Bessel, p.48.

31 Mussolini, p.246.

32 J. Gaillard, 'The Attractions of Fascism for the Church of Rome' in J. Milfull (ed.), *Attractions of Fascism,* New York and Oxford (Berg), 1990, p.208.

33 Bosworth, p.236.

34 D.A. Binchy, *Church and State in Fascist Italy*, London (OUP), 1970, p.186.

35 A reference to the occasion when a mediaeval Holy Roman Emperor had been obliged to do penance in the snow before Pope Gregory VII.

36 Cornwall, p.115.

37 J. Pollard, *The Vatican and Italian Fascism*, Cambridge (CUP), 1985, p.145.

38 Clark, p.256.

4 THE DICTATOR AT HIS ZENITH

1 Mack Smith, p.59.

2 R. Cantapulo, *Fu la Spagna. Ambasciata presso Franco Febbraio–Aprile 1937*, Verona, 1948, p.42.

3 Mack Smith, p.61.

4 Bosworth, p.184.

5 *Documents on British Foreign Policy*, Series I, Vol.XXIV, pp.1046–7.

6 *Ibid.*, p.952.

7 R. Lamb, *The Drift to War 1922–39*, London (W.H. Allen), 1989, pp.27–32.

8 S. Marks, 'Mussolini and Locarno', *Journal of Contemporary History*, Vol.14, No.3, July, 1979, p.435.

9 DDI, semitti serie 4, No.532.

10 12/9/30, Grandi Diary, in P. Nello, *Un fedele disubbidiente: Dino Grandi del palazzo Chigi al 25 uglio*, Bologna Il Mulino, 1993, pp.90–1.

11 This view is put strongly by Professor MacGregor Knox in 'The Fascist Régime, Its Foreign Policy and Its Wars: An Anti-anti-Fascist Orthodoxy', *Contemporary European History*, 4 (3), 1995, pp.347–65.

12 de Felice, *Mussolini il fascista II*.

13 Fernando Mezzosomma quote in Hibbert, p.ll; the phrase 'Sawdust Caesar' comes from the well-known 1936 biography by Seldes.

14 Sometimes fiction can also play a part in creating such stereotypes. See, for example, L. de Bernières, *Captain Corelli's Mandolin*, London (Secker & Warburg), 1994, pp.10–18.

15 Bosworth, p.215.

16 Hibbert, p.51.

17 Mack Smith, p.109.

18 Mussolini's admirer de Felice claims that the Duce worked a mere ten-hour day; see *Mussolini il duce, I*, p.20.

19 M. Sarfatti, *The Life of Benito Mussolini*, London (Butterworth), 1925; G. Pini, *Benito Mussolini: la sua vita fino ad oggi dalla strade al potere*, Bologna, 1927.

20 G. Salvemini, in A. Valeri, A. Merola and R. Vivarelli (eds), *Scritti sul Fascismo*, Milan, 1966, p.388.

21 Bosworth, p.7.

5 ITALIAN SOCIETY UNDER MUSSOLINI, 1931–39

1 Bosworth, p.235.

2 Clark, p.246.

3 Segrè, p.97.

4 Tannenbaum, p.264.

5 P. Wilson, 'Women in Fascist Italy' in Bessel, p. 79.

6 Wilson, p.82.

7 For the debate about the impact of the 1938 legislation, see Wilson, p.85, who refutes the judgement of de Grand that the 1938 law was 'draconian' (see de Grand, p.113, and also his 'Women Under Italian Fascism', *Historical Journal*, Vol.19, No.4, 1976, p.965.

8 Hibbert, p.55.

9 Mussolini's policies towards radio and the Cinema are discussed in P. Cannistraro, 'Mussolini's Cultural Revolution – Fascist or Nationalist?', *Journal of Contemporary History*, Vol.7, 1972.

10 Clark, p.245.

11 *Ibid.*, p.342.

12 Bosworth, p.344.

13 *Ibid.*, p.247.

14 N. d'Aroma, *Mussolini Segreto Capelli*, Rocca San Caseiano, 1958, p.250.

15 Clark, p.253.

16 This is the belief of Professor Bosworth (p.342).

17 Morgan, p.111.

18 Bosworth, p.260.

19 Mack Smith, pp.203–4.

20 T.H. Koon, *Believe, Obey, Fight: Political Socialisation of Youth in Fascist Italy 1922–1943*, Chapel Hill and London (University of North Carolina Press), 1985, p.183.

21 Corner, p.164.

6 THE ETHIOPIAN WAR, 1935–36

1 This is the thesis propounded by Professor MacGregor Knox in a number of publications. See, for example, his article 'The Fascist Régime, Its Foreign Policy and Its Wars'.

2 De Felice made particular use of the work of R. Quartararo. See her *Roma tra Londra e Berlino: la politica estera fascista dal 1930 al 1940*, Rome (Bonacci), 1980, p.28.

3 Bosworth, p.275.

4 I. Kershaw, *Hitler: 1889–1936 Hubris*, London (Penguin), 1998, pp.522–3.

5 E. Wiskemann, *The Rome–Berlin Axis*, London (Fontana), rev. edn, 1966, p.53. The translation from the French is the author's.

6 *Ibid.*, p.54.

7 *Ibid.*, p.57; Kershaw, p.523.

8 BMOO, Vol.21, pp.318–20.

9 Mack Smith, p.194.

10 For background material on Ethiopia, see A.J. Crozier, *The Causes of the Second World War*, London (Blackwell), 1997, pp.106–8; Brendon, pp.282–92.

11 Mussolini directive, 30/12/34, DDI, Series 7, Vol.XVI, p.358.

12 P. Reynaud, *La France a sauvé l'Europe*, Vol.I, Paris, 1947, p.157.

13 The Italian concerned was a Signor Constantini who was even invited to the coronation of George VI in 1936! See C. Andrew, *Secret Service: The Making of the British Intelligence Community*, London (Heinemann), 1985, p.406.

14 Crozier, p.108; Lord Vansittart, *The Mist Procession*, London (Hutchinson), 1958, pp.520–1.

15 Sir G. Thompson, *Frontline Diplomat*, London (Hutchinson), 1959, p.95; DBFP, Series 2, Vol.XIV, pp.220–8 and FO 401/35, PRO.

16 Mack Smith, p.193.

17 P. Aloisi, *Mia attivita a servizio della pace*, Rome, 1946, pp.57–60; E.M. Robertson, *Mussolini as Empire-Builder*, London (Macmillan), 1977, p.176.

18 Eden rejected such an interpretation of the Mussolini interview as 'pure balderdash. There was nothing in my reception at which I could have been offended even if I were an Italian and therefore susceptible to such feelings' [a somewhat odd statement], FO 371/19164. See also Lord Avon, *Facing the Dictators*, London (Cassell), 1962, pp.221–5. Mussolini ignores this meeting in his autobiography.

19 Professor Bosworth notes that 'Mussolini was certainly resolved to sound as though only war would content him' (p.302).

20 A. Mockler, *Haile Selassie's War*, Oxford (OUP), 1984, p.54.

21 *Manchester Guardian*, 10/10/35.

22 4/12/35, Mussolini to Grandi, DDI, Series 8, Vol.II.

23 Crozier, p.109.

24 BMOO, Vol.XXVII, p.203.
25 J.W. Macfie, *An Ethiopian Diary*, Liverpool (University of Liverpool), 1936, p.77.
26 Mussolini, p.337.
27 *Mussolini il duce: I*, p.642.
28 Wiskemann, pp.73–83; Robertson, pp.186–8.

7 INTO THE ABYSS: FOREIGN AND DEFENCE POLICY, 1936–40

1 G. Ciano, *Diario 1937–8*, Bologna, 1948, p.40.
2 Bosworth, p.14.
3 R. Suñer, *Entre Hendaya y Gibraltar*, Mexico, 1947, p.325.
4 Vansittart, p.503.
5 For excellent analyses of the state of the Italian armed forces immediately before the Second World War, see P.M.H. Bell, *The Origins of the Second World War*, London (Longman), 1986, pp.185–8; A. Wheatcroft, 'Italy' in R. Overy and A. Wheatcroft (eds), *The Road To War*, London (Macmillan), 1989, Chapter 5; S. Morewood, 'Anglo-Italian Rivalry in the Mediterranean and the Middle East, 1935–40' in R. Boyce and E.M. Robertson (eds), *Paths to War: New Essays on the Origins of the Second World War*, London (Macmillan), 1989, pp.167–98.
6 Bosworth, pp.371–3.
7 E. Santarelli, 'The Economic and Political Background of Fascist Imperialism' in R. Sarti (ed.), *The Ax Within: Italian Fascism in Action*, New York (Modern Viewpoints), 1974, p.177.
8 For background reading on the Spanish Civil War and Italy's involvement, see Crozier, pp.120–4; Wiskemann, pp.89–91; Bosworth, pp.316–19; Brendon, pp.331–3.
9 Ciano minute, 24/10/36, quoted in Wiskemann, p.86.
10 *Ibid.*, p.92.
11 28/9/37, R. Miller and S. Pugliese (eds), *Ciano's Diaries 1937–43*, London (Phoenix Press), 2000, p.11.
12 M. Muggeridge (ed.), *Ciano's Diary 1937–8*, London (Methuen & Co.), 1952, p.24.
13 9/3/38, R. Miller and S. Pugliese (eds), *Ciano's Diary 1937–43*, London (Phoenix Press), 2002, p.68.
14 De Felice, *Mussolini il duce: II*, pp.509–17. See also MacGregor Knox, *Mussolini Unleashed 1939–41: Politics and Strategy in Fascist Italy's Last War*, Cambridge (CUP), 1982, pp.37–8; G. Strang, 'War and

Peace: Mussolini's Road to Munich' in I. Lukes and E. Goldstein (eds), *The Munich Crisis, 1938: Prelude to World War II*, London (Frank Cass), 1999, pp.160–90; Bosworth, pp.332–3.

15 15/3/39, *Ciano's Diary 1937–43*, p.201.

16 Quoted in Wiskemann, p.180.

17 BMOO, Vol.XXIX, pp.403–5.

8 THE SLIDE TO DISASTER, 1940–43

1 This is the title of Chapter Sixteen in Professor Bosworth's book.

2 A. Horne, *To Lose a Battle: France 1940*, London (Macmillan), 1969, p.415. See also MacGregor Knox, *Mussolini Unleashed*, pp.126–33.

3 *Ciano's Diary*, 8/9/40 and 17/9/40.

4 Mack Smith, pp.256–62; Bosworth, pp.375–6.

5 Clark, p.288.

6 MacGregor Knox, *Fascist Italy and Nazi Germany*, p.129.

7 Bosworth, p.272.

8 R. Klibansky (ed.), *The Mussolini Memoirs*, London (Phoenix Press), 2000, p.235; first published, London (Weidenfeld & Nicholson), 1949. These so-called 'memoirs' are supplemented by three fragments, 'What Mussolini Told Me' by Rear-Admiral Maugeri, then Chief of Italian Naval Intelligence, 'With Mussolini at the *Campo Imperatore*' by the managers of the Gran Sasso Hotel where Mussolini was briefly imprisoned, and Cardinal Archbishop Schuster's account of his last meeting with Mussolini. The 'memoirs' cover the period 1942–43.

9 For detail on their relationship, see Hibbert, pp.181–7, and for Ciano's complaints about Petacci's extravagances, see *Ciano's Diary*, 27/4/42.

10 *Ibid.*, 20/1/43 and 21/1/43, and 22/1/43.

11 BMOO, Vol.XLIV, 11/10/42.

12 *Mussolini Memoirs*, pp.60–1.

13 *Ibid.*, pp.62–4; see also Bosworth, pp.400–1 and Hibbert, pp.209–17.

14 *Mussolini Memoirs*, pp.80–2; Mack Smith, pp.298–9; Bosworth, pp.401–2.

15 BMOO, Vol.XXXIV, p.364.

16 *Mussolini Memoirs*, p.130.

17 I. Kershaw, *Hitler 1936–1945: Nemesis*, London (Penguin), 2000, p.602; see also Bosworth, p.403 and Mack Smith, p.300. Mussolini's own account can be found in *Mussolini Memoirs*, pp.133–4; for another German perspective, there is O. Skorzeny, *Geheimkommando Skorzeny*, Hamburg, 1950, pp.135–51.

18 Compare, for example, Wiskemann, p.365 with the account in Hibbert, p.268.
19 *Goebbels Diaries*, 23/3/43.

9 THE LAST PHASE, 1943–45

1 Quoted in G. Bocca, *La reppublica di Mussolini*, Rome (Laterza), 3rd edn, 1977, p.23.
2 23/12/43, *Ciano's Diary*, p.591.
3 Hibbert, pp.280–1.
4 For this suggestion, see Mack Smith, p.310.
5 Morgan, p.185.
6 Bosworth, p.407.
7 *Ibid.*, p.24.
8 BMOO, p.255.
9 For the full text of the Mussolini–Schuster interview, see *ibid.*, pp.254–60.
10 Mack Smith, p.319.
11 Bosworth, p.32.
12 W. Audisio, *In nome del popolo italiano*, Milan (Teti), 1975, pp.376–9.
13 Bosworth, p.411.
14 Kershaw, pp.826–8.

CONCLUSION

1 Bosworth, p.419.
2 For an admirable assessment of the devastating consequences of the Second World War on European culture as a whole, see Chapter One of D. Cameron Watts, *How War Came*, London (Heinemann), 1989.
3 P. Ginsborg, *A History of Contemporary Italy: Society and Politics 1943–1988*, London (Penguin), 1990, p.92.
4 *Ibid.*, pp.92–3.
5 Clark, p.319.
6 *Ibid.*, p.321.
7 F. Lindsay, *Beacons in the Night: With the OSS and Tito's Partisans in Wartime Yugoslavia*, Stanford (Stanford University Press), 1993, p.36.
8 *Ibid.*, p.38.
9 Bosworth, p.427.

SELECT BIBLIOGRAPHY

PRIMARY SOURCES

Archive material

The main archive source on Mussolini's life continues to be the material on deposit at the Archivio centrale dello stato in Rome, which also contains the papers of leading Fascist leaders such as de Bono, Farinacci, Finzi and Volpi. There is also material on Mussolini available in the state archive at Forlì.

In London, the Public Record Office in Kew is another useful source. Of the various series available, FO 371 deals with Italy while the FO 800 series contains the papers of leading British statesmen such as Lord Halifax, Lord Templewood (S. Hoare), Ramsey MacDonald and Anthony Eden. The papers of Sir Austen Chamberlain are also available at the PRO. At Churchill College, Cambridge, the papers of Sir Robert Vansittart are available together with those of Sir William Strang. Birmingham University has the papers of Neville Chamberlain on deposit.

Printed sources

Important material on Mussolini's foreign policy can be found in:

DDI, *I documenti diplomatici italiani, semitti serie* 7, 8, 9, 10;
DBFP, Documents on British Foreign Policy 1919–39, 2nd and 3rd series;
Documents on German Foreign Policy 1918–45, Series C & D.

Biographies of Mussolini

There is a welter of biographical material about Mussolini, of varying standard. For many years, the standard reference was *Mussolini: L'uomo e l'opera* by G. Pini and D. Susmal (4 volumes, La Fenice, 1953–55). This was then superseded by R. de Felice's massive multi-volume work which appeared between 1965 and 1997. The relevant volumes are:

Mussolini il rivoluzionario 1883–1920 (Einaudi, 1965);
Mussolini il fascista: I, La conquista del potere 1921–25 (Einaudi, 1966);
Mussolini il fascista: II, L'organizzazione dello stato fascista 1925–9 (Einaudi, 1968);

Mussolini il duce: I, gli anni del consenso 1929–36 (Einaudi, 1974);
Mussolini il duce: II, Lo stato totalitario 1936–40 (Einaudi, 1981);
Mussolini l'alleato, II, 1/2: L'Italia in guerra 1940–43 (Einaudi, 1990).

In English, the 1960s saw the appearance of several titles such as C. Hibbert, *Benito Mussolini: The Rise and Fall of Il Duce* (Longmans, 1962) and I. Kirkpatrick, *Mussolini: Study of a Demagogue* (Odhams, 1964). These were superseded in 1981 by D. Mack Smith's classic study (Weidenfeld & Nicholson). Its pre-eminence is now challenged by R. Bosworth, *Mussolini* (Arnold, 2002).

Amongst the earlier material, M. Sarfatti's *Dux* (Butterworth, 1934) is worth a look, although it can hardly claim to be objective. Mussolini's own *My Autobiography* (Hutchinson, 1928) also has to carry a major health warning. There are, in addition, a number of works by members of Mussolini's family. These include: R. Mussolini, *My Life with Mussolini* (Robert Hale, 1959) and *The Real Mussolini* (as told to A. Zarca, Saxon House, 1973); E. (Ciano) Mussolini, *Mussolini, My Truth* (as told to A. Zarca, Weidenfeld & Nicholson, 1977); and V. Mussolini, *Vita con mia padre* (Mondadori, 1957).

Leading Fascists have also contributed studies of Mussolini and Fascism in one form or another. They include: I. Balbo, *Stormio in volo sull'oceano* (Mondadori, 1931); G. Bottai, *Mussolini: costruttore d'impero* (Edizioni Paladini, not dated); R. Farinacci, *Andante mosso 1924–5* (Mondadori, 1925); and G. Buffarini Guidi, *La vera verità* (Sugar, 1970). A massive additional source is also available in E. and D. Susmal (eds), *Opera Omnia di Benito Mussolini* (referred to in text as BMOO), 44 vols (La Fenice, 1951–60).

Foreign policy

In addition to the archive material and official government sources listed above, there are a number of seminal studies. MacGregor Knox's *Mussolini Unleashed 1939–41: Politics and Strategy in Fascist Italy's Last War* (CUP, 1982) is essential reading as is E.M. Robertson's *Mussolini as Empire-Builder: Europe and Africa 1932–36* (Macmillan, 1977).

In Italian, there is de Felice's *Mussolini l'alleato 1940–45* (Einaudi, 1990) and Rosara Quartararo's *Roma tra Londra e Berlino: la politicia estera fascista dal 1930 al 1940* (Editore Bonacci, 1980). More recently, there has been H. James Burgwyn, *Italian Foreign Policy in the Inter-war Period 1918–1940* (Praeger, 1997). Older studies retain their value, however, such as Denis Mack Smith's *Mussolini's Roman Empire* (Penguin, 1976), E. Wiskemann's *The Rome–Berlin Axis* (rev. edn, Fontana, 1966) and F.W. Deakin's *The Brutal Friendship: Hitler, Mussolini and the Fall of Fascism* (Penguin, 1966). *Ciano's Diary 1937–43* (Phoenix Press, 2002) remains an essential source for an understanding of Mussolini's foreign policy.

Domestic policy

Apart from the relevant volumes of de Felice's massive work, there are a number of excellent secondary texts. A selection must include M. Blinkhorn's *Mussolini and Fascist Italy* (Methuen, 1984); A. de Grand's *Italian Fascism* (2nd edn, University of Nebraska Press, 1989); A. Cassels, *Fascist Italy* (2nd edn, Harlan Davidson, 1985); and P. Morgan, *Italian Fascism 1919–45* (St Martin's Press, 1995). The sections on Mussolini and Fascist Italy in general textbooks, such as M. Clark, *Modern Italy 1871–1982* (Longman, 1984) and D. Mack Smith, *Italy: A Modern History* (University of Michigan Press, 1969), are most useful.

The rise of Fascism is especially well catered for in A. Lyttleton's *The Seizure of Power. Fascism in Italy 1919–20* (Weidenfeld & Nicholson, 1973) and A. Rossi, *The Rise of Italian Fascism* (Gordon Press, 1976). G. Carocci's *Italian Fascism* (Penguin, 1975) remains useful. Specialist studies include P. Corner's *Fascism in Ferrara* (OUP, 1984); A. Kelikian, *Town and Country under Fascism: The Transformation of Brescia 1915–26* (OUP, 1986); and F. Snowden, *The Fascist Revolution in Tuscany 1919–22* (CUP, 1989).

On Church–State relations under Mussolini, we have J. Pollard, *The Vatican and Italian Fascism 1929–32: A Study in Conflict* (CUP, 1985), while on cultural aspects of Fascism there is L. Passerini, *Fascism in Popular Memory: The Cultural Experience of the Turin Working Class* (CUP, 1987). The theoretical debate about the origins and nature of Italian Fascism is comprehensively covered in R. Griffin (ed.), *International Fascism: Theories, Causes and New Consensus* (Arnold, 1998). An interesting comparative approach is provided in R. Bessel (ed.), *Fascist Italy and Nazi Germany* (CUP, 1996) which contains a number of articles on 'The Experience of Labour under Fascism', 'Women in Fascist Italy' and 'The Crisis of Bourgeois Society in Italy'.

INDEX